FAITH IN LAW
ESSAYS IN LEGAL THEORY

Faith in Law
Essays in Legal Theory

Edited by

PETER OLIVER, SIONAIDH DOUGLAS SCOTT
and
VICTOR TADROS

·HART·
PUBLISHING

OXFORD – PORTLAND OREGON
2000

Hart Publishing
Oxford and Portland, Oregon

Published in North America (US and Canada) by
Hart Publishing c/o
International Specialized Book Services
5804 NE Hassalo Street
Portland, Oregon
97213-3644
USA

Distributed in the Netherlands, Belgium and Luxembourg by
Intersentia, Churchillaan 108
B2900 Schoten
Antwerpen
Belgium

Hart Publishing Ltd is a specialist legal publisher based in Oxford, England.
To order further copies of this book or to request a list of other
publications please write to:

Hart Publishing Ltd, Salter's Boatyard, Oxford OX1 4LB
Telephone: +44 (0)1865 245533 or Fax: +44 (0)1865 794882
e-mail: mail@hartpub.co.uk

British Library Cataloguing in Publication Data
Data Available
ISBN 1 901362–95–7 (cloth)

Typeset by Hope Services (Abingdon) Ltd.
Printed in Great Britain on acid-free paper
by Biddles Ltd, Guildford and Kings Lynn.

Table of contents

List of contributors

Zenon Bankowski is Professor of Legal Theory at Edinburgh University.

Anthony Bradney is a Professor at the Faculty of Law, University of Leicester.

Claire Davis is a doctoral student in Theology at Edinburgh University.

John Gardner is Reader in Legal Philosophy at King's College London, and a Fellow of All Souls College, Oxford.

Adam Gearey is a Lecturer at the Department of Law, Birkbeck College, London.

Timothy Macklem is a Lecturer at the School of Law, King's College London.

Maleiha Malik is a Lecturer at the School of Law, King's College London.

Peter Oliver is a Senior Lecturer at the School of Law, King's College London.

Sionaidh Douglas Scott is a Lecturer at the School of Law, King's College London.

Victor Tadros is a Lecturer at the Faculty of Law, Aberdeen University.

Introduction

PETER OLIVER, SIONAIDH DOUGLAS SCOTT and
VICTOR TADROS

T
HIS collection of essays arises out of a series of seminars which were held at King's College London in the autumn of 1997. These seminars explored the long-standing, intricate relationship between law and faith. Faith in this context is to be read in the broadest sense, as extending beyond religion to embrace the knowledge, beliefs, understandings and practices which are at work alongside the familiar and seemingly more reliable, trusted and relatively certain content and conventionally accepted methods of law and legal reasoning.

Notwithstanding the many and varied links between law and faith the subject has been curiously overlooked, especially as a matter of legal theory. We hope in this collection to remedy this neglect. The original seminars were both stimulating and extremely varied, and a good sample of that diversity is presented here. As the series progressed, we were able to isolate three broad themes, and these were the themes around which this collection was eventually formed.

The first theme[1] concerns the extent to which faith should be involved in legal decision-making. Ought decisions to aspire simply to right reason or ought faith-based models of decision-making to be incorporated into the legal system? If the latter, how is this best done? Ought faith to operate simply as a reason itself or ought it to help to structure the method by which legal decisions are reached?

The second, and perhaps most familiar theme,[2] stemming in part from rights discourse, is the extent to which law does, and ought to, respect the rights of those whose religious beliefs conflict with the dominant social norms and practices. Liberal democratic constitutions typically provide protection for religion and religious beliefs. Are these justified, and if so how? Can such protection as exists suffice from the perspective of the faithful, or does law's otherwise pervasive agnosticism make this impossible or illusory?

Thirdly, questions of identity and difference arise.[3] Assuming that most societies remain a mix of many faiths (religious and secular) and no faith, how should law and legal theory understand the varying and, it must be said,

---

[1] See, e.g., essays by J. Gardner, 'Law as a Leap of Faith' (at 19), Z. Bankowski and C. Davis, 'Living In and Out of the Law' (at 33) and A. Gearey, 'Faith, Love and a Christianity to Come: St Augustine and the Coming of Justice' (at 53) in this collection.

[2] See, e.g., essays by T. Macklem, 'Reason and Religion' (at 69) and A. Bradney, 'Faced by Faith' (at 39) in this collection.

[3] See, e.g., essays by V. Tadros, 'A Comfortable Inauthenticity: Post-Theological Law' (at 107) and M. Malik, 'Faith and the State of Jurisprudence' (at 129) in this collection.

conflicting claims for recognition. Many different approaches are possible. Should we encourage conformity in the hope of reducing friction, or should we preserve and promote difference, seeking to understand others, whether groups or individuals, without removing that which makes them distinct? More radically and controversially, should we be more sceptical of individual and group claims to authenticity and see them rather as strategies in an ongoing power game? Faith after all, like reason and law, has never been far from politics and intrigue, especially in its institutional representation.

The role of this introduction is therefore to explore these themes and to attempt to show the relationship between them. In the first part of the introduction we attempt to expose questions about law, faith and reason which current legal theoretical writing often fails to consider. The second part of the introduction relates more closely to the questions and approaches set out by the contributors to this book. Here again, we try to trace the series of main themes which connect the different essays, and we also deliberately, but we hope not unfairly, try to tease out some of the more controversial or contestable arguments that their authors have proposed.

Given the inevitable diversity of approaches to law, legal theory and legal reasoning, each reader, like each of the editors and contributors, will no doubt react very differently to the topic and to these essays. Some will reinforce their belief that law's usual professed agnosticism and insistence on clear, reasoned, open justification are vital qualities which should not be lightly adjusted, much less abandoned. Other readers, perhaps not professing (or, perhaps just as likely, rejecting) a formal religion, may nonetheless recognise in the affirmation of faith the need to protect a space in which identity, difference and non-conformity resist being appropriated, denigrated or otherwise manipulated by the dominant discourse of law and society. Readers who hold to a religious faith will not find here arguments for imposing the teaching of one religion via law. They will, however, find in some essays an understanding of how a supposedly 'neutral' legal system imposes a distinct range of contestable values on those who are within its jurisdiction, and how this presents a challenge to those who hold to faiths which depart from the societal norm.

This last observation points to considerations which we hope will interest all readers. The essays on *Faith in Law* present an opportunity to consider whether law, despite its professions of objectivity, rationality, certainty, coherence and the like, is not also based on faith, be it secular or religious. And, if so, we may wish to consider whether faith should come within the compass of legal theory, or whether, being that about which nothing can be said, nothing should be said.

In the present era, many of us may be largely unfamiliar with the concept of faith. We attempt in the next part to explore the nature and potential interest of faith, notably by contrasting it with a more familiar concept, within and without law, that is, reason.

I

The concept of faith is difficult to define. It reflects our deepest commitments, concerns and experiences. Sometimes faith appears to refer to the transcendent and ineffable domain that is so difficult to capture in language. Consequently, decisions, beliefs and actions of the faithful can often appear unjustifiable, obscure and irrational to those who do not share this faith. It may even be that the faithful can *never* explain their actions and beliefs to others. Hence Norman Malcolm argues that:[4]

> "You may invite someone to see the world as a heartless mechanism or, on the contrary, as throbbing with love. Once a person has the beginnings of such a vision you may strengthen it for him by means of luminous examples. But unless he already shares that vision in some degree, he will not take your examples in the way you want him to take them. It may be that your conviction, passion, love, will move him in the direction of religious belief. But this would be speaking of causes, not grounds."

It is in spite of this dimension of faith that this collection of essays is presented. In exploring the relationship between faith and law we hope to show that, despite this ineffable quality, or perhaps even because of it, faith may still have an important role to play in the theory and practices of the law.

In the first part of the introduction we hope to clarify some of the different aspects of the concept of faith by showing the ways in which it can be related to the familiar concept of reason. The relationship between faith and reason clearly has many different aspects. For example, faith may be seen as directly opposed to reason, justifying and identifying with reason, personalising reason, operating as one reason among many, regulating, qualifying and supplementing reason, or completely structuring reason. The list is by no means exhaustive. By understanding these different aspects of the relationship between faith and reason we may be able to see more clearly the ways in which faith impacts on law. We will begin by developing two extreme positions concerning the relationship between faith and reason before moving on to consider possible intermediate positions.

At one extreme, then, the concept of faith may be seen as radically opposed to reason. To act or to believe out of faith in this conception is to act or to believe *without* reason or *for* no reason. As Timothy Macklem puts it in this collection:[5]

> "When we say that we believe in something as a matter of faith, or to put it the other way round, when we say that we have faith in certain beliefs, we express a commitment to that which cannot be established by reason, or to that which can be established by reason but not for that reason."

---

[4] N Malcolm, *Thought and Knowledge* (Ithaca, Cornell University Press, 1977) 216.
[5] See Macklem, *supra* n. 2 at 83 .

Plato, it seems, was in agreement with this view, at least in the *Phaedrus*. We may expect Plato, as an ultra-rationalist, to reject the idea of divine inspiration in favour of right reason. On the contrary, he thought that it was those that appear as mad to the rationalist who have truly captured the essence of the divine: "madness is a nobler thing than sober sense . . .; madness comes from God whereas sober sense is merely human."[6] The virtue of faith, he thought, was that it reflected a truth unavailable to reason and which those who are too tied to reason cannot possibly comprehend. It is possibly for this reason that faith cannot be explained to those without faith. For those without faith demand reasons where the faithful can give none that will satisfy. Perhaps this stark opposition between faith and reason provides faith with both its obscurity and its power.

Reflecting this first extreme conception, faith is sometimes used to describe acts or beliefs which are without or beyond reason. Hence the phrase "act of faith" is used to describe acts where the agent has little or no conventional reason to anticipate success and which are not done *for* the reason that one calculated that one will succeed. An individual who crosses himself before jumping into a raging fire does so as an act of faith, it may be said, if he has no reason to anticipate that he will be saved from the flames. It is an act of faith precisely *because* he does not believe that he will be saved, at least *in the same way* as he believes in ignition, combustion and the effects of heat. The difference is that one may ask for the agent's reasons for believing the latter whereas it would be inappropriate to ask for equivalent reasons for the agent's faith. Faith is its own source of explanation and justification and provides its own structure to action and belief. Furthermore, for the faithful, it may be that one not only *can* act out of faith but that one *must*, even where faith requires that which our conventional reason would reject.

At the other extreme, it is possible to conceive of faith as having no active, practical or ongoing role to play in deciding what to believe or how to act. It may be that the only extent to which we are entitled to show respect for faith is to show respect for right reason, thus exhausting faith's role in decision-making. For, it may be said, reason is itself that which is given to us by God. This position was defended by Immanuel Kant. Kant, apparently here in accordance with Aristotle's maxim that the life of reasoning is the most divine life,[7] regarded reason and faith as entirely reconcilable. This was so, he thought, by virtue of the fact that our reason was given to us by God. In fact, our knowledge that God is the highest form of good, according to Kant, can only be established to the extent that the commands of God are in accordance with the commands

    [6] Plato *Phaedrus* (London, Penguin, 1973) 47.
    [7] *Nicomachean Ethics* (trans. T. Irwin; Indianapolis, Hackett, 1985) book *x*. In general, Kant was critical of Aristotle's *eudaemonism*. He thought that Aristotle was subordinating reason to pleasure. On this question see T. H. Irwin "Kant's Criticism of Eudaemonism" in S. Engstrom and J. Whiting, *Aristotle, Kant, and the Stoics* (Cambridge, Cambridge University Press, 1996).

of right reason.[8] Consequently, one's duty to lead a religious life is only a duty insofar as it is in accordance with right reason:[9]

> "Again, we have a duty *with regard to* what lies entirely beyond the limits of our experience but whose possibility is met with in our ideas, for example, the idea of God; it is called the *duty of religion*, the duty 'of recognising all our duties as (*instar*) divine commands.' But this is not consciousness of a duty *to God*. For this idea proceeds entirely from our own reason and we ourselves make it. . . . We do not have before us . . . a given being to whom we would be under obligation; for in that case its reality would first have to be shown (disclosed) through experience. Rather, it is a duty of a human being to himself to apply this idea, which presents itself unavoidably to reason, to the moral law in him, where it is of the greatest moral fruitfulness. In this (practical) sense it can therefore be said that to have religion is a duty of the human being to himself."

Hence, for Kant, it is reason and reason alone that ought to guide us. To act solely by virtue of right reason is not to reject faith. In the Kantian scheme at least, it is the only way in which one can truly be faithful.

At one extreme, then, we have a conception of faith that would require us to act in a way that is radically opposed to that dictated by reason. In adopting this conception of faith we may be required to act out of faith and faith alone, even where our faith tells us to do that which is radically opposed to the guidance of right reason. At the other extreme we have a conception that gives faith no role to play in deciding what to believe or how to act: reason is sufficient.[10]

However, we may still accept the force of the requirements of faith even if we take neither of these extreme positions. It may be possible to identify a role for faith within the processes of deciding how to act or what to believe that neither encourages us to embrace the irrational nor relegates faith to reason.

First, we may find a role for faith in determining when we ought to act according to the reasons that *we* respect and when we ought to substitute the reasons that come from another source. We can see this version of faith if we consider what we do when we "put faith in another". To put faith in another is to forego acting or reasoning entirely for oneself by leaving a task in the hands of another. For example, I may acknowledge that one of my colleagues is a better judge of character than I am. After seeing all of the candidates for a particular job, through my own process of reasoning I may be inclined to the view that A is the best. One of my colleagues, whose ability to judge character I trust more than my own, may think that B is the best. I may now be inclined to argue for B even though, through my own reasoning, I think that A is the best. In this case, I have faith in my colleague's judgement more than in my own. But in this case, my

---

[8] *Grounding for the Metaphysics of Morals* (3rd edn, trans. J. Ellington; Indianapolis, Hackett, 1993) 21.

[9] *The Metaphysics of Morals* (trans. M. Gregor; Cambridge, Cambridge University Press, 1996) 193.

[10] It should be noted that this description does not entirely capture Kant's position. Kant thought that the *idea* of God was essential for us to treat the universe as purposive.

putting faith in another may be *for a reason*. The phrase "putting faith in another" expresses the concept of having a reason (one's belief in the other's wisdom) to ignore one's other reasons (one's judgement concerning which candidate is best).

It may be thought that putting one's faith in another is to move towards irrationality. But this is not necessarily the case. One may have perfectly good reasons for relying on the reasons of another rather than relying on one's own reasons. For example, my colleague may have made judgements which, in the short term, I consistently disagreed with but which, in the long term, I have come to adopt. This may make it reasonable for me to trust her judgement over mine.

This idea of having faith in another is not necessarily an all or nothing affair. At the extreme, it may be that one forgoes reasoning for oneself entirely. In such a case, faith in another results in absolute obedience. However, one's faith in another may also affect one's reasoning without foregoing reasoning for oneself. For example, suppose that my friend thinks X to be a reason where I do not think that X is a reason for action. Having faith in my friend, I may adopt X as a reason for action even where I do not see why I ought to regard this as a reason. Furthermore, if my friend thinks that X is of great importance whereas I think that X is only of minor importance I may begin to attach greater importance to X even where I do not understand the reasons for doing so. In each case, I still reason for myself. But my reasoning process is affected by my faith in my friend.

A second, less extreme conception of the relationship between faith and reason, and one which also indicates how faith may become important in one's reasoning process, is to treat *faith itself* as a reason for which one ought to act. The fact that one is faithful may be considered a virtue in itself. Consequently to regard one's faith as a reason to pursue a particular course of action is to respect this virtue. To act in accordance with one's faith may not be justified merely because one has good reasons to be faithful. It may be justified because one has good reason to respect one's faith as an important element of the good life. Hence, the guidelines that are provided by one's faith gain their force not merely to the extent that one's faith is justified by right reason but also to the extent that it is a virtue to be faithful.[11] And to act against the guidelines that are provided by one's faith impacts not merely upon the rightness of one's decision but also upon the other dimensions of one's faith. To act against a principle that is derived from one's faith is to reject, in that instance at least, not only the reasons that may justify that principle but also to reject one's faith *per se*.[12]

However, the role of faith need not be restricted to what counts as a reason and to what weight to give to various reasons. Faith may also have an effect on the *style* of reasoning that one adopts and the *structure* within which reason

[11] Gardner, *supra* n. 1, argues along these lines.
[12] This problem is particularly acute in the case of obdurate religious believers. See Bradney, *supra* n. 2 for further discussion.

finds its place. Practical reasoning involves discovering which reasons one ought to adopt, identifying what weight to give to those reasons and determining which actions best reflect the weight of those reasons. Hence practical reason is unlike mathematical reasoning, for example. Trying to identify reasons and balance them is not merely a question of logic; it is a question of wisdom, care, sensitivity and courage. Furthermore, adopting the right reasons involves having due respect and regard for the values of others. Whether or not there are right answers to hard cases, either in law or in morals, it is difficult to resist the claim that practical reasoning lacks both the clarity and the rigidity of mathematical reasoning. Because there is a limit to the extent to which practical reasoning can achieve clarity, a wise judge cannot rely merely on her powers of logic. She must also adopt the care, sensitivity, courage and humility that are appropriate to an uncertain but powerful science. These concerns, it may be argued, are brought to bear most forcefully through faith. For care, sensitivity, courage and humility are central to many accounts of a faithful life.[13]

Of course, with this style of reasoning comes an ambiguity that may seem unpalatable in a social practice such as legal decision-making. At least since the nineteenth century, certainty has been a central tenet of modern law. Few would challenge the principle that certainty is a virtue of law. But insofar as certainty is unattainable, at least without a cost to justice, we ought perhaps to develop a style of legal decision-making that is sufficiently sensitive to prevent injustice through inflexibility. As we have noted, faith, whether that term is understood in its religious or secular sense, is the paradigmatic way in which the uncertain and ineffable aspects of our lives become a part of our concerns. Consequently, faith may have a role to play in just decision-making.

Finally, faith may play a role in determining the structure of one's life. Faith may play a role not merely in determining *how* to reason but also in determining *when* one ought to use one's reason. Reasoning itself may only find its appropriate place when it is adopted as a part of a coherent life. For Kant, as we have seen, it is reason and reason alone that ought to provide the guiding principle in one's life: if faith is to play a role in decision making, it is only insofar as faith is in accordance with right reason. However, one may also argue that it is reason that requires a proper place or a guiding principle. Hence, for Augustine, Anselm and Aquinas, one ought always to begin with faith. It is only within the framework of faith that reason or philosophy finds its place. As Frederick Copleston writes of Aquinas, to take but one possible example of this type of argument:[14]

> "[R]eason can indeed apprehend basic ethical principles. Philosophical ethics, however, if taken completely by itself, knows nothing of man's supernatural end and of the life in Christ by which it is to be attained. Although therefore reason is valid in itself, in that it demonstrates the rational bases of the moral life, it is limited in a variety of ways and needs to be subsumed in Christian ethics."

---

[13] This theme is developed, e.g., by Bankowski and Davis, *supra* n. 2.
[14] F C Copleston *A History of Medieval Philosophy* (London, Methuen, 1972) 183.

The system of faith could include reason within its structure. But reason could not provide the structure. That was left to faith and faith alone.

From this discussion we can see a dilemma emerging: even if one is faithful, ought one's faith to be adopted within a life of reason or ought one's practical reasoning to find its place within a life of faith. This dilemma between faith and reason provided the foundation to Kierkegaard's *Fear and Trembling*: ought we to be knights of faith and adopt the life of the faithful or ought we to adopt right reason as the guiding principle of our lives? To accept the former it not necessarily to reject reason but to relegate reason to its place. To accept the latter is not necessarily to reject faith but to relegate faith to its place. This is a dilemma which concerns those propositions which we are to consider as axiomatic in deciding how we ought to live. Decisions, argument and reason can only take place on the back of certain axioms. The axioms that we use decide which system, discourse or language-game we are operating in. But the axioms of the system themselves cannot be grounded.[15] Given that one cannot ground the axioms with which one operates, how is one to decide which kind of life to adopt? It is with this dilemma in mind that these essays are introduced.

II

Kierkegaard's discussion of the dilemma between faith and moral reasoning is the starting point for John Gardner's essay. However, Gardner's construction of the dilemma is somewhat different from the dilemma with which we concluded the first section. In our discussion, the fundamental dilemma was between whether one ought to adopt a life of faith or a life of reason; whether it is reason that ought to guide one's life and define the role for one's faith or whether one ought to adopt a life of faith within which one may find a place for reason. For Gardner, on the other hand, the dilemma between faith and the moral law is a dilemma between competing reasons. This is most clearly illustrated by the biblical story of Abraham and Isaac, a recurring theme in this collection. In our construction, Abraham's conflict is a conflict between whether to follow his faith or whether to follow reason. For Gardner, on the other hand, the dilemma is one between *different reasons*: there are reasons to act which are provided by one's ordinary moral reasoning and reasons to act that are provided by the religious point of view. The dilemma, for Gardner an ordinary moral dilemma, concerns *which* of these reasons ought to be given priority.

Gardner's point is that *within* a system of moral reasoning, faith can make a constitutive difference to the way in which one ought to act. For faith itself has

[15] See, e.g., Malcolm, *supra* n. 4, ch 9. In a legal setting, see N. MacCormick, *Legal Reasoning and Legal Theory* (2nd edn, Oxford, Clarendon Press, 1994) ch.10 and N. Luhmann 'Legal Argumentation: An Analysis of its Form' (1995) 58 *Modern Law Review* 285. See also M. Foucault, *The Archaeology of Knowledge* (Routledge, London, 1972) and L. Wittgenstein, *Philosophical Investigations* (2nd edn, trans. G.E.M. Anscombe; Oxford, Blackwell, 1976) 5 *et seq.*

value within the scheme of morality. One's reasons for becoming faithful may be "modest", but once one is faithful, one has a strong reason to act in accordance with the dictates of one's faith. As being faithful may be regarded as having moral value in itself, at least in some circumstances it may be *morally* correct to act in accordance with one's faith even where one's faith commands one to do what, aside from one's faith, would be morally wrong. Consequently, he shows that one need not present the dilemma of Abraham and Isaac as a dilemma between the "realm of faith" and the "realm of reason"; rather one can present it as a dilemma *within the realm of reason*. And within this realm the commands of God need not be considered redundant. For what one has reason to do *aside from one's faith* is not the same as what one has reason to do *given one's faith*.

For Gardner, there is a parallel between the role that faith may have in practical reasoning and the role that the *Grundnorm* may play in legal reasoning. Just as the fact that one is faithful may make a difference concerning what it is morally right to do, the fact that one is a judge, a member of the legal system, and consequently an adherent to the *Grundnorm*, may make a difference as to the decision one ought to reach legally:[16]

> "Just as those who have faith in God thereby automatically acquire new moral reasons irrespective of whether their original reason for having faith in God was a moral reason, so those who ally themselves with the *Grundnorm* automatically acquire new moral reasons irrespective of whether their original reason for allying themselves with the *Grundnorm* was a moral reason."

Allying oneself with the *Grundnorm*, for Gardner, does not mean abandoning the requirements of practical reasoning. It means giving special weight to the reasons that the law dictates, whether or not they are reasons that one would accept as valid aside from one's allegiance. The decision that one ought to reach *given* one's allegiance to the *Grundnorm* may be different from the decision that one ought to reach aside from that allegiance. That is not to say that those that ally themselves with the *Grundnorm* ought always to follow the dictates of the law. Just as Abraham, in Gardner's terms, was in an ordinary moral dilemma, so the judge may be in a dilemma where ordinary morality conflicts with the requirements of the legal system. Such dilemmas require resolution through the balancing of reasons. They cannot be dismissed in favour of *blind* faith in the law.

For the theological philosophers, Gardner's resolution of the dilemma between faith and moral reasons would be problematic. Whilst Gardner has found a role for faith within practical reason, he has clearly prioritised practical reason over faith. Faith, whilst it may make a constitutive difference to one's decisions, does not play *the* constitutive role in guiding one's life. One only ought to act in accordance with faith, in Gardner's reading, to the extent that it is in accordance with right reason to do so. But, some of the faithful may object,

---

[16] Gardner, *supra* n. 1, 27.

this is already to fail in one's faith. For it is faith, they may argue, that ought to be the guiding principle in one's life and it is only through faith that one can find the correct role for practical reasoning. Hence in some forms of monasticism it is only once one has learned to be obedient and faithful that one can learn the correct role for independent reasoning in deciding what to believe and how to act.[17] We may introduce Kierkegaard's dilemma at a higher order: the knights of faith are those that determine the role of reason within a faithful life, and they can be contrasted with Gardner's moralist who determines the role that faith can play within practical reason. This second order dilemma may be important as far as judging goes: ought we, in allying ourselves with the *Grundnorm*, to accept the dictates of the law, which defines the limited role for independent reasoning (say in the interpretation of the meaning of laws) or ought we to act primarily out of moral reasoning, within which we may find a special place for *legal reasons*. Which of these is the correct way to see faith in law?

For Zenon Bankowski and Claire Davis neither solution would seem to be correct as they perceive the relationship as far more fluid and overlapping. They point out that the tension between the ineffable spirit of faith and the clear articulation of reasoned law is already present in both the Judaic and Christian traditions. The tension between law and love, they suggest, is often presented as a tension between Judaism and Christianity, but it is in fact a tension within each faith. The aim, for Bankowski and Davis, is to show that this tension is not a problem to be resolved; it is both inevitable and necessary. "One should not be forced to choose between a nomian and an anti-nomian way of life . . . [as] they are dependent on each other."[18] Drawing on the work of Gillian Rose, they try to show that the apparent polar opposites of law and love (which may be supplanted by the terms "reason" and "faith" that we have used here) are in fact more intimately connected than the tradition may have suggested. It is not that law and love collapse into each other, but rather that they inform each other. Love's recognition of the particular and the contingent introduces uncertainty into the calculable world of law, and law introduces a rule into the ineffable domain of love. To collapse ethics into the world of law or into the "nihilism of love" is to retreat from the essential place in which just decisions must be reached. It is to abrogate responsibility either by making decisions in machine-like fashion or by denying the necessity of being able to justify one's decision altogether.

Whilst Adam Gearey's argument is quite different in its sources, style and content, there are parallels with the approach of Bankowski and Davis. Like the latter authors, Gearey seeks to provide a version of legal decision-making that would incorporate faith and make the legal decision "more than a balancing of power and an algebra of property rights."[19] Furthermore, like these authors,

---

[17] Cf. M Foucault "Technologies of the Self" in *Ethics: The Essential Works 1* (London, Penguin, 1997).

[18] Bankowski and Davis, *supra* n. 1, 34.

[19] Gearey, *supra* n. 1, 55.

though in a different way, Gearey asserts that decisions in reason are thought to be founded in a relationship with undecidability. For Gearey, this is the meaning of a term popularised by Jacques Derrida: "aporia": "Thinking the aporia might show that reason itself is founded on what it would like to expel; the undisciplined, shocking and radical interpellation of alterity.'[20] Consequently, these authors think that the dilemma facing Abraham is irresolvable, and, *contra* Gardner, not because there are competing reasons the merits of which are difficult to evaluate. For Bankowski, Davis and Gearey the difficulty comes in the dilemma between the demands of reason and the demands of the ineffable realm of faith and love which exists at the limits of reason.

It may be said that the difficulty with these last-mentioned approaches is that the extent to which a decision-maker relies on faith is also the extent to which his decision is incapable of explicit or satisfactory justification. Hence the extent that a judge has relied on faith is also the extent to which it cannot be *demonstrated* whether or not the decision was a just one. To this extent the decision can appear arbitrary, notably to those who do not share the judge's understanding of that which faith or love require. Hence Bankowski and Davis suggest that "we have to take responsibility, without the ethical to guide us. We have to create and recreate it with that mysterious act which appears arbitrary and for which we need both faith and courage."[21] And Gearey argues that "justice will always be in excess of any human or positive manifestation."[22] One can only act. One cannot justify the action through reasons for the act is singular and unrepeatable.

But this suggests a reason for which it may be inappropriate to replace or even to supplement the demands of reason with the demands of faith for the purposes of the law. After all, legal subjects demand not merely a just decision but one that can be explained to them in terms which they can relate to and understand.[23] A significant part of the force and the justice of the law would be lost if decisions could not adequately be explained to those before the law. The ability to give adequate reasons is an important dimension of a legal decision. As the old adage goes, it is important both that justice is done and that justice is seen to be done.

It is this singular and personal nature of faith that provides a distinction between Abraham and the judge in the modern legal system. Abraham is both judge and defendant. The only consideration for Abraham in acting is that he acts *as he ought*. There may be a conflict between acting out of reason and acting out of faith. Both of these "points of view" may inform what he *ought* to do. However, the judge needs to do more than act *rightly*, to decide correctly, justly

---

[20] *Ibid.*, 57.

[21] Bankowski and Davis, *supra* n. 1, 44.

[22] Gearey, *supra* n. 1, 65.

[23] For example, an important part of the punishment of offenders is communication to her about the nature of her wrongdoing. See, for example, R. A. Duff, *Trials and Punishments* (Cambridge, Cambridge University Press, 1986).

or wisely. He needs to do this for other members of the community, not just for himself. The system of law is as much about the appearance of impartiality as it is about decision. Consequently, there is a reason not to treat one's faith as fundamental to legal decisions. The enduring question is whether this always (or ever) leaves sufficient material for the judge to arrive at such decisions.

Hence, there may be a dilemma between the activity of *doing* justice and the requirement that one's decisions are in need of explanation. Whereas reasons at least make an appeal to that which is objectively acceptable, the demands of faith are often singular and highly personal, whatever their ultimate alleged grounding. It may be true that faith can be brought more openly into the decision-making process but, unless the judge is asked to prefer the tacit faith of the majority, her judgment is likely to appear highly partial. It may be no comfort at all for the defendant to be told that this is an inevitable part of the human process of judging.

Does this mean that we must revert to law as a grand calculating machine in which the responsibility of the judge is entirely abrogated to the rules of the law? But questions of this sort arguably misunderstand the nature of practical reasoning that is at work in the law. Putting considerations of faith aside for the moment, it may be said that the point of a legal decision is not just to discover the truth of a situation but to make the best decision on the balance of reasons. The process of balancing is not one whose outcome is determinable. The reasons that the judge refers to must be valid reasons for the purposes of the law. But the weight that is given to them, their applicability and their appropriateness in a particular case cannot be decided in advance. Whether or not this entails that legal decision making ought to involve an expression of faith depends upon which conception of faith one adopts. If faith is taken as the extreme opposite of reason, there are clear reasons to be sceptical about the role of faith in legal decision making. After all, in this sense at least, relying on faith would also be to deny one the ability to explain adequately to those who do not share this faith. However, if one adopts a conception of faith as a way of altering the *style* of practical reasoning, one need not accept these concerns. For faith, in this conception, need not deny one the power of explanation.

The question of whether one's faith can be given special protection from the principles of secular law is considered in this collection by Timothy Macklem. This is the question of the extent to which we should protect religious freedom in law. The root of Macklem's argument concerns the question of the nature of value. Macklem believes that those who defend freedom of religion have done so inadequately in that they have tended to adopt an inadequate account of the nature of value. As Macklem demonstrates, one's understanding of the value of religion has a practical effect not just on whether freedom of religion is to be protected but, more importantly, on the extent and nature of this protection. In particular it affects which set of beliefs and activities that may want to call themselves religions will receive the special protection adopted under the label of freedom of religion.

Macklem identifies a strategy to ground his account of freedom of religion in an argument from morality rather than an argument from semantics. He describes the latter argument as follows. There is a core to the way in which we use the concept of religion in ordinary language. Whether or not a particular set of beliefs and practices can call itself a religion for the purposes of the law would be determined according to whether or not those beliefs and practices fall within our ordinary use of the concept "religion". However, as Macklem notes, this provides "a semantic response to what is apparently a moral question. We are concerned here, not to know how the term religion *is* used . . . but to know how the term religion *should* be used."[24] Consequently, Macklem argues, what these accounts lack is a connection between the fundamental reasons to protect freedom of religion and the question of whether or not a particular set of beliefs and practices deserves that protection.

We may immediately note a risk in Macklem's argument. The problem may be that the reason to protect religions also amounts to a reason to protect a wholly different set of ways of life. And these may also receive special protection from the law. Consequently, tying the limitation on freedom of religion to the reasons for which religion ought to be protected may also entail losing any distinctiveness that religion has within the law. And this loss of the *distinction* between practices which one would call religious and other practices which deserve protection may amount to a loss of value as far as the faithful are concerned: in particular the preservation of their identity within the legal system. Furthermore, this may result in a further alienation of the secular law from religion that is described by Anthony Bradney in this volume. The gains that one achieves at the level of plurality may also amount to losses at the level of the distinctive identity that the law seeks to protect.

Macklem is quite happy to wear his plurality on his sleeve. He suggests that traditional accounts of freedom of religion, by focussing on the core semantic use of the concept of religion result in an overly restrictive account of the rights to be protected. Hence he argues that "conventional accounts of freedom of religion exhibit an overly restrictive view of the kinds of belief that may underpin or at least nourish the pursuit of a successful human life."[25] However, this does not mean that he accepts any form of relativism. He rejects the claim that an account of freedom of religion can only be acceptable on the grounds that it will protect *whatever* is the "ultimate concern"[26] of any individual. This, he thinks, can be rebutted: "the bare fact that a belief or practice is of ultimate concern to someone is no reason for any other person to regard that belief or practice as valuable, and, more pertinently, no reason for any other person to respect it."[27] Hence to his plurality he adds objectivity.

---

[24] Macklem, *supra* n. 2, 70.

[25] *Ibid.*, 76.

[26] Macklem draws this psychological account of religion from the writings of William James. See Macklem, *ibid.*, 76–77.

[27] *Ibid.*, 79–80.

Macklem bases his alternative account of religious freedom directly on the concept of faith. Faith, Macklem suggests, can have us believe and act in ways for which there are insufficient reasons to act. Sometimes these beliefs or acts are essential to our "well-being", the latter being a crucial (and potentially problematic) concept for Macklem. Consequently, there is an extent to which faith is essential to well-being: "faith is valuable where the inability to make the commitments that faith makes possible would have a negative impact on well-being, both because the commitments in question are potentially valuable and because failure to make them would be harmful."[28] Hence the argument runs as follows: religious freedom is important insofar as it is reliant on faith because insofar as it is reliant on faith it *may* provide an essential condition of our well-being. And it is only to this extent that religious freedom ought to be protected.

Nevertheless, we may suspect that in this case, the label "religious freedom" means *nothing more* than the protection of well-being in general. For, we may think, the reason to protect faith is just the reason to protect any mode of life that concerns the agent's well-being in a fundamental way. Macklem provides no reason to respect religion in particular over any other form of well-being. But surely an argument for *religious* freedom, as opposed to freedom *in general*, is dependent on some particular value in protecting the particular over the general. And this can only be so to the extent that we accept that religion provides a distinctive mode of life over and above the general category of well-being. This, it seems to us, stands and falls on the *social* role of religion rather than its contribution to individual well-being. For surely this is an important way in which the faithful mark their faith out from other ways of achieving well-being.

Whether or not Macklem is right, the feasibility of adequately determining whether or not a particular set of beliefs ought to be protected under the concept of religious freedom, or indeed any other concept, depends upon those beliefs being adequately represented to the court. It is only if the individual or group concerned has a fair opportunity to represent themselves before the court that this can happen. Furthermore, it is important that legal discussion is conducted in such a way that certain social practices are not excluded from the concept of religion simply by virtue of their difference as opposed to their ethical inferiority.

This problem is extremely acute at a practical level as can be seen from Anthony Bradney's essay in this volume. Through three cases, Bradney shows the way in which beliefs which do not conform to the major belief systems that are recognised by English law have not adequately been understood by the courts who have made decisions concerning their validity and worth. The problem, Bradney suggests, appears to stem at least in part from a lack of sympathy and knowledge on the part of the courts. However, there is also a deeper pessimism in Bradney's work. Even improved sympathy and knowledge, Bradney thinks, cannot cure the fundamental conflict between the law and certain types

[28] *Ibid.*, 86.

of religious belief, particularly that of those he refers to as "obdurate believers". Obdurate believers are believers whose religion fundamentally structures their existence. They have "faith in the timeless and boundless significance of their religious system".[29] Conflict between obdurate believers and the law is inevitable. For, Bradney argues, such believers "can never win on their own terms and, wanting to live their lives only on their own terms, will always be disappointed in the law".[30]

We may question whether all aspects of Bradney's pessimism regarding legal treatment of religion are justified. Is it necessary to eliminate the fundamental conflict between law and certain types of religious belief in order to improve this treatment? Is it essential for "obdurate believers" to win on their own terms, or would it be sufficient that they win for different reasons — judicial self-restraint, for example? Some of the preceding discussion in this introduction has suggested that even if the legal system does not share the faith of each of the individuals and groups (religious and secular) within that system, legal practitioners can be made more aware of the role that faith may be playing in their own decision-making. This awareness may not allow "obdurate believers" to win regularly, much less on their own terms, nor would such believers expect that. Conflict with the values of mainstream society is probably a fundamental aspect of their day-to-day existence. However, it could have the effect of moderating law and lawyers' occasional inflexibility when it comes to dealing with unfamiliar attitudes and beliefs, and this may in turn lead to a greater number of decisions in favour of those on the fringe of society.

Bradney himself recognises that the facility for the representation of religious minorities in the law could be improved. However, he does not sustain an account of how this may best be done. Some of the space created by Bradney's recognition of the problem of the failure of the legal system to represent all of its subjects is covered by the analyses of Maleiha Malik and Victor Tadros. Both writers consider the extent to which adequate representation of the beliefs and identity of legal subjects is possible in a modern system of law. The role of faith in their arguments is quite different, however.

Malik's argument is focussed on the problem of providing those who value faith with adequate representation within the legal system. In order to pass judgement, the law must find a way of understanding and representing the interests, identity, belief structure and practices of those before the law. As Anthony Bradney's essay reveals, the understanding that legal practitioners have of a particular faith inevitably affects their ability to represent individuals and groups in the legal system.

As far as representing a religion is concerned, this consists in providing an adequate way of representing a *social* practice. However, representing a social practice is fraught with difficulties. Unsympathetic description of a social practice may also alter that practice: "reflecting back to an individual a distorted or

---

[29] Bradney, *supra* n. 1, 91.
[30] *Ibid.*, 105.

demeaning image of themselves will influence not only the perception of out-siders, it also impacts on the self-understanding of 'insiders' ".[31] To this extent, a partial or false representation of the faith of a legal subject may *directly* harm those for whom faith is vitally important. The harm caused is not solely in the unjust decision that may result from such misrepresentation.

The question is, then, the degree to which it is possible accurately to represent particular social practices within law. As Tadros suggests, this problem is not related simply to representing faith. The general question of how best to create the social conditions within which individuals before the law receive adequate representation of their beliefs, practices and selves is one that has been at the margins of traditional legal theory. For Malik there is a serious problem to be confronted here concerning the adequacy of ordinary legal analysis. Neutrality and certainty, Malik contends, are two cornerstones of legal analysis. These principles are intended to allow the legal practitioners to occupy a position in which their own perspective on the question of faith does not corrupt the theo-rists understanding of those of a different faith: "the theorist is encouraged to break free of his own perspective and to adopt a neutral point of view as a pre-requisite to study; thereby using a method for the study of human conduct which avoids the dangers of uncertainty, evaluation and subjective interpreta-tion."[32]

However, Malik argues, this strategy must fail. For it is dependent upon ren-dering human conduct amenable to this form of analysis. This can only be done through a process of abstraction whereby the "internal" aspect of faith drops out of the picture. The external conduct of the believer is represented. However, the internal set of motivations behind that practice and which may be essential for its legitimation are inadequately represented. Furthermore, even where there is an attempt to represent the beliefs of the agent, the objective neutrality pre-sents these beliefs in the realm of fact rather than meaning.

For Malik, this provides a special problem when the law is confronted by the faithful. For the conduct of the faithful to be at all intelligible, Malik suggests, it is essential to attempt to adopt an internal point of view. It is insufficient to treat a belief as having a causal relationship to an action, which is the way in which alternative faiths tend to be represented in modern law. One must see belief as being a reason or explanation for an action. Furthermore, as the intel-ligibility of one belief is dependent upon a whole system of beliefs, so the intel-ligibility of an action is dependent on that system of beliefs. Hence an adequate appreciation of what makes the action intelligible, will not be gleaned unless a point of view internal to the system of beliefs of the faithful is adopted.

Before moving from representation to understanding, and thereby consider-ing Malik's hermeneutic solution to this problem, it is worth taking a detour into Tadros's essay. Like Malik, Tadros is concerned with the problem of ade-quate representation. And like Malik, he suggests that traditional methods have

[31] Malik, *supra* n. 3, 138.
[32] *Ibid.*, 138–9.

shown themselves to be inadequate. Tadros is not primarily concerned with the representation of the faithful but representation of legal subjects in general. For him, modern practices of law are characterised by their movement away from the attempt to represent subjects in an authentic manner through confession. Confession, he suggests, was a tool by which the authentic subject was supposed to be made into the subject of analysis. It created a text which various interpretative practices could work upon. Hence confession was considered as outside the boundaries of strategy.

Modern law, on the other hand, has been characterised by a recognition that confession itself is strategic, that the ways in which the subject represents itself are as much imbedded within the operations of power as any other element of discourse. Consequently, what is represented by confession is not an authentic subject but a strategic subject. The creation of the self, Tadros argues, is manipulated for political purposes.

Again, like Malik, Tadros rejects traditional solutions to this problem. He attacks the work of Drucilla Cornell in particular. Cornell reconstructs an argument from liberalism to solve the problem. The liberalism of Mill suggests that each individual ought to be permitted to pursue his or her own version of the good. Consequently, liberal political theory is concerned with creating and protecting the space within which one's life-projects can be pursued. Similarly, for Cornell, the politics of identity ought to be concerned with creating and protecting the space within which the subject can represent himself or herself in whatever way he or she sees fit. Tadros, on the other hand, argues that it is impossible to create such a space which is free from the operations of power. Consequently, the creation of the self will not primarily be an ethical or aesthetic act but a political one.

It is at this stage that we may find a disagreement between Malik and Tadros. Tadros argues that the inevitable relationship between the representation of oneself by oneself and one's strategic ambitions prevents the possibility of the just representation. The fact that representation cannot be authentic is present to the law and is utilised by the law for its own ends. The legal system has become aware that its version of reality is partial and can never be better than partial. The representation of this idea has become important for the autopoiesis of the legal system.[33] This condition of modern law, Tadros suggests, cannot be overcome. This is because solutions in ethical theory "do not anticipate the way in which freedom can be utilised by the legal system within the 'rights' discourse to attain ends that are directed against those anticipated by the rights-strategists."[34]

Malik, on the other hand, thinks that the inadequacy of liberal theory as far as the question of representation is concerned, can be at least partially overcome by adopting hermeneutic techniques of understanding. This perspective, Malik

---

[33] On autopoiesis see, e.g., G. Teubner, *Law as an Autopoietic System* (Oxford, Blackwell, 1993).
[34] Tadros, *supra* n. 3, 126.

argues, allows different parties within the legal system to adopt the perspective of each other through their own perspective, thereby making the practices of each party intelligible to the other. "Rather than merely noticing that the [faith-based] action is different and alien, the theorist can attempt to comprehend the meaning of the action from the perspective of the subject. It is only from this perspective—from trying to grasp the significance of the external conduct for the agent—that the action can be made more intelligible."[35] Whether it is Tadros or Malik who is correct depends upon the extent to which hermeneutic practices must be regarded as inherently strategic. If hermeneutics can operate without the inappropriate corruption of strategy we may agree with Malik. Otherwise Tadros's scepticism would prevail. This is a question which must be addressed by legal practitioners—judges, legislators and lawyers—as well as legal theorists.

This collection examines a number of different aspects concerning the relationship between faith and law. The ambiguous question of faith may be seen as anathema to the lawyer who desires certainty. What some of these writers show is that certainty may also entail a departure from justice. They show that the rigours of legal argument ought not to obscure the difficulties in understanding others and administering a justice which will be acceptable to individuals and groups within the community who have very different structures of belief and action. The role of legal theory in mapping out the relationship between faith and law in the present era has only just begun. Some of the questions that this collection has considered are relatively new. We sincerely hope that this will be a starting point for further theoretical work to be done in the field.

---

[35] Malik, *supra* n. 3, 145.

1

Law as a Leap of Faith

JOHN GARDNER*

I

"*Euthyphro*: I would say that what all the gods love is holy . . .

Socrates: The point which I want to resolve first is whether the holy is beloved of the gods because it is holy, or holy because it is beloved of the gods."[1]

SOCRATES' challenge is not merely diverting sophistry. It seriously threatens the fabric of theism. The threat becomes particularly clear if we translate the underlying puzzle into the Judaeo-Christian idiom of a single all-powerful and all-knowing God.[2] On the one hand, we are told that whatever this God commands is the right thing to do by virtue of God's commanding it. This is an aspect of God's omnipotence. On the other hand, we are reassured that whatever this God commands is commanded because it is the right thing to do. That is an aspect of God's omniscience. But these propositions about God and His commands surely cannot both be true at once. Either this God makes a constitutive[3] difference to what we should do or He does not. So which is it to be?

* This essay was prepared especially for the King's College London Legal Theory Seminar 1997, and, liking its pace and structure, I have left the text largely as I presented it then. However a variety of small changes and extra footnotes proved necessary to deal with objections and queries raised on that occasion and at a later meeting of the University of London Political Philosophy Discussion Group. Many thanks to everyone who grappled with the piece, and especially to Peter Oliver and Tim Macklem who gave me generous written comments to the quality of which I have not done justice in my revisions. For many years of insightful instruction on Kelsen's work, and countless words of wisdom on many other philosophical topics represented here, I owe a special debt of gratitude to my great friend Tony Honoré.

[1] Plato, "Euthyphro" in Benjamin Jowett's edition of the *Dialogues* (Oxford, Clarendon Press, 1871), ii, 84.

[2] I apologise in advance for adopting all the trappings of this tradition here and throughout, notably the capitalisation of God and the use of male pronouns to identify Him.

[3] Here and elsewhere in the essay I ignore the possibility that God makes a merely *epistemic* difference to our reasoning, i.e. merely assists our *knowledge* of what we should do without affecting what we should do. I ignore this possibility because (a) it entirely eliminates God's practical authority (in favour of purely theoretical authority) and therefore makes a mockery of God's supposed omnipotence; (b) it takes all the force out of the Biblical example of Abraham and Isaac (discussed below) which illustrates nothing worth dwelling on unless it illustrates that God can command what would be, apart from his commands, truly abhorrent actions; and (c) there is no obvious reason to believe that a believer's knowledge of God's commands is generally more reliable or less vague than

For obvious reasons, neither alternative is wholly appetising for theists. Either God's commands are supposed to make it right to do what would, apart from God's commands, be wrong, in which case we may ask why we are supposed to give God's commands any rational credence, or else God's commands only make it right to do what is right anyway, in which case God seems to be condemned to rational redundancy. Faced with these apparent alternatives, Christian theologians have gone to tremendous and sometimes to my mind preposterous lengths to shake off the Socratic puzzle. Kierkegaard, for example, began boldly enough by grasping the first horn of the dilemma, holding that God's commands can make it right to do what would, apart from those commands, be wrong. The crux of the matter, he explained in *Fear and Trembling*, lies in understanding the difference between two points of view. For Abraham to kill Isaac was wrong from the *moral* point of view, but nevertheless right from the *religious* point of view, in virtue of the fact that God commanded it.[4] When the question arises whether someone should take the religious or the moral point of view, however, that question is not open to rational deliberation. Within each point of view there are reasons, but there are no further independent reasons to take one or the other point of view. It is a non-rational although (and thus?) courageous leap which brings a person to one or the other, and from the one to the other.[5] Neither position is absolute except in its own relative eyes, and neither therefore answers absolutely to the other. Nevertheless those who make the courageous leap to occupy the religious point of view, albeit without independent reason to do so, now find themselves paradoxically within grasping distance of an absolute or non-relative position. This absolute position, occupied only by those whom Kierkegaard dubs "Knights of Faith", is a position in which "my contrast to [finite, moral] existence constantly expresses itself as the most beautiful and secure harmony with it".[6] For the Knight of Faith, in other words, the rational struggle between the moral and the religious is extinguished, nay *transcended*, in the condition of divine grace. The Knight:

> "has felt the pain of renouncing everything [for the sake of religion], even the most precious thing in the world, and yet the finite [mere morality] tastes just as good to him as to one who never came to know anything higher . . . he has this security that makes him delight in it as if finitude were the surest thing of all. And yet, yet, the whole earthly figure he presents is a new creation . . . He resigned everything infinitely and then he grasped everything again by virtue of the absurd."[7]

The promise here seems to be that the dilemma to which Socrates draws attention is dissolved if and only if one can reach that true oneness with God, which,

his or her knowledge of what he or she ought to do apart from God's commands, and so the general case for treating God as a theoretical authority in such matters is hard to grasp.

[4] *Fear and Trembling* (1843; trans. H Hong & E Hong, Princeton, NJ, Princeton University Press, 1983), e.g., at 55 and 68–9.

[5] *Ibid.*, 48–9.

[6] *Ibid.*, 50.

[7] *Ibid.*, 40.

as the ultimate absurdity of life, no investigation that would satisfy Socrates or any mere philosopher can reveal or explain or accept. Reasoned argument is useless in the sight of God; only faith will do. And where reason ends and faith begins even the truly contradictory can be the case: as a Knight of Faith, Abraham can fully reconcile the rightness of his act with its wrongness, without sinking back into relativity. There is no more struggle between competing points of view. The very categories of right and wrong are transcended in the absoluteness of God. It is probably already clear to you from the difficulty I am having in expressing this idea that I find it painfully obscure. But then again, approaching the issue by reasoned argument, presumably I am *bound* to find it painfully obscure. That is Kierkegaard's whole point. The obscurity of it all to me only goes to show that I am no Knight of Faith, for Knights of Faith glory in the absurd rather than shrinking from it in Socratic bafflement and disdain.

On his way to this extraordinary dissolution of the Socratic dilemma, Kierkegaard quickly dismisses a simpler dissolution. One might argue that God is none other than a personification of goodness, and His commands therefore none other than imperatively-expressed encapsulations of rightness. It is true, therefore, that God's commands are right. But they are neither His commands because right, nor right because His commands. There is no explanatory order to be found, no possible logical priority as between these apparent alternatives identified by Socrates, because a command's being God's is exactly the same property as its being right. God's command is therefore right *in being* God's and God's *in being* right. Kierkegaard rejects this dissolution on the ground that, in his view, it fails to save God from redundancy. In this solution "God comes to be an invisible vanishing point, an impotent thought; His power is only in the ethical, which fills all of existence".[8] But I think that Kierkegaard is too quick with this dismissal. In fact I think he is too quick, in general, to anticipate imminent news of God's moral redundancy. Here is the explanation.

Pace Kierkegaard, it does not follow from the fact that God has the power to command us to do *what would otherwise be* wrong that God has the power to command us to do wrong. The mere fact that, but for God's commands, Abraham is wrong to kill Isaac does not show, as Kierkegaard assumes it does, that God commands Isaac to do wrong. One need not change from one point of view to another, nor embrace the absurd, to believe that killing Isaac is wrong if God did not command it and right if God did. Both of these propositions may be ordinary moral propositions and both may be sound without paradox or absurdity. The temptation to doubt it comes of an underestimation of the sheer totality of God's omniscience. God, being omniscient, knows not only what is the right thing for His people to do independently of His commands, but also what is the right thing for them to do *given* His commands. He also knows that these two need not be identical actions. He knows, for example, that there may be value, on occasions, in people showing that they have faith in Him through

---

[8] *Ibid.*, 68.

obedience to His commands, even commands to do what would otherwise be wrong. This expressive value may tip the balance, making an action that would otherwise be wrong into a right action. It would be wrong for Abraham to kill Isaac if God did not command it, but remember that God's command to kill Isaac is a test of Abraham's faith. If it is valuable for Abraham to show his faith then it may be right for him, now that God has commanded it, to kill Isaac. All of these may be regarded as ordinary moral propositions. There is no logical discontinuity requiring a shift from one point of view to another. If Abraham does shift into a religious point of view for the purposes of identifying and acting on God's commands this does not mean he has abandoned the moral point of view. For the moral point of view may itself require him to take the religious point of view, given the moral value of faith.

If this is so, then the Socratic dilemma may be dissolved in the simple way that I indicated, and without Kierkegaard's extraordinary manœuvres. God is none other than a personification of goodness, His commands are rightness itself. Being omnipotent, God may command any action and thereby make it right for those commanded to do it. But, being omniscient, He commands only what is right. It does not follow that His commands are redundant, merely highlighting what would be right anyway, quite apart from His commands. Because God does not only command what would be right apart from His commands. He commands what is right *given* His commands, and that, as I have explained, need not be the same thing at all.

You may object that the key move here lies in the assumption that faith in God can have moral value, and that this assumption is self-undermining in view of the other elements of the picture I presented. God tells Abraham to kill Isaac as a test of faith. The command, I am saying, is right taking account of the value of that faith, although wrong without it. But why, given that He commands something that would apart from His command be wrong, does God *deserve* this faith? What can be the moral value in having faith in a God who commands, effectively, that one have faith in God? Indeed what can be the *rationality* of this? Aren't we forced back to Kierkegaard's manœuvre of making Abraham's rectitude depend on a *non-rational* leap of faith? Doesn't the Socratic dilemma therefore simply reassert itself in a new guise?

I do not believe so. Many moral reasons share the following structure: Being a friend is a reason for acts of friendship, being a judge is a reason for judicial acts, being a citizen is a reason to do one's citizenly duty, etc. These reasons may appear to lift themselves by their own bootstraps. But of course they do not quite do so. They presuppose that one may have a reason for being someone's friend, or for being a judge, or for being a citizen. But that reason may be something quite modest. One has a reason to make friends with someone just in case, for example, one enjoys his or her company. One has reason to be a judge just in case it would be a good career move. One has reason to become a citizen just in case this will allow one to escape persecution elsewhere. This need not be a moral reason. Nor need it be a reason to perform, separately, any of the partic-

ular acts which, as a friend or as a judge or a citizen, one must then go on to perform. These further acts are made rational, and indeed in some cases morally
required, by the fact that one is a friend or a judge, not by the reason one had to
become a friend or a judge in the first place.

   Things are no different with faith in God. It is true that apart from his faith
in God Abraham is morally wrong to kill Isaac, and with it he is morally right
to kill Isaac. But his reason for having faith in God need not be, as it stands, a
reason to kill Isaac. His reason for having faith in God may be something quite
unrelated to Isaac's living or dying. He may have escaped from some terrible dis-
aster or plague by apparently miraculous means. More prosaically, he may have
witnessed the long and successful life which faith in God brought to someone
else. This is a reason for having faith in God. And given that one has faith in God
for this reason, God's commands are reasons for doing what is commanded
even though, apart from God's commands, the fact that faith in God could bring
a long and successful life would not have been any kind of reason for doing the
thing that God commanded (e.g. killing one's son). Thus God's commands are
not morally redundant for those who have faith in Him, and yet the leap of faith
which gives God's commands their constitutive importance in determining what
is the right thing to do need not be unsupported by reasons. Faith in a God who
sometimes engineers a test of one's faith by commanding one to do something
awful, which apart from that command one has absolutely no reason to do and
every reason not to do, can therefore be fully and normally rational. This does
not mean that Abraham himself faces no dilemma, that rationality all points one
way for him. It does not mean, for example, that there are some extra moral reasons to prefer his faith in God over his love for his son. There are reasons for his
faith in God, I am sure, and reasons, I am equally sure, for him to love his son.
Given that he has faith in God and love for Isaac, his is an ordinary moral
dilemma, in which two incommensurable moral duties are pitted against one
another, one a requirement of faith in God and the other a requirement of love
for Isaac.[9] That is the whole point of God's test: it is to place Isaac in this moral
dilemma and see whether he chooses faith in God over the love of his son. If
Abraham chooses faith in God he is not transcending moral reasons. He is acting on moral reasons, reasons which his faith gives him, a faith he holds, no
doubt, for reasons. If the reasons for his faith are undefeated by his reasons for
loving his son—and since the two are *ex hypothesi* incommensurable the answer
is that they cannot but be undefeated—then he is morally right to kill Isaac in
view of the fact that God commanded it, and God commanded it in view of the

   [9] In discussion of this essay, some people thought that I was presenting Abraham's dilemma as a
struggle between "Faith" and "Reason". Not so. The dilemma as I present it is even-handedly rational, i.e. both alternatives in the dilemma are supported by reasons. As I say, Abraham has reasons
to love Isaac as well as reasons to have faith in God. For those reasons he has faith in God and loves
Isaac. The resulting dilemma is *within* rationality, between the duties of faith and the duties of love.
As for "Reason" with the God-like capitalisation, I do not know what this is unless it is just rationality, i.e. the capacity and propensity to be guided by reasons, including those mundane ones I have
just been discussing—reasons for faith and reasons for love, reasons of faith and reasons of love, etc.

fact that, for Abraham as a faithful subject of God, it is morally right. Of course if the test leads Abraham, on the contrary, to abandon his faith, then he is wrong to kill Isaac: whatever else it can do, on the argument just sketched out, faith cannot lend its justifications to the faithless.

II

The Socratic challenge to theism should strike a chord with legal theorists. Its logic is replicated every year in a thousand undergraduate examination essays pitting the tradition of legal positivism against the natural law tradition. In the tradition of legal positivism, law is binding because it is posited. In the natural law tradition, on the other hand, law is posited because it is binding. Since it surely cannot be both, one must choose between positivism and natural law (thus far the second-class candidate). Or else one must revel in law's ultimate absurdity, its fundamental contradiction, as Kierkegaard gloried in religion's (a first or a third depending on whether the contradiction is made apparent on purpose or by accident). But are these truly the alternatives? Or can we have law on the same terms as, according to my explanation, we can have God, namely without contradiction as both the (positive) source of right and the (natural) repository of it?

You will not be surprised to learn that I believe we can. And I believe that Kelsen already gives us the key to understanding the law in this way. At first sight this may seem surprising, because of all modern theorists of law Kelsen came the closest, in his official account of the relationship between law and morality, to Kierkegaard's view of the relationship between religion and morality. Kelsen describes law and morality as constituting distinct and independent rational points of view. When the question arises whether someone should take the legal point of view or the moral point of view, however, Kelsen can see no overarching rational point of view from which the question should be asked or answered. One might expect it to be a moral question whether one should take the legal point of view. But for Kelsen it might as well be a legal question whether one should take the moral point of view.[10] Officially, Kelsen makes no point of view answer to any other, rationally speaking. I say "officially" because, as Raz has shown, Kelsen was not able to honour this doctrine consistently with his analysis of the legal point of view.[11] In an attempt to honour it he was apparently drawn more and more towards a Kierkegaardian glorification of the absurd in his later work, at the expense of his earlier, and more Kantian, exegesis of the Pure Theory.[12] This later work, in which law was said

---

[10] *General Theory of Law and State* (trans. A. Wedberg; Cambridge, Mass., Harvard University Press, 1945) 374.

[11] *The Authority of Law* (Oxford, Clarendon Press, 1979) 134–7.

[12] For the full story see I. Stewart, "Kelsen and the Exegetical Tradition" in R. Tur and W. Twining (eds.), *Essays on Kelsen* (Oxford, Clarendon Press, 1986).

to be based upon a *fiction* of its own rightness,[13] to my mind clouded Kelsen's earlier insights. For those insights depended on the fact that, in the earlier exegesis of the Pure Theory, what is commanded by law is ultimately identical with what is right. Therefore, just as a theist may dissolve the Socratic dilemma of theism by holding that God just is goodness personified, so a Kelsenian resolves the structurally identical dilemma of positivism and natural law by holding that law is rightness institutionalised. The question whether legal rules are posited because right, or right because posited, thus ultimately evaporates without absurdity in the logic of the earlier Kelsenian legal system.

It is important to stress the word "ultimately" here. That is because it is well known and cannot be denied that all individual laws, for Kelsen, have whatever normative force they have merely because posited. Regarding individual laws, Kelsen subscribes to a particularly rigorous version of positivism's definitive "sources thesis",[14] according to which the bindingness of a law is entirely a matter of its being made by an official authorised to make it by a higher law. Thus Kelsen is rightly associated by many with the view that we lawyers should grasp the first horn of the Socratic dilemma, and hold that law is binding because posited, not posited because binding. But Kelsen is also famous for the thesis that the ultimate source of validity for any legal system is what he called the system's *Grundnorm*, its basic norm. It is ultimately by the grace of the *Grundnorm* alone that all positive law is valid. And the *Grundnorm* is neither right because posited nor posited because right, for it is not posited at all. Its validity is, rather, a presupposition of those who treat posited law as valid *qua* law.

So what exactly is this presupposition? As Kelsen often stated it, it is the presupposition that the historically first constitution is valid.[15] But "valid" here is a notoriously problematic term. This validity cannot *ex hypothesi* be validity endowed by some further authorising norm. For *ex hypothesi* we are talking of the historically first constitution, and this cannot, by its very definition, take its validity from any other positing act. It cannot take its validity from its sources. It must, instead, be valid *on its merits*. For "sources" and "merits" exhaust the possible ways of validating anything. The *Grundnorm* must therefore be interpreted as the presupposition that the historically first constitution is meritorious, and that this merit is inherited by whatever positive law the first constitution authorises. The presupposition of the *Grundnorm* therefore brings might and right into a necessary, definitional alignment. Like the *Grundnorm* itself, what is authorised by the *Grundnorm* is neither right because authorised nor authorised because right. Again there is no explanatory order to be found. For in the presupposition of the *Grundnorm* is the identification or fusion, in the

---

[13] Kelsen, "The Function of a Constitution", written in 1964 and translated by Iain Stewart for *Essays on Kelsen, ibid*. See especially the discussion at 117: "A fiction in this sense is characterized by its not only contradicting reality but also containing contradiction within itself". Similarly: Kelsen, "On the Pure Theory of Law" (1966) 1 *Israel Law Review* 1 at 6

[14] On which see Raz, *supra* n. 11, ch. 3.

[15] E.g., *supra* n. 10 at 115.

juristic consciousness, of authorisation and rightness. The *Grundnorm* is, in this sense, the juristic God.[16] Under the authority vested by the *Grundnorm* we must, of course, often do what, apart from that authority, we should or need not do. In law, the sources therefore often seem to require us to depart from the merits. But with the *Grundnorm* presupposed the merits are brought back into line. For the *Grundnorm* by its nature lends its merit to whatever sources it authorises. Like God, the *Grundnorm* can make it right, by its demands, to do what would otherwise be wrong.

Kelsen himself had notorious difficulty conveying this point. On the one hand he was anxious to distance himself from the natural law tradition by denying that the *Grundnorm* is a moral norm. On the other hand his normative rationalism prevented him from denying that the *Grundnorm*'s validity turns on its merit or value by shifting instead to a practice-based or empirically-grounded foundation for the legal system of the kind that Hart later endorsed.[17] Although this led to some wavering on Kelsen's part throughout his career, there is an important passage in the *General Theory of Law and State* in which he steers a course between empiricist positivism and natural law in the following terms:

> "The essential characteristic of positivism, as contrasted with natural law theory, may be found precisely in the difficult renunciation of an absolute, material justification, in this self-denying and self-imposed restriction to a merely hypothetical, formal foundation in the basic norm. . . . Any attempt to push beyond the relative-hypothetical foundations of positive law, that is, to move from a hypothetical to an absolutely valid fundamental norm justifying the validity of positive law . . . means the abandonment of the distinction between positive and natural law."[18]

This passage is easily misconstrued. One may think it cuts against my claim that the *Grundnorm* is a juristic God—for after all, God is surely absolute if He exists? But this passage in fact captures Kelsen's affirmation of what I said. In legal science or legal theory, which is Kelsen's subject-matter in this passage, the *Grundnorm* is a mere hypothesis. But in the juristic consciousness it is not a hypothesis but a presupposition. Studying the nature of law theoretically we must understand how it looks from the inside, but that is different from actually standing inside it. What is relative in legal science is absolute in law itself. What legal science interprets as a norm which is valid hypothetically—i.e. only if one presupposes the *Grundnorm*—is, from the perspective of one who *does* presuppose the *Grundnorm*, simply right. What is hypothetical in the view of legal

---

[16] Kelsen himself makes the comparison very briefly in *ibid.*, 110–11. I think he errs (theologically) in regarding God as more akin to the first Constitution, and therefore as having a basic norm presupposed behind Him, which says something like "the commands of God are valid". See sections III.3 and III.4 below for closer consideration of this difficult point. And see J Raz, *The Concept of a Legal System* (Oxford, Clarendon Press, 1970), for the argument that there need be no *Grundnorm* behind the first Constitution either, i.e. that the most basic legal norm can itself be a positive norm of the system. I cannot pursue here my reasons for disagreeing with Raz on this point.

[17] See Hart's famous note comparing his "Rule of Recognition" with Kelsen's *Grundnorm* on pages 245–6 of *The Concept of Law* (Oxford, Clarendon Press, 1961).

[18] *Supra* n. 10 at 396.

theory is absolute in the view of law. It is exactly the same as with theism. What is relative for me as a student of theism, namely the presupposition of the existence of God as a personification of goodness, is necessarily absolute in the view of the faithful whose faith I am studying. So rather than driving a wedge between positivism and natural law the *Grundnorm* ultimately reconciles them. With the presupposition of the *Grundnorm* merely hypothesised, law is valid on its sources alone. With the *Grundnorm* presupposed those sources necessarily have absolute merit. By virtue of the *Grundnorm*, their authorisation entails their rightness and their rightness entails their authorisation. For the two properties are one and the same.

And just as the question arises whether God deserves one's faith, so the question arises whether the *Grundnorm* deserves one's allegiance. Just as one may have reasons for faith in God, so one may have reasons for allying oneself with the *Grundnorm*. Just as one's reasons for having faith in God may be non-moral reasons, so one's reasons for respecting the law may be non-moral reasons. Just as those who have faith in God thereby automatically acquire new moral reasons irrespective of whether their original reason for having faith in God was a moral reason, so those who ally themselves with the *Grundnorm* automatically acquire new moral reasons irrespective of whether their original reason for allying themselves with the *Grundnorm* was a moral reason. Therefore, just as the faithful may have moral reasons to do on the basis of God's commands what, apart from God's commands, they would have no moral reason to do, so those who ally themselves with the *Grundnorm* may have moral reasons to do on the basis of legal rules what, apart from these legal rules, they would have no moral reason to do. And just as the moral reasons mentioned here to do what God commands have no application to the faithless, so the moral reasons mentioned here to follow legal rules have no application to those who do not ally themselves with the *Grundnorm*, or who, to put it another way, do not have faith in law. My own belief is that such faith need not be irrational or arational any more than faith in God need be irrational or arational. It may be straightforwardly rational. People may have faith in the law for the simple reason that it once endeared itself to them by determining a case in their favour. If they do then, other things being equal, their law-abidingness may be justified. But by the same token lack of faith in the law may be rational for those who had unfortunate dealings with it, and to that extent a general attitude of law-abidingness need have no rational attraction for those who lack faith in law.

III

Lest too much is made of these similarities between theistic and legalistic belief, I should end by identifying five important and closely interrelated dissimilarities between God (seen as goodness personified) and the *Grundnorm*, dissimilarities which the above remarks inevitably tended to suppress.

1. Where God is concerned, it can be morally right to do on His command what would be morally wrong without it, *only* if one is faithful. Only faith can fill the apparent logical gap. One may, of course, have instrumental reasons for becoming faithful (e.g. fear of eternal damnation) but once one is faithful the logical gap can only be filled non-instrumentally by the expressive value of faith itself. Regarding the law things are more complicated. Faith in the law, held for whatever reason, is one of the things which can fill the apparent logical gap between what one should do apart from the law and what one should do in the light of it. But instrumental considerations can also fill that logical gap in part. The classic (although not the only) case is that of the co-ordination problem in which any one of several alternative actions would be justified apart from the law but only one of these is justified given the law. Here it is the law's ability to eliminate transaction costs by getting us to act in harmony which fills the apparent logical gap.[19] This does not depend on faith in the sense that I have been discussing above, or anything analogous to it. Of course these co-ordination-based reasons arise only if people in general have faith in the law as a way of solving problems—otherwise the law will fail to establish a co-ordinating practice. But given that people in general do have this faith in the law, its instrumental co-ordinating reasons apply even to those who are faithless, who do not ally themselves in the slightest with the *Grundnorm*. They too should join in the law's solution, where applicable, to reduce transaction costs. Of course these considerations do not apply across the whole body of the law. Not everything which the law does is an example of successful co-ordination, or of some other instrumental achievement. But my view is that these considerations do not apply *at all* in the case of God. Only those who have faith are, to my mind, ever affected by God's commands. God's authority, to put it another way, is exclusively inspirational rather than instrumental. If one is not inspired by God then God has no authority over one at all. Not so the law, where some authority is instrumentally justified and other authority expressively justified, i.e. justified as an expression of the faithful's faith. In this respect an atheist is in a different moral position from an anarchist. An anarchist is morally permitted to deny authority to the law where, were she to have faith in law, that fact in itself would lend the law its authority over her actions. But the anarchist is morally wrong to deny authority to the law where its authority over her is instrumentally justified, e.g. through the benefits of co-ordination. But it seems to me that an atheist, even if she is wrong to deny God's existence, is morally permitted to deny Him any authority over her actions at all.

2. In the case of God, to know Him is to love Him. Cognition of God entails moral commitment. Not so the *Grundnorm*. Kelsen struggled with this point throughout his career.[20] He struggled to find a way in which lawyers, for example, could enjoy cognition of the law without any personal commitment to it. He

---

[19] See e.g. J. Finnis, "Law as Co-ordination" (1989) 2 *Ratio Juris* 97.
[20] See his testimony to his own problem with this in the notes of *The Pure Theory of Law* (2nd edn., trans. Knight, Berkeley, Cal., University of California Press, 1967) at 204.

clearly believed that this was possible. He believed that one could be an anarchist who is a perfectly competent lawyer, or at any rate a perfectly competent scholar or teacher of law.[21] So, fundamentally, he needed to find two different ways in which the *Grundnorm* could be presupposed—fully, if you like, and on the other hand merely *arguendo*. He never quite succeeded in this, although successors like Raz and MacCormick have fared much better.[22] The point I am making is merely that this divide cannot even intelligibly be sought in the case of God. The reason is not simply that God is goodness personified in the eyes of the faithful. After all, as I argued, something very similar is true of the *Grundnorm* in the eyes of its faithful. The reason, rather, is that of God's comprehensively overarching role in the universe, if He exists. This role is such that merely recognising His existence amounts, necessarily, to laying oneself down before Him. Nobody need feel the same about a legal system. One may see that a legal system exists, and what it involves, without in the slightest laying oneself down before it. For example, one may look up French law to discover how things are done in France. When one does so, to borrow Raz's terms, one presupposes the *Grundnorm* in a detached rather than a committed way, or, to borrow MacCormick's terms, one has the cognitive internal attitude to law without the volitional internal attitude. To know the law is not to love it even though the *Grundnorm*, if for any reason we *do* come to love the law, necessarily fuses for us the merits and the sources of law.

3. The *Grundnorm* does not command directly, for it is not an agent but a norm. It merely authorises agents to command. All legal authority, even constitutional authority, is thus for Kelsen legally subordinate authority. God, on the other hand, commands directly. There is disagreement among faiths and among interpreters of faiths about whether He also commands *in*directly, e.g. through His officers on earth. Some hold that these officers are merely conduits through whom God issues His own commands. Others hold that these officers issue their own commands, by delegated authority from God. Still others hold that God's officers are fallible interpreters of God's commands. The question is interesting and important because it bears on the relationship between the merits and the sources of religious doctrine. If God delegates authority, does it follow that His officers on earth also share, by God's authority, the definitional goodness which He personifies? Are they, within the scope of their offices, likewise personifications of goodness? The matter bears on the Kelsenian view of law because, given that the *Grundnorm* does not command directly, we need to know whether those whom it authorises to command are always necessarily commanding meritoriously just because of their authorisation. Kelsen's very appealing answer is that they are. Within the law, by virtue of the *Grundnorm*, source-based authority is the only merit that counts. The *Grundnorm* makes legal officials infallible

---

[21] *Ibid.*, 218n.

[22] Raz, *supra* n. 11 at 137ff, N. MacCormick, *Legal Reasoning and Legal Theory* (2nd edn., Oxford, Clarendon Press, 1994) at 275ff (discussing Hart rather than Kelsen, but to much the same effect).

when they act within the scope of their authorisation, even though what they command was, for example, in their own discretion rather than dictated by the first constitution, and whether or not what they commanded is a matter of interpretation of some existing law. It does not of course make legal officials infallible regarding what should be done apart from what they command. They often make mistakes in determining where the merits of the case lay before they gave judgment, or issued their instructions etc. The *Grundnorm* makes them infallible regarding only what should be done given what, with the *Grundnorm*'s authorisation, they command. Their lawful rulings are, to put it in simple terms, dispositive in the eyes of the law.

4. The fact that legal authority is all more or less subordinate opens the way, you might say, for selective faith in law. Couldn't one have, for example, faith in the courts but none in the legislature, or faith in old law but not in newer law? I think that one may. The question is whether this makes the *Grundnorm* drop out of the picture. For the importance of the *Grundnorm* surely resides in the fact that it entails the coincidence of all sources and all merits, so that on the doctrine of the *Grundnorm* one would expect faith in the law, like faith in God, to be an all-or-nothing affair, in which picking and choosing is unintelligible? Doesn't the possibility of picking and choosing in one's faith make the *Grundnorm* redundant? I think this is a premature conclusion. The fact that, as I explained, one may through the detached presupposition of the *Grundnorm* know law without loving it is what explains the possibility of picking and choosing where one will put one's faith. Cognition of the *Grundnorm* with detachment allows one to identify laws and understand them complete with their claim to meritoriousness *in advance of commitment to them*. Not so God and His commands. Since to know God is to love him, one has no logical space to pick and choose with His commands. His role in the life of the faithful is, for that reason and that reason alone, all or nothing. It is not that He would be redundant if we could pick and choose. It is that He would be something much less extraordinary than what, if He exists, by His nature He must be.

5. You may say that now we have come, at last, to the crunch. Law plainly exists. But God's existence is everywhere and always in doubt. In admitting that there are cases in which faith in God is rational I surely assumed God's existence. For there can be no reason for anyone to have faith in a non-existent God. In case of a non-existent God, faith is reduced to superstition. Of course such superstition may be excusable. People who act on justified but false beliefs can often be excused their consequently erroneous actions.[23] But the issue here is whether faith in God can lend *justification*, not mere excuse, to the faithful. There is a short answer. The short answer is that I *obviously* assumed God's existence. After all, the Socratic puzzle with which I started assumes God's existence. For if God does not exist, then God does not command, and if God does

---

[23] See my "Justification and Reasons" in A.T.H. Smith and A. Simester (eds.), *Harm and Culpability* (Oxford, Clarendon Press, 1996).

not command then there can be no puzzle about the constitutive difference that his commands make. So there was never any hesitation in this discussion so far as the assumption of God's existence is concerned. But personally, as I am sure I have made tolerably clear, I think the assumption is false. I do not believe that goodness is personified anywhere in the universe. I have, in that sense, no knowledge of God. But of course I can grasp the *idea* of goodness personified, and hence hypothesise the presuppositions of a believer in such a thing. It is no different from what I do as a philosopher of law when I daily hypothesise the presuppositions of lawyers. One must be careful not to confuse detachment and hypothesis. I claimed (III.2 above) that one cannot presuppose God's existence in a detached way as one can presuppose the *Grundnorm* in a detached way. But it does not follow that, as a philosopher, one cannot hypothesise the believer's committed presupposition of God in the same way that one hypothesises the lawyer's detached presupposition of the *Grundnorm*. The capacity of the human intellect for hypothesis and its capacity for detached presupposition are quite different. Ronald Dworkin's *Law's Empire* tells us that, as lawyers, we cannot presuppose the validity of the first constitution non-committally—we must be committed to the whole history of the constitution. The same book tells us that, as legal theorists, we cannot hypothesise the presuppositions of lawyers without endorsing them.[24] So not only lawyers but also legal theorists can only talk about law while being committed to it. I think Dworkin is wrong even on the first point. Law is not God, and happily lawyers need not, in their professional capacity, be true believers. But Dworkin's error is deepened by his failure adequately to distinguish the two points. Even if law were God, so that lawyers would have to be true believers, it would not follow that only true believers could be *philosophers* of law.

---

[24] The essential moves are laid out in *Law's Empire* (Cambridge, Mass., Harvard University Press, 1986) 11–15.

2

Living In and Out of the Law

ZENON BANKOWSKI and CLAIRE DAVIS

"Und sehe, daß wir nichts wissen können!
Das will mir schier das Herz verbrennen."[1]

INTRODUCTION

LAW and love seem to exclude each other. Love is arbitrary in the sense that it cannot be constrained or predicted by law; it knows no reason—the demands of law and rationality fall before it. How can one capture something like welfare in law when it must depend upon the necessarily contingent situation? An individual's need will necessarily be its and its alone. A rule such as "give everyone what they need" will depend upon individual and contingent judgements. Love is anti-nomian because its demands will lead to places that will be impossible to capture and predict by law. Law, on the other hand, claims that it cannot be treated as one reason among many. Its very nomianism demands that it excludes other ways of looking at the matter; one cannot pick and choose which law to follow.

These extremes seem to capture two images of the moral life. The relation between them is mirrored in one view of the relationship between Christianity and Judaism. Here Judaism is seen as a nomian religion, whereas Christianity was to liberate from the narrow conformism of law following to a religion of the heart: the anti-nomian religion *par excellence*. Empirically, of course, this has never been the case, and Christianity has been as legalistic as Judaism is supposed by it to be. However, in principle at least, it was seen as the defining feature of the relationship. That image can be summed up, in the Christian Gospels, in the following quotation from the St Matthew's Gospel:[2]

> "Woe to you, scribes and Pharisees, hypocrites! for you tithe mint and dill and cumin, and have neglected the weightier matters of the law, and mercy and faith; these you ought to have done, without neglecting the others. You blind guides, straining out a gnat and swallowing a camel!"

[1] J.W. Goethe, *Faust* (Munich, Goldmann, 1956):
  "All I see is that we cannot know!
  This burns my heart."
[2] Matthew 23: 23–4.

Looked at in this way, then, the answer seems to be that one can only have one or the other, the normative vote here clearly going to a form of Christian anti-nomianism. But this does not seem accurately to reflect the Christian message itself. For was not law an essential part of that message also? Thus, again from St Matthew's Gospel:[3]

> "Think not that I have come to abolish the law and the prophets; I have come not to abolish but to fulfil them. For truly, I say to you, till heaven and earth pass away, not an iota, not a dot, will pass from the law until all is accomplished."

Thus, from the Christian side at least, the identification of Judaism with law and Christianity with love or grace fails to pay sufficient heed either to Jesus' teachings on the law or to his life as a Jew under the law. Moreover the problem with the relation of law and love, with nomian and anti-nomian tendencies is the same in Judaism, as Gillian Rose shows.[4] The tensions that seem to be between both great systems are in fact tensions within each.

So it is not a matter of choosing the one form of life or the other, Judaism or Christianity, since both have the tensions between law and love within them. The idea that Judaism and Christianity were opposed in this way made it easier for people to think of law and love as being contradictory; as there having to be a choice between the one and the other, even within Christianity or Judaism. Our aim in this essay is to say that there is no such contradiction, that one should not be forced to choose between a nomian and an anti-nomian way of life, but that they are dependent upon each other. To live the life of rules implies being able to step out of them when necessary, and to break the rules implies being able to follow them. There is no easy resolution. The tension between law and love will always be there; there is no reconciliation or transcendence. What we want to do in this essay is to ask what it means to live lawfully, a question that is central to the Gospels. It is perhaps best to use the rather old-fashioned "righteous" here, since that more closely approximates what we are trying to get at: how to live the tension between law and love; how to live in and out of the law.

THE MIDDLE

It can be said, however, that a new way of looking at this problem is emerging. This can be described as the attempt to overcome a dichotomous mode of thinking based on the polarisation of seemingly opposite principles: universal/particular, knower/known, object/subject, mind/body, male/female, law/love. This new way of looking begins with a recognition of the interdependence and mutually constitutive existence of the dichotomies opposing terms. It goes on to explore a new construction of the space within and between, which resists the

---

[3] Matthew 5: 17–8.
[4] G. Rose, *Judaism and Modernity* (Oxford, Blackwell, 1993) chs. 1–3.

temptation either to make the distance absolute and unbridgeable on the one hand, or to overlap completely and reduce to sameness on the other. The space described traces instead the choreography of an erotic relationship in which difference and distance remain, without precluding intimacy. It is a space in which two terms co-exist with paradox but without logical contradiction. This space is similar to what Gillian Rose[5] calls "the middle", where the contingent outbreak of love breaks the boundaries of law, while at the same time, love's transgression finds meaning only by virtue of its resonance against the backdrop of the law itself. There is no love without law, no law without love.

For Rose there is no easy retreat from the one to the other. The promise of modernity is the promise of universal reason, and that promise is forged in the encounter between Athens and Jerusalem, transforming both. There is no going back; this is our inheritance, Christian and Jew alike. Christianity cannot abandon the law; Judaism is not confined to Jerusalem. We are disillusioned with this promise because we have refused to inhabit the tension between particular and universal, autonomous and heteronomous, law and love, Athens and Jerusalem. We have found, however, that philosophy without revelation and tradition is as empty as Judaism outside time and history is fantastic. The answer lies in finding the courage and the faith to live in the present, informed by past and future but not subsumed beneath them. Only then is it possible to engage as participant and not as historian or utopian dreamer.[6]

> "Reason in modernity cannot be said to have broken the promise of universality—unless we have not kept it; for it is only we who can keep such a promise by working our abstract potentiality into the always difficult but enriched actuality of our relation to others and to ourselves."

Part of what happens in modernity, according to Rose, is that we see the tension-laden space of the middle as impossible to occupy and try to theorise it away. This contributes to a false and distorting polarisation of law and love; a polarisation which, in modernity, leads on the one hand to the soulless force of instrumental rationality and, on the other, to the always frustrated search for immediacy.

For Rose it is this middle space that must be protected, as it is there that, for her, politics occurs. Without this space the polarities collapse into each other and do not give room for the "third", or "singular", which for her is the product of politics. Without this space, you get, in the religious context, a sort of transcendence or "holy middle" which in reality is the collapse of the universal into the particular. She shows that the Christian sect as a form of Christian communism was both the universality of the Christian community and the totalitarianism of an individual. She documents how sects which start off with some form of collective ideal end up by being run by one person as embodying that ideal. The certainty of the universalistic ideal is embodied in the leader of the

---

[5] G. Rose, *The Broken Middle* (Oxford, Blackwell, 1992).

[6] Rose, *supra* n. 4 at 9.

organic community who can do no wrong for he speaks for that community and in fact is it. Once the community becomes identified with the individual, the normal practices of democratic politics go by the board and everything that the individual does is right because that individual *is* the community. One can also see this in modern-day religious sects. But one does not have to look to the esoteric world of religious cults. This was also clearly embodied in Nazi Germany and the "cults of personality" in the former communist countries. Further, one can also see it in the 1960s fashion for community work. The world of the community worker often hid much highly undemocratic activity since everything was being done in the name of the "community" by that worker as part of the community.

The response in the flight to some form of individualism shows the converse situation. There everyone is seen as a unique individual. There everyone becomes equal for the purpose of organisation of the political sphere and the market in the process that Marx calls commodification. So, as there is in principle no distinction between them, they can all be lumped together in a collective way. Thus utilitarianism does not care for the individual so much as for total happiness, the individual being lost in the collective. It is worth noting that the *Leviathan* of Hobbes, that acme of totalitarianism, stems at base from the fact that all men are more or less equal and not that they are different. In this way one might say, with John Milbank,[7] that these sorts of societies are basically collectivist.

The middle then holds concepts apart so that they can be used without sliding into an unreflective mass. The middle is for Rose an ambiguous place. In it law defines what power we already possess. That in itself is liberating, but it is also the beginning of anxiety, for in the middle we have to confront the possibilities of failure. Indeed, we may say that part of the reason the middle collapses into one or the other polarity is precisely because we busy ourselves in trying to construct a society or place where there will be no possibility of failure, where there will always be a calculable answer. Afraid of the complexity and difficulty of decision-making and judgement, what is desired is simplicity and clarity, something to make the world simpler than it is.

Martha Nussbaum's[8] reading of *Antigone* makes this point well. Nussbaum shows how both Creon and Antigone can be seen as making the same moral mistake, even though one can say that Antigone is morally the better. Both run away from the tension and anxiety of the middle. They do not know where to begin, so what they do is to deny that there is any conflict. For Creon there is no conflict between the demands of piety and love and the demands of justice for the city. Everything, including piety and love, is to be understood as pertaining to the city, so everything must refer back and be seen under the optic of the good of the city. For Antigone everything is seen, as Nussbaum points out, not out of

[7] J. Milbank, "Socialism by Gift and Socialism by Grace" (1996) 77 *New Blackfriars* 632.

[8] M. Nussbaum, *The Fragility of Goodness* (Cambridge, Cambridge University Press, 1986) ch. 2.

love but rather the *philia* of the family. So again there is no conflict; rather, everything is seen as referring back to, and through the optic of, family duties. Love becomes duty and a relationship founds an obligation regardless of the feelings involved. Love in the play is better exemplified by the love of Ismene and the passion of Haemon for Antigone. What appears to be the love of Antigone is rather the view that the answer lies in the eternal laws of the gods and that, in some way, Antigone is the sole interpreter of them. Here again we can see Rose's point. For the particularity of love (Antigone's) collapses into a universalism of laws of which she is the sole interpreter, just as Creon turns the universalism of the city's laws into the particularity of his anger and lust for power. But part of the driving force of all of that is the need for certainty, the need to eschew that idea that we can hold values that are radically incompatible with each other and engender difficult, if not impossible, choices.

The condition of modernity is to seek a "comfort zone"—either by the soulless application of universalism (by just applying law and accepting that this necessitates forgetting the impulse to love and welfare, which is seen as dangerous and arbitrary), or by recognising the "violence" behind the law and going over to the nihilism of love. The results, as we saw in the example above, are very similar. For Rose the product of acting in the middle is the singular which is the fruit of the encounter of the polarities and which also acts to keep the space of the middle open and available for acting in this way. But we saw how the theorisation of the impossibility of this middle and the desire to take one or other side of the polarity, or transcend it, stems from the desire for certainty, the difficulty of dealing with the anxiety that must always (since we can never really *know*) accompany the middle. So the middle is for Rose the beginning of anxiety because it is always risky and unsettled. It is there that we have to stake ourselves. But it is also the anxiety of beginning *because* it is in the middle. There is no end because the middle is the place that we always inhabit. Even as there is no end, neither is there a beginning. We must guard against inventing mythical beginnings which make things easier for us. The way we go forward is by "suspending the ethical" which in this context means refraining from seeing something as an incarnation of the universal.

One might understand the above in the following terms. When I ask the question, "Should I obey the law?", I might ask it in terms of some mythic "state of nature" and original social contract. However, in making a decision in this way, I am not really abolishing the ethical and making a risky judgement about obedience to this law, for I am bringing the ethical back in the guise of social contract theory. Thus we get the reason for Hume's attack on the social contract, which roughly argues that one cannot have the notion of the (social) contract without positing civil society first. So when I ask whether I should obey a law, I have to start from the here and now, from where I am in a complex society; from why this particular law should be obeyed. My decision will be the fruit of an encounter with all sorts of reasons, including the universal ones. Thus our political life is realistic because it recognises that we inhabit the middle; but it is risky because it is shaped by the mystery of the beginning, the risky arbitrary act that we have always to recreate anew. The point about that beginning is that ultimately we have no beginning or end to guide us in safety and certainty. We have to commit and stake ourselves to a decision which, *ex hypothesi*, we will not know is correct until we see what happens. But is it not a consequentialist decision, nor is it one that is guaranteed the certainty of, for example, the Kantian categorical imperative. It is not, however, a nihilist way of looking at things, with each judgement guaranteed by nothing at all.

Part of Rose's argument is to defend law and universalism against the cry that "Love is all you need". Law is something that we need and must be part of our decision-making processes. Though we have to suspend it at times, we do so to recreate it. Though we deny it, we have faith in it. But the point is that we can never know if that decision, as we have taken it, is right. We cannot hide behind the mythical certainties of the universal law or mythical beginnings or ends. We might say that our decisions whether to apply the law or not are always going to be arbitrary, in the sense that they will not be constrained by law. For though law ultimately is not self-applying, that should not diminish our faith in it. But we will never know for sure whether we are right; we cannot build a society, machine-like, where there is no possibility of error. When we try, law and love collapse into each other and give us, as we have seen, the totality of the individual and the group in one. We must realise that our life is never clear-cut and clean and is always something of a mess. But we must get hold of it as it is. We have to confront ourselves as we are and live our life from the middle. That place is always anxious and creates the conditions of anxiety and error (sin). We can only be seen when we eat of the tree of knowledge; but that is what we must eat, and we must use that anxiety creatively.

JUDGEMENT AND THE ENCOUNTER

The way we have gone about using Rose here might seem to be getting away from her project, which is not one about the problems of decision-making, both personal and political, but rather a historical thesis about modernity and the way that the risky space of the middle is closed down. What we intend to do now is to put some of this analysis into the context of legal decision-making. First then, accepting that this is not part of her project (though it does feature, brilliantly and movingly, in *Love's Work*[9]) we must ask how we are to decide in the middle. How are we to know what to do, except for the fact that we are to stake ourselves? What sort of principle is that, if I am faced with a conflicting decision about whether I should go off with my lover or stay with my spouse, for example? Both courses of action might be risky and move away from the comfort zone. Going off with the lover is risky and might fail; staying with my spouse is

---

[9] G. Rose, *Love's Work* (London, Chatto & Windus, 1995).

also risky because I have to accept that my relationship there will always be problematic and fraught, and will not necessarily give me peace. But both choices could also be seen as seeking security. Stay with what one knows (at least there is security in the relationship however problematic) or go off with the lover who offers the prospect of secure love.

Conscience, some idea that you know this is the right thing to do, cannot do the work, for that is merely doing what one thinks is right, and this collapses into existential nihilism: that everything is all right as long as one is sincere; that all that counts is ones authenticity. That seems like no principle at all. This is in fact precisely what Rose wants to avoid and what is for her the consequence of a completely jettisoning nihilism. The anxiety that accompanies these decisions cannot help us either, though it can be creative as well as destructive. The fear of failure makes for a debilitating anxiety which prevents my doing anything at all. But it can also be creative since it means that one is not complacent in deciding what to do and rightly recognises the possibility of failure, the difficulties ahead, and the possible necessity of picking oneself up and starting all over again. This does not so much tell us what to do as give us the "adrenaline rush" necessary for the journey ahead. It is something that concentrates the mind but does not tell us how to make the judgement in the first place. The obvious answer seems *phronesis* and a balancing of the various reasons that we might have for making a decision. But how do we avoid that collapsing into either the particularity of law or the universality of love?

We can encounter this problem in legal reasoning also. To explore this fully we must start with a distinction that Klaus Günther makes between justification and application.[10] He, following Habermas, makes a distinction between the justification of norms and their application. In order to justify a norm we use universalistic criteria. But it is another matter when we come to apply that norm which we have justified in a universalistic way. Here we have to attend to the particularities of the case. If we transpose this into the realms of legal reasoning, we can say that legal decision-makers have to do two things when they stand before law. First, they have to decide what that law means, and then they have to decide whether or not the law applies in the particular case, and how. The criteria will be different in each case. For the first, the criteria will be universalistic, and for the second, since they have to do with the particularities of the case, they will be more particular. This latter will be the case because a potential subject of the law could always ask of the rule, "why me?". The answer must always attend to that subject. One can, however, deny that one needs separate criteria by saying that the meaning determines the application. Thus the question is always that of interpreting the rule in such a way that it qualifies the facts before it. This is the universalistic answer that, for example, MacCormick makes in his controversy with Jackson about whether or not one can see law as a deductive

[10] K. Günther, *The Sense of Appropriateness: Application Discourses in Morality and Law* (trans. J. Farrell; Albany, NY, State University of New York Press, 1993).

system. Jackson[11] accuses MacCormick of thinking of law as in principle calculable, as a large machine-like system which always churns out the answers that its programme ordains and which admits of no exceptions. But how does one decide on the particularities of the case? Even some who accept the justification/application distinction have problems. Thus Klaus Günther,[12] though he makes a distinction between justification and application, appears somewhat to nullify it. For the application discourse is characterised by what can be seen as similar universalistic criteria as the justification discourse. Universalisation is the criterion of the former, and the idea for application is that the judgement must fit and be coherent with all similar instances, which at least on one of the ways he interprets it in his book is just another version of the justification criterion. Again, Peczenik and Alexy,[13] in their analysis of what counts as weighing and balancing reasons, end up with a criterion which is coherent and universalistic in the Günther manner.

We can take this argument further when we think of the middle as what Michael Detmold[14] calls the "particularity void". Again for him it is the space that exists between the rule and its application. There is for him a difference between deciding whether something is reasonable to do and whether some rule is reasonable to apply. It might, for example, be reasonable to apply some rule that is in itself unreasonable or it might be unreasonable to apply a reasonable rule. Thus the rule against murder might be perfectly reasonable but it might be unreasonable to apply it in a mercy killing situation. Alternatively, it might be reasonable to apply a decision made wrongly in a previous case because the advantage of the precedent outweighs the wrongness of the decision. Even though this latter example appears to tend towards the universalistic, it must be noted that it is in the particular instance that judges have to see it as reasonable and not in all other instances. Judges have this responsibility; they cannot get away from responsibility for their decision by hiding behind the rules. Judges must think it is right for them to apply that law now, and they must have the courage and integrity to do so in this particular instance. This is the meaning of the strange argument that Detmold[15] gives for the inseparability of law and morality. He says that judges, if they have integrity, cannot meaningfully say that they sentence someone to death but do not support the death penalty. This is because in that particular instance they judge that it is morally right to sentence someone to death while thinking it to be wrong in the abstract. *This* person ought to be so sentenced by *this* judge because in *this* case the demands of the law, the judicial role, the particular deeds of the accused, and many other reasons mean that on the balance of reasons this should be the case. Notice that

[11] B.S. Jackson, "Semiotic Scepticism: A Response to Neil MacCormick" (1991) 4 *International Journal of Semiotics* 181.

[12] *Supra* n. 10.

[13] R. Alexy and A. Peczenik "The Concept of Coherence and its Significance for Discursive Rationality" (1990) 3 *Ratio Juris* 130.

[14] M. Detmold, "Law as Practical Reason" (1989) 48 *Cambridge Law Journal* 436.

[15] M. Detmold, *The Unity of Law and Morality* (London, Routledge and Kegan Paul, 1984).

what Detmold is saying is that judges must take responsibility for the decision. They cannot escape behind the fact that they are simply applying the law. But *a fortiori* it works the other way around, that is, in not applying the law. Thus in a answer to one of the classic Diceyan assertions of Parliamentary sovereignty— that Parliament could validly and enforceably enact legislation to kill blue-eyed babies—he asks whether this is a realistic example, not because it is implausible, but because, if judges were to have to decide such a hypothetical case, they might, taking responsibility for their decision, decide not to apply this rule. It would be unreasonable to apply the rule for a host of particular reasons even though, in terms of the procedures of its promulgation etc., it was a reasonable rule.[16]

Let us look at the "particularity void" further. For Detmold[17] there are certain problems that cannot be answered by universalistic reasoning, and in those we have to pay attention to the particularity of the case. His example is taken from the confrontation between Pierre and Davout in *War and Peace*. Davout does not shoot Pierre as a Russian spy, even though those are the orders, because he looks at him, hesitates, and does not shoot. Tolstoy here says that, at this moment, many things passed through their minds, and they saw they were both human and both brothers. Now one might cast this as a form of universalistic reasoning, and Tolstoy, in writing about it, appears to cast it as such.[18] However it is the hesitation and the action that is important, and this comes from the realisation that this person feels pain, and is afflicted (we come to that notion later). At this moment, according to Detmold:[19]

> "I, the judge, and Davout, at the moment of practicality entered the unanswering void of particularity, the realm of love, about which only mystical, poetic things can be said . . . or nothing. . . . Judges enter this realm everyday."

But, as soon as that is the mystical solution that is posited, then it appears that one can do nothing, that one can only swing from one polarity to the other, law-like regularity or mystical particularity. As Gillian Rose shows, this tends to dissolve into forms of totalitarianism or nihilism. To put it in terms of reasoning, the problem is that the universal normative propositions would seem to be unable to refer to the particular prospective instance; and reference by the user would seem to lack universalistic justification. Various solutions take one or the other side of the divide, and we are left sliding from an insulated decision where we cannot connect with the substantive, to a substantive one where we cannot connect with the universal. So we go for one or the other because, though we can see the problem, we do not know how to stand in the middle.

To occupy the middle one needs courage to take responsibility for judgement and action that might go wrong; to eschew the safety of universality and yet

---

[16] M. Detmold, *Courts and Administrators* (London, Weidenfeld and Nicholson, 1989).
[17] *Supra* n. 14.
[18] See S. Veitch, "Doing Justice to Particulars" in E. Christodoulidis (ed.), *Communitarianism and Citizenship* (London, Ashgate, 1998) 220.
[19] Detmold, *supra* n. 14 at 457.

have the faith that reason and the law will not be subverted in the particularity of one's actions but will be continually recreated by those acts. How do we do that? How do we find the faith for that?

We will again be helped if we take a theological example. From the perspective of Rose's "middle", the problem of faith must be recast not as the problem of belief or disbelief, but as the problem of recognition and discernment:[20]

> "God tested Abraham, and said to him, 'Abraham!' And he said, 'Here am I.' He said, 'Take your son, your only son Isaac, whom you love, and go to the land of Moriah, and offer him there as a burnt offering upon one of the mountains of which I shall tell you.' "

According to Kant, Abraham should be condemned as a murderer and criminal, not hailed as the father of faith. Kant's judgement is as follows:[21]

> "Abraham should have replied to this putative divine voice: 'That I may not kill my good son is absolutely certain. But that you who appear to me are God is not certain and cannot become certain, even though the voice were to sound from the very heavens'. . . . [For] that a voice which one seems to hear cannot be divine one can be certain of . . . in case what is commanded is contrary to moral law. However majestic or supernatural it may appear to be, one must regard it as a deception."

Abraham's dilemma is precisely that he is asked to go beyond the law, to go beyond what is publicly articulated and understood, and in that sense certain, and therefore to open himself to misunderstanding and misrecognition. As Kierkegaard argues:[22]

> "Abraham cannot be mediated, which can also be put by saying he cannot speak. The moment I speak I express the universal, and when I do not no one can understand me."

How does Abraham know that God is speaking to him? What makes him recognise and distinguish this voice as God's voice? Is he more accurately described as a murderer or a lunatic?

We want to suggest that recognition is the defining practice and dynamic principle of Rose's "Middle"; that what emerges from a held tension between particular and universal, law and love, individual and society is a means of discerning the path ahead. But it is a means which is paradoxical: only by obeying the law will one know when the law is to be disobeyed or suspended, and it is only in this suspension that the law itself is continually renewed. Recognition, however, is not a universal. The ability to recognise emerges from within particular traditions and remains tied to the cultivation of particular perceptions and sensibilities. In other words, there is more than one law. A Christian perception is not the same as a secular humanist or a Moslem one.

---

[20] Genesis 22: 1–3.

[21] I. Kant, *The Conflict of the Faculties* (trans. M. Gregor; London, University of Nebraska Press, 1992) at 63, quoted by Rose, *supra* n. 5 at 12.

[22] S. Kierkegaard, *Fear and Trembling* (trans. A. Hannay; Harmondsworth, Penguin, 1985) at 89, quoted in Rose, *supra* n. 5 at 18.

The implication of these insights for Christian theology points to the need simultaneously for greater humility and more courage. Much Christian theology has been guilty of appeal to a Divine power in defence of both intellectual and institutional claims which could not otherwise be justified. On the other hand, and at the same time, as John Milbank has argued,[23] Christian theology has been too willing to surrender to a secular reason which necessarily and by definition undermines the possibility of a distinctive Christian contribution. To lay claim to a distinct perspective is not the same as to accord an absolute or privileged position to the insights which emerge therefrom.

The law, or those publicly acknowledged ways of acting which constitute society, is what forms individuals. The individual, in this sense, is created by the law. On the other hand, once formed, the individual is itself a vehicle of the law which it has appropriated and will deploy in new and original ways in the diverse situations which it encounters. The individual, therefore, in turn, becomes a lawmaker. This encounter between the law and the particular situation, if it remains a real encounter, is what Gillian Rose calls the singular: the particular is neither simply subsumed beneath the law, universally applied, nor is the law abandoned. The encounter depends upon the individual's ability to recognise the particular instance as both consistent with and different from previous instances. Appeal to any authority, including God, external to this encounter and applied as a principle which determines its outcome, is illegitimate. The only legitimate authority is the authority of recognition which arises from the encounter itself. This is not to say that perceptions cannot be warped and corrupted or to deny the need for critique. But critique and judgements about the authenticity of encounter presuppose the encounter itself and cannot be made in advance. Any perspective on the encounter's meaning can often only be gained on the basis of its outcome and, even here, no ultimate perspective is available. Our understanding is contingent and limited, continually subject to the revision and rearticulation afforded by fresh encounter.

Abraham's recognition of God's voice is set within the context of a life of faithfulness and obedience. It is only in relation to this setting that Abraham is able to make the leap of faith which propels him outside what is already publicly understood and accepted. Paradoxically, however, this step outside the law, or what Rose calls the suspension of the ethical, is what in turn transforms and redeems the law, such that Abraham is recognised not as a murderer or a lunatic, but as "father of the faith".

But one cannot completely abolish the ethical because then there is no context at all. The action taken when I suspend the ethical is not one of self- assertion but of self-renunciation because it renounces the self-possession associated with never failing. And it is that self-possession that we suspend.[24] There is no final judgement; I can always be wrong. Violence is interwoven in the ethical,

---

[23] J. Milbank, *Theology and Social Theory: Beyond Secular Reason* (Oxford, Blackwell, 1993).
[24] R. Williams, "Between Politics and Metaphysics: Reflections in the Wake of Gillian Rose" in L.G. Jones and S.E. Fowl (eds.), *Rethinking Metaphysics* (Oxford, Blackwell, 1995).

according to Rose, and we cannot isolate it as a basic action without suspending it. Thus the law is suspended when Abraham tries to kill Isaac, and we have what she calls the anxiety of authorship; that is, we have to take responsibility without the ethical to guide us. We have to create and recreate it with that mysterious act which appears arbitrary and for which we need both faith and courage. The point here is that we cannot seek to insure ourselves from failure by retreating to a "holy" place and having nothing to do with the world. We cannot think of the world as violent and evil and have nothing to do with it or its institutions. We have to work from where we are. We cannot refuse to sully ourselves with the dirty business of "politics" (in Rose's sense) and keep ourselves pure by seeking a false utopianism or by becoming cynical and not caring at all. We have to engage and take responsibility.

We hope that by now it will be clear how one might apply the above in looking at the life of the law from the perspective of the "middle". What law does is set standards and give calculable results. It shows us how to judge situations and precludes the possibility of error as long as we apply these standards correctly. The downside is that it drives out the particular and love—"Hard cases make bad law". This is expressed in law in the desire to make legal reasoning universalistic, to encase it within a predicate logic, which, though in many of its nuanced versions it gives room for some flexibility, is at base trying to say that there are calculable answers within certain perimeters. The opposing camp takes an epistemological and a normative view here. Part of the latter stems from the hope that love will drive out law, the opposite view of those who support the law. Part of the reason for that is epistemological in that it is claimed that the law is inevitably indeterminate, made up of principles and counter-principles, and that there can be no rational way of finding a conclusive answer, there being no principle of judgement. This conclusion is seen as no bad thing, because then we can concentrate on the particularity of the situation and on love. But, then, we enter the "particularity void" of Detmold and what is the way out of that?

Our encounter with Gillian Rose gives us a clue about the way out of the "particularity void". It has shown that it is the encounter that is important, and it is in that encounter that law and love meet. What makes law indeterminate is not the flexibility of its meaning but the fact that in the encounter we enter the place where we have to decide whether to apply it or not. That is a particular decision which will stem from the particularity of the encounter, and we take responsibility for it. We might try to evade responsibility by saying that we are only applying the law, but we have, as we saw, to take responsibility for that as well as for suspending it. So, one might say that it is in application that we make the law and not in the determination of its meaning. If we make the application a function of its meaning, as MacCormick does,[25] or if we see the criteria of the

---

[25] D.N. MacCormick, "Notes on Narrativity and the Normative Syllogism" (1991) 4 *International Journal for the Semiotics of Law* 163.

application discourse as being universalistic, as Günther does, then we deny the encounter and the fruit of that encounter. We impose a universalistic view on the particularity of the situation, thus losing that situation. But that encounter is not nihilistic in that it does away with the law and, as a consequence, "anything goes". It must be seen within the context of the law as the act that stems from living in the law but whose product is not the unthinking application of a rule; rather, it is an encounter with the particularity of the situation which might result in applying or not applying the rule. In this way the "particularity void" is not mystical, but rather a statement of the fact that we have to start from the particular situation and not let the rule make us forget it. Thus Davout does not start from the rule "Spies are to be shot". Instead, by paying attention to his encounter with Pierre, he sees his affliction and does not shoot him, in a sense recreating the law as "All men are brothers and are not to be shot".

ATTENTION AND THE JOURNEY

What is important here is paying attention to the story; looking at all the empirical details; following it all along its sometimes strange pathways and not necessarily judging its meaning by the application of a pre-determined rule. From that one will come to judgement, and it is in that way that meanings will come which we will be able to use, and perhaps discard, in other situations. But this attention will always be something done within the context of the law. The encounter is a journey which we cannot prejudge although we have a context within which to understand.

Let us look at an example of what we mean here by considering the sacred parables. One might think of the parables of Jesus in two ways. First of all, we can think of them as things that impose meaning on a situation and thus provide us an answer. In this way we can view them, as Jülicher did,[26] as simple stories which have been made more complex by the Synoptic Gospels. What they do is tell us simple platitudes which neither show us their mysterious complexity nor disturb what MacKinnon calls the "cake of custom".[27] In this way they tell us nothing that we do not already know, since the stories are merely ways of making that simple message clear to the listeners. Jülicher, then, fights against the ideas of the parables being allegories, as wanting to move beyond themselves. He reduces them, in the second volume of his work, to, as it were, a moral message for each—as though one could reduce, as White[28] points out, the dark and complex parable of the Good Samaritan to the banal aphorism, "Love knows no limit". But the point of the parables is not to impose meanings on the situation.

---

[26] A. Jülicher, *Die Gleichnissreden Jesu* (Freiburg, J.C.B., 1889).

[27] D. MacKinnon, *The Problem of Metaphysics* (Cambridge, Cambridge University Press, 1974) chs. 6–7.

[28] R. White, "MacKinnon and the Parables" in K. Surin (ed.), *Christ, Ethics and Tragedy: Essays in Honour of Donald MacKinnon* (Cambridge, Cambridge University Press, 1989) 49.

As Donald MacKinnon stresses, they are telling us something, not through a general point or some universal principle to be applied rigidly; rather they are an invitation to explore a radically different perspective on a familiar terrain. In that sense they invite us on a journey "beyond". But how can that be? As Roger White points out:[29]

> "The parables are very far from the innocuous little anecdotes that Jülicher made them out to be: if we are to say something better about them than he did, then we must be prepared, with Donald MacKinnon, to confront them in their strangeness, to embark on an exploration, and [sic] exploration which leads to the heart of the divine even if it goes along routes that we would not of ourselves have dared to take."

It is this theme of journey that is important. Expressed in a different way, Hillis Miller says that parables are performatives in that they make things happen:[30]

> "A parable is a way to do things with words. It is a speech act. In the case of the parables of Jesus, however, the performative makes something happen in the hearts and minds of his hearers, but this happening is a knowledge of a state of affairs already existing, the Kingdom of Heaven and the way to get there."

Now the idea of the journey is all-important here, for it is right that the sacred parables are there to do something to the listeners. It is to get them on and ready for a journey where the destination is not really given; the kingdom is something that is to guide them on the way. What the parables do not provide is moral certainty. MacKinnon examines the apocalyptic parable of the Last Judgment (Matthew 25: 31–46) in which Jesus describes the separation of the sheep from the goats. MacKinnon points out the strangeness of this parable, residing in the fact that neither the righteous nor the cursed know who they are. Both are equally baffled by the judgement passed upon them. They both must ask of the Christ, "When did we feed, clothe, welcome, or visit you?" or, "When did we fail to do so?". The point is not that one can establish those to whom one owes an obligation and dutifully fulfil it in the certain knowledge that one has observed the demands of the law. Nor is the point that one has an indiscriminate and boundless obligation to everyone whom one encounters. The point is that one cannot rest secure in knowledge.[31]

> "Watch therefore, for you do not know on what day your Lord is coming. But know this, that if the householder had known in what part of the night the thief was coming, he would have watched and would not have let his house be broken into. Therefore you also must be ready; for the Son of man is coming at an hour you do not expect."

[29] R. White, "MacKinnon and the Parables" in K. Surin (ed.), *Christ, Ethics and Tragedy: Essays in Honour of Donald MacKinnon* (Cambridge, Cambridge University Press, 1989) at 69.
[30] "Parable and Performative in the Gospels and Modern Literature" in J. Hillis Miller, *Tropes, Parables and Performatives: Essays in Twentieth Century Literature* (Hemel Hempstead, Harvester Wheatsheaf, 1990) 135.
[31] Matthew 24: 42–4.

"If a man or woman supposes that he or she can provide exhaustive and definitive criteria for distinguishing "the least of these my little ones" from the rank and file of humanity he has evacuated the parable of its irony. He has indeed converted it from a parable into a recipe whereby he can achieve a certain moral security, even play in his own eyes the elevating role of the saviour of mankind, the one on whose service the outcasts depend."[32]

We have to risk the journey, guided but in the dark.

We might say that the parables are the meeting ground of the law and love, the particular and the universal. Parables are true only to the extent that they create and maintain a tension between law and love, between the received wisdom of tradition and the often shattering demands of a particular encounter. Law and love are not in opposition; rather, each provides the possible conditions of existence for the other. Without law one has no discernment, no powers of articulation, no means of recognising the situation which calls the law into question. Without love, law is empty and meaningless. The parabolic discourse is the discourse of this mutuality. Thus they do not do away with law; they are recounted within a setting framed by the law. "Who is my neighbour?", "Why does your teacher eat with tax collectors and sinners?", "Why do we and the Pharisees fast, but your disciples do not fast?", "Is it lawful to heal on the Sabbath?", "Why do your disciples transgress the tradition of the elders? For they do not wash their hands when they eat", "Lord, how often shall my brother sin against me, and I forgive him?". These questions are legal questions posed as challenges to Jesus' observance or non-observance of the law. He responds to such challenges with parables. The answers that he gives are not, however, saying that we must abolish the law and have love instead. Instead, as we have shown, in the act of love he re-establishes the law anew.

We will return to these themes in our conclusion, but at the moment we turn to explore some common law reasoning in this light. Bernard Jackson in *Law, Fact and Narrative Coherence*[33] explores the law from the point of view of narrative and of story telling. Part of his point is that it is attention to the *stories* of the cases which leads to an understanding of the result, rather than the rules which give these cases a pre-ordained meaning. By looking at a collection of similar but not identical contract cases,[34] he provides an example of how attention to narrativity can help us to understand common law decision making. The basic scenario is as follows. Someone offers to buy something from a seller, while holding himself out to be someone he is not, someone respected and creditworthy. He gets the goods and pays for them with a bad cheque (or something similar) and then sells them on to an innocent third party. The original seller discovers the fraud and wants his goods back. The question rests on whether title has been passed, and that in turn rests on whether the contract was void or

[32] D. MacKinnon, *supra* n. 27 at 86.
[33] B. Jackson, *Law, Fact and Narrative Coherence* (Merseyside, Deborah Charles Publications, 1988).
[34] *Ibid.*, 101–6.

voidable. If the contract was voidable, then title has been passed, and the seller is unlucky because the fraudster has already passed the (valid) title on. The criterion of whether the contract is void or voidable depends on whether the seller is taken to be selling it to the person with whom he has the face-to-face encounter or the person who he claims he is. In the former, the contract is merely voidable and title has passed.

In *Cundy* v. *Lindsay*[35] the fraud was done by letter. One Blenkarn claimed to be "Blenkiron & Co." (an existing and reputable firm). It was held here that the seller intended to contract only with the firm and therefore the contract was void *ab initio*, and title had not passed. This was distinguished in the case of *Phillips* v. *Brooks Ltd.*[36] There, someone went to a jeweller representing himself as Sir George Bullough and signed, in exchange for some jewels, a cheque in that name. The shopkeeper checked to see if there was a Bullough living at the address given. Here it was held that title had passed as the shopkeeper had intended to sell to the person in his shop. Jackson now asks us to consider the case of *Ingram* v. *Little*.[37] Here the fraud was perpetrated by someone who claimed to be one P.G.M. Hutchinson. The sellers checked in the telephone book to see if there was such a person living at the address claimed, and when they saw there was they sold their car to him in return for a bad cheque. Here the contract was declared void and no title passed.

Jackson points out that there was no real difference between the last two cases: both are face-to-face encounters. He says that you can understand the different decision only in terms of paying attention to the story. In the former, the story is about a shopkeeper, a jeweller, who would be presumed to expect at least some fraud; and, in the latter, it was a private transaction with two old ladies. In terms of our argument, one might say that the courts were paying attention to the empirical detail and, in hesitating to apply the law under the old rule, recreated it as, according to Jackson, "the consequences of a mistake as to creditworthiness differ according to whether the party is a retailer or a private individual".[38]

Jackson then goes on to look at the next case in line, *Lewis* v. *Averay*.[39] Here the fraudster posed as Richard Greene who was a well-known film actor. He produced proof of his identity with admission passes to a studio and a car logbook in that name. The car was duly sold for a bad cheque. This time the contract was held voidable and, accordingly, title had passed. This is confusing since it appears not to be different from *Ingram* v. *Little*. However if we pay attention to the details of the story then we do see, according to Jackson, why the decision went the way that it did. Jackson suggests that, in *Lewis* v. *Averay*, the story was told in such a way as to indicate that the seller was fooled rather

[35] [1873] 3 AC 459.
[36] [1912] 2 KB 243.
[37] [1961] 1 QB 31.
[38] Jackson, *supra* n. 33 at 104.
[39] [1971] 3 All ER 907.

than defrauded. In this case, the seller and the innocent third party were both young and clever (they were students), so the choice in respect of distributing the loss between them was marginal. Therefore, since the seller had behaved stupidly (who would have believed the fraudster's story?), the loss was left with him. In the former case, of course, the story was entirely different. We were dealing with little old ladies (it is amazing how the old are judged not as smart as the young), and the loss for them would have been greater.

Jackson uses these examples to put forward a particular semiotic view of law. What is important for us, however, is to see other elements: how the fact of getting immersed in the practical details and cross-currents of the story drives the judgment on; how the judges are standing in the ground where the law meets the particular; and how one might theorise this as being in the middle. Of course, judicial decision-making does not always work in this way, and judges often use more (in terms of our argument in respect of parables) of a Jülicher way of looking at the decision, that is to say, looking at it from the perspective of a rule without going into the particularity of the case. One needs the rules or principles, but it is in the particularity of the actual case that they meet.

This way of looking at things—from the middle—helps us in understanding one of the problems about arguments from analogy in the law. The approach proceeds roughly as follows. If arguments from analogy work by saying that one thing is similar to another by reference to a general principle that fits them under one category, then why is it necessary to have the analogy when deduction from a principle will do? The answer would be that the principle is necessary, but in the end it will be the encounter with the case itself that will determine whether the principle will be applied. It will be in that act that the law is suspended and recreated anew on the model that we saw of the encounter between Davout and Pierre. And so one is living in and out of the law but denying neither.

CONCLUSION: THE GOOD SAMARITAN

On one occasion a lawyer came forward to put this test question to him: " 'Master, what must I do to inherit eternal life?' Jesus said, 'What is written in the Law? What is your reading of it?' He replied, 'Love the Lord your God with all your heart, with all your soul, with all your strength, and with all your mind; and your neighbour as yourself.' 'That is the right answer,' said Jesus; 'do that and you will live.'

But he wanted to vindicate himself, so he said to Jesus, 'And who is my neighbour?' Jesus replied, 'A man was on his way from Jerusalem down to Jericho when he fell in with robbers, who stripped him, beat him, and went off leaving him half dead. It so happened that a priest was going down by the same road; but when he saw him, he went past on the other side. So too a Levite came to the place, and when he saw him went past on the other side. But a Samaritan who was making the journey came upon him, and when he saw him was moved to pity. He went up and bandaged his wounds, bathing them with oil and wine. Then he lifted him on to his own beast, brought him to an inn, and looked after him there. Next day he produced two silver pieces and gave them to the innkeeper, and said, 'Look after him; and if you spend any more, I will repay you on my way back.' 'Which of these three do you think was neighbour to the man who fell into the hand of the robbers?' He answered, 'The one who showed him kindness.' Jesus said, 'Go and do as he did.' "[40]

The parable of the Good Samaritan is a good way to finish this discussion of living in and out of the law. Let us turn to explore just a few of its complexities. Though this parable might be seen as an example of "Love no knows limit" (and therefore as a wider definition of neighbour), it would be a mistake to see it as merely a definition. We can say that Jesus is not just giving us a rather wide definition of neighbour and telling us to love him; rather he is saying that those to whom you act in a neighbourly manner you make your neighbour and tie them to yourself through the bonds of law and obligation. In this sense, then, the violent explosion of love has within it, and inscribed in it, the bonds of the law. It is the way that in each application we extend and recreate the law. We can thus see parallels with the sacrifice of Isaac and our application of it which we discussed above. It is important to note that both the Priest and the Levite had reasons under the law for not going to the help of the injured man, for they would thereby be defiled. We can thus see the suspension of the law and its re-creation. Again we can see that the individual explosion of love is not arbitrary; it is done in the context of the law. For the context of the parable is that Jesus is seen as going outside the law and consorting with sinners, tax collectors etc. He is tested on this by the lawyer and asked what one should do to gain eternal life. The answer that is given is impeccably within the law: "love God and thy neighbour as thyself". The parable is then given in response to the question, "Who is my neighbour?", asked by the lawyer, and it is there that we see the suspension and recreation of the law.

But here our analogy appears to break down, for the one who suspends the law is not like Abraham (one in possession of the law and who lives the life of faith) but the Samaritan. Let us go deeper into the story. First of all, the man we are urged to love is not the injured man but in fact the Samaritan. The parable is told in answer to the question, "Who is my neighbour?", and the answer is: the Samaritan. Why should this be? Surely we are not being told to love the rich and strong? Jesus is here telling us to imagine that when we are in the direst need, as is the injured man, that we are to accept help, extend the bonds of community to those whom we consider our deepest enemies (as the Jews did the Samaritans). In other words, Jesus is also giving us a clue about the identity of those to whom we should act in a neighbourly manner, for he asks us to think of ourselves as equal in weakness. Christianity is not a religion of the strong, but one of equality in weakness and vulnerability. In the parable, in answering the lawyer, Jesus is asking him to consider himself in this position. We see here how this shows the point of the encounter between Davout and Pierre, in which Davout hesitates, and in that hesitation sees the humanity of them both. It is in

---

[40] Luke 10: 25–37.

that hesitation that we see his attention, the ability to let the truth of the particular encounter come to him, make him take pity. At that moment he sees that, like Pierre, he is afflicted; he is weak and vulnerable. So what is also being said is that the law is not to be privileged, that being in possession of the law, like the injured man on the road (he was a Jew) will not make you strong. The law needs love to sustain it. But that does not thereby make love the stronger, for in the gift of love it receives the weakness of the law. (The gift of the Samaritan was dangerous, in that the man lying injured could have been part of a ruse to rob the unwary traveller.) Law and love are dependent on each other in their mutual vulnerability.[41]

So in looking at and paying attention to this dark tale we can see how law and love are mutually dependent. We see that law is continually being made and remade in the encounter with the particularity of the decision, and that all this is done in the context of the law itself. This is how we live both in and out of the law.

[41] See C. Davis, "Who is my Neighbour" (1997) 48 *The Furrow* 583.

3

Faith, Love and a Christianity to Come: St. Augustine and the Coming of Justice

ADAM GEAREY*

How can St. Augustine be read in our dark times? Any questioning of St. Augustine and his masterwork, *De Civitatae Dei, The City of God*,[1] is inseparable from a broader and no less pressing question: to what extent can faith be seen as a central aspect of a critical philosophy of law?[2] This essay offers a reading of Augustine that takes seriously the deployment of "postmodern" thought within Christian theology. Central to the argument will be a focus on Augustine's understanding of love. Love is the definition of the human; there is no one who does not love: *nemo est qui non amet*.[3] However,

* Thanks to Robert Cartledge, Piyel Haldar, Pannu Minkkinen, Maria Drakopoulou, Peter Oliver, Sionaidh Douglas Scott, Victor Tadros and M.C. Grenham.

[1] St. Augustine, *The City of God against the Pagans* (Harmondsworth: Penguin Books, 1972).

[2] The idea of critical legal studies is problematic. Critical Legal Studies (CLS) is traditionally traced back to scholarly activism in American Universities in the 1970s. Drawing on Marxism and phenomenology, CLS scholarship was first marked by an attack on what was perceived to be the inherent contradictions of the prevalent liberal theory and practice of the law, and a critique of the reification of human relations in legal discourse. Gary Minder in *Postmodern Legal Movements* (New York, New York University Press, 1995) at 116–27, proposes a second wave of CLS that engaged to a greater extent with deconstruction and other forms of poststructuralist thought. For a critique of American CLS from the perspective of an English critical scholar, see Peter Goodrich, 'Sleeping with the Enemy: An Essay on the Politics of CLS in America" (1993) 68 *New York University Law Review* 1013. British critical legal studies seems to thrive on its impossibility: see Peter Goodrich, "Critical Legal Studies in England: Prospective Histories" (1992) 12 *OJLS* 195: rather than being a unified movement, it is fragmentary and draws on a variety of critical and theoretical paradigms. See also P. Fitzpatrick and A. Hunt (eds.), *Critical Legal Studies* (Oxford, Blackwell, 1990). An essential text for any attempt to read Augustine's work as a critical philosophy of law is A. Hirvonen (ed.), *Polycentricity: The Multiple Scenes of Law* (London, Pluto Press, 1998). In particular see Hirvonen's essay "After the Law", *ibid.*, 239–45. See also P. Minkkinen, *Correct Law: A Philosophy of the Aporetic* (Helsinki, Basileus, 1998) for a consideration of the philosophy of the aporetic and legal theory.

[3] Hannah Arendt, quoting St Augustine in *Love and St Augustine* (Chicago, Ill., University of Chicago Press, 1996) at 259. This essay represents an early stage in Arendt's writing; it reads as a working through of her various intellectual debts and the search for her own authentic voice. A more conventional introduction to St Augustine is E. Gilson, *The Christian Philosophy of Saint Augustine* (London: Gollancz, 1961). Gilson presents Augustine as a "true philosopher" whose philosophy "implies an act of adherence to the supernatural order which frees the will from the flesh

this definition is built on an unresolvable contradiction between its pagan roots and its incorporation into Augustine's theology. Augustine attempts to elaborate a Christian celebration of *agape* from a pagan concern with *eros*, the body and its desires. Tracing the disruptive implications of this contradiction will allow a re-reading of *De Civitatae Dei* as a description of law's illegitimacy. Faith is an essential aspect of this project.[4] The strange nexus between love and faith (or, to put it in other words, the separation Augustine describes between The Heavenly City of *Civitas Dei* and The Earthly City), opens the possibility of a far-reaching critique of state law. State law can be questioned from the perspective of a more profound provocation of a justice whose arrival in the affairs of the world is always imminent.

This political atheology[5] is not an attempt simply to revive law's theological foundations by reference to a source of divine purity. It is an expression of the need to think of the law and the human subject as resting on a contradiction that needs to be sustained rather then resolved; a contradiction that is necessary for a critical thinking of justice. Political atheology can be described as a thinking that operates from within legal traditions and genealogies, but suggests that law's future might always be different from its past; or that the future might be contained within a past which is still to come.

through grace and the mind from scepticism through revelation" (235–6). This essay will problematise the autonomy and sufficiency of Gilson's terms without rejecting them completely.

[4] The question of faith in Augustine's thought is a subject of great complexity. A useful introduction is provided by A. Dulles, in *The Assurance of Things Hoped For* (Oxford: Oxford University Press, 1994), especially at 25–8. Dulles argues that Augustine's earliest writings, with their Neoplatonic influence, conceive of the subject trapped in a world of empty appearances that prevent any knowledge of divinity. Asceticism becomes a necessary element of faith. In *The Confessions*, faith is achieved through obedience to the word of God and a denial of the world and the sensuous. The later works move more towards a conjunction of faith and charity. Moved by the spirit of charity, the believer can find an intimation of God. The essential problematic is one of knowledge of God in the darkness of the fallen world. Augustine thus repeats the basic Christian foundation of faith in a testimony to Christ as the Son of God. To witness Christ is to have faith; a faith that although it operates through reason must go beyond the rational and act out of belief. As belief involves the will, and the will is motivated by love, the essential conjunction between faith and love is stressed. Dulles quotes a passage from *De Moribus Ecclesiae* (Book 1, ch.17, 26, n.31): '[i]t is love that asks; it is love that seeks; it is love that knocks; it is love that makes one adhere to revelation, and it is love that maintains the adherence once it is given". There is also an interesting sense in which faith involves the play between the hidden and the revealed: "[f]aith prepares us for the vision of that which we do not see. Its merit consists in believing that which remains hidden . . ." Dulles, *ibid.*, at 27. Dulles goes on to argue that faith thus has to work in time, although its object is eternity. As this correlates with the problematic of love and the world to be developed in this essay, the notion of time and faith will serve as the guide through the complexities of Augustine's thought.

[5] Political atheology is a reworking of political theology from the perspective of postmodernity. This term gestures towards the idea of a political theology and also Mark C. Taylor's atheology: M. Taylor, *Erring, A Postmodern Atheology* (Chicago, Ill., Chicago University Press, 1984). For a review of ideas of political theology see J.H. Burns (ed.), *The Cambridge History of Medieval Political Thought* (Cambridge, Cambridge University Press, 1988). This return to political theology opens questions about the construction of law: see P. Haldar, "Synchronoi Dike, On the Question of Dissemblance in Medieval Political Theology" (1996) 7 *Law and Critique* 85.

THE RETURN OF ST. AUGUSTINE

Augustine has become the lodestar for an attempt to create a "postmodern (or post liberal) theology".[6] Moving away from those readings that see Augustine as an anticipator of dialectical method,[7] "postmodern theology" is concerned with locating an incorrect appropriation of Christian theology as a fault-line of modernism. John Milbank's work is exemplary of this search as it critiques modernism as an unsuccessful realisation of a humanism that banishes the sacred to the purely private realm and understands revelation as a "positivistic concept . . . interrupting the normal self sufficiency of reason".[8] Elaborating this position is a critical approach to the separation of law and value that is similar to the postmodern analysis of the diremption of ethics and law.[9] At stake is a vision of a different future where the law has to become more than a balancing of power and an algebra of property rights. Underlying the re-thinking of law is a revision of traditional Christianity. Revelation and any praxis drawing on Christian faith must be understood as historically situated but interpreted in historical circumstances in a way that is not closed and eschatological but open to the changing interpretation of the Christian message through time. In a memorable phrase this process is described as "the continuing story of the Church, already realised in a finally exemplary way by Christ, yet still to be realised universally, in harmony with Christ, and yet differently, by all generations of Christians".[10] Milbank's postmodern re-interpretation of Gospel narrative can form the basis for the appropriation of Augustine. It is from within the dynamic and updating narrative that the resource for a reinvention of *Civitas Dei* can be drawn.[11]

---

[6] J. Milbank, *Theology and Social Theory* (Oxford, Blackwell, 1990) at 382.

[7] See E. Alliez, *Capital Times* (Minnesota: University of Minnesota Press, 1996), at 92–6.

[8] *Supra* n. 6 at 19.

[9] G. Rose, *The Broken Middle* (Oxford, Blackwell, 1992) at 277–84. Although Rose addresses the separation of law and ethics, she does so from a perspective very different from that of Milbank. She is critical of Milbank's self–proclaimed postmodernism. For Rose, the postmodernists have been too "hasty" in announcing the end of metaphysics and philosophy; postmodernism cannot conceive of its own complicity in the unresolved problems of modernist thought. The whole attempt to utilise a discourse of love or holiness ignores a different approach that would posit a "political history" which would approach the *agon* of a philosophy which has constantly to repeat and rewrite itself. The problems of freedom and unfreedom, universality and singularity, and the problem of an originary violence cannot be avoided. The present essay might save a "postmodern political theology" by arguing that the "aporia" is precisely the point which philosophy and theology repeat without comprehending. This is not a break with either theology or philosophy, but the realisation of the contradictions existing in these traditions of thought. Rose writes that Revelation might enter philosophy as "the incursion of the incomprehensible" (at 18). The aporia of *eros* and *agape* is perhaps a similar problematic. A reinvention of *De Civitate Dei* would leave "the ethical open and unresolved" in much the same way as Derrida's discourse on faith and the gift beyond exchange (discussed *infra*). See also M. Mack, "Law and Charity" in A. Gearey and J. Butler (eds.), *Law Text Culture* (Motus, Chippendale, Australia), v, no. 1, summer 1999.

[10] *Supra* n. 6, at 386.

[11] *Ibid.*, at 402.

Civitas Dei can be actualised in the community of a Church that does not inhabit a terrestrial territory, but through its offer of salvation for all victims, gives the hope of an alternative to the power of secular law. Christianity opposes the construction of the legal subject as a possessive individual. This model can be traced back to the inherent individualism of Roman law. The classical vision conceives of law as based on economy and exchange organised around a mean. Underpinning this world view is a community predicated on a search for worldly honour and glory that is profoundly alien to the Christian vision of just order. With its concept of *dominium*, where goods and slaves can be owned and freely exchanged by economic actors, Roman law offers a proto-model of the market form that has dominated liberal and modernist thought. A Christian critique would specifically reject the *phronesis* of political man, who, blind to revelation, can use his wisdom only to distribute economies in the temporal world. In the place of the individual as economic actor, the Augustinian understanding of law is profoundly social. Essential here is the mystic notion of the body of Christ as the symbol that holds the Church together:[12]

> "Augustine allows us to see many forms of the "the social" beyond the political, and so implies that the political is necessarily imperfectly social . . . True society implies absolute consensus . . . and entire harmony amongst its members, and this is exactly . . . what the church provides, and that in which salvation, the restoration of being, consists."

In the space of the *eschaton*, whilst the return of the rule of divinity is awaited, the government of men by men is made necessary, but is always more or less illegitimate. The necessity for discipline in the world is a tragedy, which the Church copes with as best it can. Providing a living practice of forgiveness, the Church acknowledges that any form of discipline or punishment has a tendency to fall into sin itself, as it derives from the human urge to power and control. It is as if the Church must oppose discipline with a counter practice that recognises the inherent illegitimacy of state power in the face of love.

Although certain disagreements with this version of "political Augustinianism" will be elaborated in the present essay, the orientation of the argument will be to sustain what Milbank describes as the "path of a peaceful flight".[13] Before postmodern theology can become useful to critical legal studies, it is necessary to face two related problems. Given the commitment of critical legal studies to plural modes of thought, there has to be a defusal of an imperialistic Christianity that assumes jurisdiction over the "truth".[14] Related to this problem is the need to resist pessimistic Christian tendencies that deny the body and

---

[12] *Ibid.*, p. 406.

[13] *Ibid.*, at 434.

[14] For a particularly insightful consideration of this problem, see D.H. Lawrence, *Apocalypse* (Penguin, Harmondsworth, 1986). *The Book of Revelation* is seen as representative of a kind of Christianity: "[w]hat we realise when we have read the precious book a few times is that John the Divine had on the face of it a grandiose scheme for wiping out and annihilating everybody who wasn't of the elect . . ." (at 9).

materiality in recompense for a life hereafter. How can Augustine's thought be opened to reinvention?

The philosophy of alterity offers itself as an important ally.[15] Scholars of legal theory have drawn on the thinking of alterity to articulate a theory of ethics as a critique of the orthodoxies of legal philosophy and practice. It would be wrong, however, to see the philosophy of alterity as presenting another set of theoretical "tools" for legal analysis. Alterity is not a concept; it cannot be reduced to an object of knowledge or a methodology. At best it could perhaps be described as a provocation. Thinking alterity makes for a restatement of an ancient problem which returns to Plato and the roots of the tradition. To be human is to desire the just, but to find that determinations of justice as secular and positive laws do not satisfy the yearning. This yearning for justice has been described as an ethics.[16] From this ethical perspective the problems haunting modernist legal thought can be reappraised. Despite the attempts to found law in its purity as an autonomous and self-regulating body of rules, the problem of ethics remains. Law has frequently disassociated itself from the ethical, and yet the need for "justice" has never quite been satisfied by its determination as rule-based or administrative procedures.[17]

[15] A key text here is C. Douzinas and R. Warrington, *Justice Miscarried* (London, Harvester Wheatsheaf, 1994). The work of Douzinas and Warrington represents a particularly productive tracing of what is occulted in the Western tradition of legal philosophy. As there can be no return to a golden age where law and justice were united, the responsibility of critical thought is to reassess the legacy of the Western tradition in the light of the postmodern condition, or "the exhaustion of the exalted attempts to ground action upon cognition, reason or some a priori stipulated conception of the good" (at 160). Although the Socratic dialogues determine justice as the quest for the just community, these foundational texts cannot offer a definition of the just. Justice is a desire that "must be accepted before any final rational justification of [its] desirability" (at 135). This is an awakening to a new beginning that is already ancient, the revivification of a "Law of law" deep within the archives of Western thought. Although Douzinas and Warrington open up legal philosophy to alterity, they tend to reject or denigrate the Christian tradition and the possibilities it offers for critical thought. See also M. Davies *Delimiting the Law: "Postmodernism" and the Politics of Law* (London, Pluto Press, 1996). For Davies, alterity names a way of thinking against imposed limits; it offers a form of immanent critique which borrows the deconstructive notion that no tradition or text is ever closed. It cannot be a question of simply rejecting the law in the name of a moment of liberation. The "struggle between necessity and possibility"(at 16) is the paradoxical position of the critical account of the law, which operates within a field both limited by its conceptual resources and open to trangresssive or subversive interpretations of those resources. Any transgression is, however, a re-affirmation of the boundary in the very act of acknowledging that it needs to be transcended. This is no cause for despair: "a transgression is a challenge that demonstrates the permeability of our frontiers, and may in the process weaken or otherwise alter their rigidity" (16) Thinking differently effectively reinscribes the limit. It relates to a critical conception of justice which is not reducible to a specific content, as "[i]t remains a projection beyond law, a 'beyond' which is opened up continually" (at 8).

[16] See Douzinas and Warrington in *Justice Miscarried*, *supra* n. 15.

[17] A key text here is J. Derrrida, "The Force of Law: The 'Mystical Foundations of Authority' " in D. Cornell, M. Rosenfeld and D.G. Carlson (eds.), *Deconstruction and the Possibility of Justice* (New York, Routledge, 1993) 3. See also Douzinas *et al.* (eds.), *Politics, Postmodernity and Critical Legal Studies: The Legality of the Contingent* (London, Routledge, 1994). For a consideration of the disturbance of ethics in the common law, see M. Drakopoulou, "Dangerous Liaisons? The Relationship of Equity and the Common Law", *Law Text Culture*, forthcoming. For an elaboration of a similar perspective on the English constitutional tradition, see A. Gearey, "Towards a Feminist Critique of Sovereignty" in N. Whitty and S. Millns (eds.), *Feminist Perspectives on Public Law* (Cavendish, London, 1999).

Certain correlations can thus be traced between the philosophy of alterity and postmodern Christianity. The shared critical perspective suggests that an alliance between these trajectories of thought could be productive; especially as there is a need to engage with the "genealogy" of western law which is unthinkable without the influence of Christianity. There is also the important sense in which the problems encountered in political Augustinianism outlined above could be addressed from this different perspective and a reinvention of Augustine's thought made possible. However, bringing together a postmodern Christianity and a thinking of alterity would mean negotiating one of the most intractable problems of philosophy and theology: the complex relationship between Christian revelation and the philosophy of reason.[18] How can these two opposite ideas be brought into communication with each other? Again, it is possible to borrow from the philosophy of alterity and to utilise the notion of the aporia. At a general level thinking aporetically involves the radical reappraisal of relationships that were thought to have been settled; in this sense it is coherent with Milbank's project: man, community and the certainties of the sociological tradition are opened to the most profound questioning. At its deepest level, the aporia names the simultaneous existence of "two different, even antagonistic or incompatible relations".[19] The aporia describes the contradic-

---

[18]   The complexities of this issue can only be hinted at in this essay. For an overview of the problem, see N.H.G. Robinson, *The Groundwork of Christian Ethics* (London, Collins, 1971). Robinson concentrates on modern Protestant theology, but locates it in relation to Augustine and Aquinas. Robinson presents Augustine as "superimposing" a Christian "insight" onto Platonic ethics, thus suggesting, but not elaborating, the difficulties that are attendant on this conjunction of reason and faith. The problem is nevertheless well illustrated in a quotation from D.M. Baillie, who describes the "all round paradox of . . . Christian faith and experience" (*ibid.*, 14–15). A particularly acute working through of reason and revelation can be found in the work of the German theologian, Helmut Thielicke, whose encyclopædic *Theological Ethics* (London, Adam and Charles Black, 1966) presents an articulation of ethics from the perspective of "being in the world" (*ibid.*, p. xxiii). This work contains many interesting parallels with an ethics of alterity. Thielicke writes that "[t]he believer cannot . . . believe "in" God without believing "against" the reality in which he finds himself [a reality to be interpreted through the use of reason, inductively and deductively], the reality which seems to be opposed to God and in the face of which he must struggle through to the "nevertheless" of faith" (*ibid.*, p. xviii). The believer thus struggles with both faith and the demands of the world, which pull in opposite directions; the believer suffers a "fall" in fulfilling divine mandates as there are opposing commitments in the world which need to be honoured. Derrida is struggling with a similar problem in *The Gift of Death* (Chicago, Ill., Chicago University Press, 1985). This text will be considered below. Thielicke's concept of the "borderline situation" where the commands of God and the demands of the world come into conflict is similar in some respects to Derrida's aporia; but for Thielicke there is hope that ethics can be organised dialectically into a coherent structure. Derrida's meditations on Kierkegaard, also in *The Gift of Death,* might present a way into a reappraisal of this approach to Christian ethics.

[19]   J. Derrida, "Acts of Literature" in D. Attridge (ed.), *Jacques Derrida and the Questioning of Literature* (London: Routledge, 1992) at 2. For a useful discussion of what is placed in question by the aporia and the deconstruction of theology, see K. Hart, "Jacques Derrida, The God Effect" in Philip Blond (ed.), *Post-secular Philosophy* (London, Routledge, 1998) at 259. Hart argues that Derrida never quite makes an assertion of faith, nor declares himself to be an atheist. Commenting on the notion of the gift beyond exchange, Hart writes that it is a "scandalous thought because it is, at heart, a thought of faith, maybe *the* thought of faith, the thought that only faith can give" (*ibid.*, 261). This strange faith is tracked through Derrida's commentaries on negative theology, and Hart "concludes" that Derrida's work helps to draw attention to the necessary tensions, the "aporias"

tory relationship of terms that have been thought of as separate and autonomous. Thinking the aporia might show that reason itself is founded on what it would like to expel; the undisciplined, shocking and radical interpellation of alterity. There is a great deal at stake in this dislocation of divinity in alterity. In the encounter between alterity and Christianity, any divinity becomes strictly unknowable, irreducible to human reason; but nevertheless it continues to enter the world, and to surprise with a responsibility that could articulate the problematic relationship between reason and revelation. Jacques Derrida has seen the "sacrifice" of Isaac as a traumatic moment when a rational Kantian ethics of duty comes up against a limit:[20]

> "In order to assume his absolute responsibility with respect to absolute duty . . . [Abraham] must also in reality remain a hateful murderer . . . In both general and abstract terms, the absoluteness of duty, of responsibility, and of obligation certainly demands that one transgress ethical duty, although in betraying it one belongs to it. The contradiction must be endured in the instant itself."

As Kant has been hailed as possibly one of the greatest "Christian moralists",[21] this engagement with a Kantian vocabulary can perhaps best describe the coming together of alterity and Christian ethics. The categorical imperative is refigured as an interpellation of a radical otherness that resists reduction to thought; it is thus a re-appraisal of an ethic in which the rational subject gives himself the law. As its very title suggests, the categorical imperative places an irresistible demand on the moral agent. It makes the agent's will both the rational producer of the law and subject to that law which is binding because it is rational. The appeal of the other is a "dissymmetry".[22] It prompts a refiguring

---

(*ibid.*, 278) that must be kept at play in theology. See also J.D. Caputo, *The Prayers and Tears of Jacques Derrida* (Bloomington and Indianapolis, Ind., Indiana University Press, 1997) 57. Caputo describes deconstruction as a "*fin de siècle* faith" (*ibid.*, 57). His concern is to outline the way in which deconstruction does not replace faith but re-orientates the discourse of faith: the deconstructive deployment of "indefiniteness" and "undecidability" is merely one way of approaching the conditions of "the decision" and the statement "*je ne sais pas, il faut croire*" (*ibid.*, 338). Caputo's rhapsodic conclusion, which reads rather like Kerouac's memorialisations of Neal Cassady, implies that St. Augustine is a vital figure to establish a "religion without religion".

[20] J. Derrida, *The Gift of Death* (Chicago, Ill., Chicago University Press 1985) 66.

[21] Robinson, *supra* n. 18 at 73. Also, see E. Cassirer, *Law and Grace* (Edinburgh, The Handsel Press, 1988). Cassirer's study of Kant, St Paul and the Hebrew prophets reads as the spiritual biography of a disgruntled Kantian. The key to the argument is a comparison of St. Paul's rejection of the old law with Kant's insistence that it is only through conformity of will with law, that the human subject is made free from self-destructive passions and impulses. Kant's view of law and freedom forces man to rely on reason, but this cannot free the human subject from the influence of evil. Cassirer maintains that it is only through commitment to a notion of the revelation of law rather than its rational discovery that the problems inherent in Kant's understanding of moral law can be addressed. Although the present project is not in touch with this form of argument, the notion of revelation as a source of law, and the limitations of reason could have certain resonances within postmodernism and critical legal studies.

[22] In *The Gift of Death* (Chicago, Ill., Chicago University Press 1985), Derrida has approached this problem through the story of Isaac in Exodus. The command of the other is always specific: a demand to a particular person at a particular time. It must disrupt any universal moral system. Derrida describes Abraham's response as responsible because he answers for himself before the

of Kantian ethics where respect for the other is conceived on the basis that the other is also subject to a categorical imperative that reflects the universalising principles of reason. The appeal of the other does not relate back to the ego or the will of the rational subject. In this figuring of responsibility the categorical imperative acts "as if" it was revelatory, an inbreaking of what is both beyond and fundamental to reason.

If this reinscription of ethics were acceptable, the next problem would be the need to find in Augustine the bringing together of an ethical interpellation that is "revelatory" with a sense of a location in the world that is not dismissive of materiality and hence does not make Christianity a religion of a world denying spirituality.

FAITH AND LOVE IN ST. AUGUSTINE.

Augustine's thought cannot be read in a vacuum, and so to appreciate his deployment of faith it is necessary to begin with the Bible. Given the constraints of this paper, an exhaustive review of the Biblical literature is not possible; it does however, seem sensible to start with St Paul. Augustine's awakening was provoked by the Pauline texts, and the central concept of *De Civitatae Dei* can be traced to the writings of the apostle.

In *The First Letter to the Corinthians* (13:3), Paul writes of faith, hope and charity. This nexus represents the linkage at the core of Christianity between love and the law. Arguably, it is here that thinking of the aporia of ethics can begin. The love that relates man to God, the law that is written on the heart, is love as *agape*. Anders Nygren in his account of the Christian notion of love presents *agape* as the reworking of Jewish legal righteousness from the perspective of a principle of excess, a lack of proportion in God's dealings with men. It is impossible to try to extract from this theory of *agape* that which appears excessive from the perspective of sober legal theory. The viewpoint is unable to describe the relationship between God and man, as the originating of the law in an absolute epiphany, a moment that is strange, disturbing and beyond proportion or reason.

It would be possible to find in this epiphany of *agapaic* interpellation a resonance with the ethics of alterity developed above. The aporia emerges in the relationship with another manifestation of love, *eros*. Plotting the disruptions of the aporia in Augustine's thought necessitates a brief detour through the

"absolute other" and yet "paradoxically irresponsible because it is guided neither by reason nor by an ethics justifiable before men or before the law of some universal tribunal" (*ibid.*, 77). The demand to be responsible is impossible to satisfy in that one cannot be responsible both before the other and before others: if God names the inaccessibility of the other, and others are seen as equally inaccessible it "implies that God, as the wholly other, is to be found everywhere there is something of the wholly other". This means that Abraham's relationship with God is equally that of the relationship to any other. The excessiveness of this relationship cannot be made present, cannot appear as revelation or the privileging of a single unproblematic term.

secondary literature on his theology. In Anders Nygren's major study of love in the western tradition,[23] *eros* is opposed to *agape*. *Eros* is a motif of pagan thought. It describes a *eudaemonism*, an ethics that is unfamiliar to Christian revelation. Augustine's *Confessions* describe the influence of a particular passage from *The Symposium*, the "right way of *eros*".[24] The lover of the world is led upwards towards a knowledge of beauty itself. Cicero's *Hortensius*, another profoundly influential text for Augustine, concerns a similar quest for eternal philosophical wisdom. *Eros* is linked to the notion of reason and to the self-fashioning of the philosopher. In another sense, *eros* is "boundless"[25] or "excessive"[26] desire. Involved in the world, in the fleshy desires of lovers and the caress of bodies, *eros* is discovered in physical intimacy and immediacy.[27] Even if *eros* ultimately moves beyond the economics of desire in physical love, it is precisely in the embrace that we achieve an intimation of heaven.[28]

In Augustine's though *eros* as love of the world has to become transfigured to *agapaic* love of God. The ecstatic or visionary elements of *eros* have to become overdetermined by *agape*[29] in a fusion that is given a new name, *caritas*.[30] Augustine sees *caritas*, or charity, as the root of good, just as the desires of the flesh are the root of evil. Caritas carries with it the *agapaic* notion of God's freely given love or grace and man's response to this love. In *caritas* God becomes the object of man's love. Augustine would like to demarcate the lines of *eros* and *agape*, but *eros* remains difficult to discipline. Augustine's strategy is to link *eros* with the transient, with the world that passes away. *Eros* is rein-

[23] A. Nygren, *Agape and Eros: A Study in the Christian Idea of Love* (London, SPCM, 1930) 465.
[24] See Nygren, *ibid.*, 246.
[25] D. de Rougement, *Passion and Society* (London, Faber and Faber, 1951) 61.
[26] T. Chanter, *Ethics of Eros* (London, Routledge, 1995) 160.
[27] I. Singer in *The Nature of Love* (New York, Random House, 1966) describes how in pagan thought *eros* is "primarily an attribute of man" (*ibid.*, 166).
[28] *Eros* itself has an aporetic structure. Singer, *ibid.*, describes the myth in *The Phaedrus* which presents human nature as a pair of winged horses who pull the charioteer in opposite directions: towards heaven and towards earth. Plato describes the contrary impulses which define human nature as both body and soul. Likewise, the madness associated with *eros* can also be divided into a divine madness and a debased madness. Singer suggests that this is a psychosis that results from contrary impulses to sexual desire. In *The Symposium*, this association with physical love continues, and *eros* love is linked with sexual union and with reproduction. *The Symposium* and *The Phaedrus* in *The Collected Dialogues of Plato* ed., E. Hamilton and H. Cairns (Princeton, Princeton University Press, 1961).
[29] Nygren, *supra* n. 23, identifies a lurking dialectical vocabulary in this reading; a portrayal of a "synthesis" which does not destroy the pre-existing elements, but brings them to a higher resolution. Augustine represents a coming together of Christian and pagan attitudes to love; indeed he is a figure who stands on the "frontier" (*ibid.*, 451) between Greek and Christian world views, his work is a "renewal" (*ibid.*, 250) of the tradition which brings with it a reappraisal of *agape*.
[30] Underlying *caritas* is a theory of the human subject as a desiring subject which Augustine inherited from the Greek tradition where love is described as craving, or in the Latin translation, *appetitus*. The goal of human life is happiness, or the satisfaction of craving. Man is destined to desire, constantly to have needs which demand satisfaction: to be human is to strive for objects in the world. Just as man cannot escape from desire, he is haunted by fear of loss once he has obtained the desired object. It was from this torment of worldly desire that Augustine looked to God for release. It was a release bound up with the notion of love understood as *caritas*. It is this definition of the desiring subject that reveals a way of reading the aporia in Augustine.

terpreted as *cupiditas*: "in *cupiditas*, man has cast the die that makes him perishable. In *caritas*, whose object is eternity, man transforms himself into an eternal, non-perishable being."[31] Why does this strategy fail?

The distinction between *caritas* and *cupiditas* is difficult, because, fundamentally, they are both forms of appetite or desire. *Cupiditas* is "love of the world" or a seeking for what remains outside the subject. It is a drive away from oneself, which risks loss of self in the dispersion, distraction and ultimate escape of the world from the lover. Augustine would like to oppose *cupiditas* to *caritas* as a love for God, a point of inner stability that creates a unified loving subject who finds completeness in God. As much as Augustine wants to believe in the exteriority of God, the supra mundane, the principle of love has to remain in the world, in the mundane, which is the province of *eros*.[32] God cannot be purified of the material and an ontology of love sustained. Although the writing of the law of *caritas* on the heart of the believer *could* be described as a foundational moment, to try to read Augustine through this interpretative grid would be dishonest, as it would attempt to impose a consistency on thought that is inherently aporetic and contradictory.

A postmodern atheology that brackets any ultimate revelation of a unitary truth finds in this problematic conjunction a source of hope for a critical theory of law. It might be possible to imagine an aporetic "foundation" for a law of love. As a thinking of law this discovers the "source" of obligation neither in the command of the sovereign nor in the faculty of human reason. Derrida's terminology of the secret could be used to describe the moment when this law is impressed on the heart. "Divinity" interpellates the individual, calling beyond the world with a voice within the world. The voice of "God" might echo in this provocation to act justly, but it is groundless, impossible to locate or describe in the language of reason.

If this is the "structure" of the law of love, what is the relevance of faith, given the intimate connection between these terms in the Pauline verse? Faith is an

---

[31] Quoted in Arendt, *supra* n. 3, at 18.

[32] A variation on this argument is Arendt's suggestion, *ibid.*, that the main problem for Augustine is that the definition of love as desire is Hellenic and pagan and cannot be easily developed in a Christian paradigm. Both *cupiditas* and *caritas* are merely ways of "mediating" between gods and men. Such a mediation is, from a psychoanalytic perspective, essential to the function of law. See P Legendre, "An Introduction to the Theory of the Image" in P. Goodrich (ed.), *A Legendre Reader* (Macmillan, Basingstoke, 1997) at 211–55. Legendre explains how the law must provide a series of images which allows it to speak for the absent divinity in whose name law operates. To uncover this complex would involve tracing the roots of law to the theological discourses that tied the soul of the faithful to the Church through ritual and doctrine which represented the presence of an absent God. The very notion of faith was founded on symbols. The same concerns lie at the base of civil law. Justinian's *Institutes* suggest that behind the letter of the law is the presence of an occulted other in whose name the law binds. In the same way that the image or the icon spoke to the believer and brought them into the community of the Church in the celebration of an absent God, the institution of the law attempted to take hold of the soul and to connect it to the institution of the law. Law becomes the very possibility of institutional being; images and rituals the possibility of its perpetuation.

attitude towards time that is central to the flawed ontology of love.[33] Presently this conjunction of love and faith will be shown to open a space where state law can be shown to be illegitimate. The next stage of this essay, however, will develop the problematic interface between love and faith.

Faith is directed towards a necessary futurity, a looking towards an anticipated satisfaction in the union with God. However, faith also directs attention firmly towards the human community and the world of finitude and time. Has this tension always infested this key term? Christ's coming makes the possibility of salvation an event in the world, a present reality, but also, as true judgment must await the end of the world and Christ's return, the Christian is suspended between a "now already" of the Christ event and the "not yet" of the coming *parousia*. Faith is the difficulty of remaining in[34] the indicative "now already" of salvation and the "not yet", the ongoing process of existence and the anticipation of future salvation. There is a further difficulty with faith. If *eros* is part of *agape*, *cupiditas* integral to *caritas*, then, as an anticipation of fulfilment, faith always involves the world of flesh and the body. As Luce Irigaray has commented, the notion of the word become flesh is a potentially profoundly disruptive idea, because divinity involves itself with the world, with fallen matter.[35] In other words, faith could have a location in what could be described as a space where God appears not as a certainty at the end of time, but an uncertainty within time, a further development of the aporia of love. As a subject of love and faith, the puncturing of divinity into the quotidian is a profoundly unsettling experience that connects the subject with the secret that provokes a love for the fellow man in the absence of certainty, in the absence of ground.

LAW, JUSTICE AND CIVITAS DEI

It is now necessary to trace the implications of the aporia of love and faith into Augustine's descriptions of human sociability and his justification of the state

---

[33] It is argued by Arendt, *supra* n. 3, that the key problem for Augustine was the problem of being in a world which was constantly decaying. The human subject, the subject of *appetitus*, is thus always bound to a fear of loss. This deplorable state can be remedied only by Christian faith. Faith is an attempt to transcend time and discover an eternity that is modelled on a notion of an eternal present. In *The Confessions*, Augustine writes passionately of a knowledge of God that is associated with a time out of time. Knowledge of God is predicated on a catching of the "glory of that ever fixed eternity" (*De Civitate Dei* , XI, 13).

[34] These terms are developed within contemporary theology. Schmithals describes the "dialectical connection of the indicative and the imperative". See W. Schmithals, *Introduction to the Theology of Rudolf Bultmann* (London, SCM, 1968) 111. The 'kingdom of God' comes in a future time which is "entirely future". "The kingdom of God is genuinely future, because it is not a metaphysical entity or condition, but the future action of God, which can be in no sense something given in the present. None the less this future determines man in his present, and exactly for that reason is true future—not merely something to come 'somewhere, sometime', but destined for man and constraining him to a decision": *ibid.*

[35] L. Irigaray, *The Irigaray Reader* (Margaret Whitford (ed.), Oxford, Basil Blackwell, 1992) 23.

and positive law.[36] After outlining the conventional interpretation, the disturbances of the aporia will be plotted.

Love implies an ontology of communal living[37] where the state and its institutions are always required, but are more or less illegitimate. Throughout *De Civitatae Dei*, Augustine refers to the Biblical creation story. Man may have been created as an individual, but this was not an indication that he was to remain a solitary being; men are bound together by feelings of human kinship.[38] The human creature is destined to live in communities. A sense of human limitation also feeds into the Augustinian *mythos*. Man is a creature hopelessly divided between an angelic part[39] that is an echo of his creation in the likeness of God, and a fallen animal self, that is mired in the lusts of the world and separated from divinity. Augustine understands the original disobedience of Adam as a rejection of God in favour of self-serving lusts: "there is nothing so social by nature, so anti social by sin as man".[40] As human government is also a product of the fall it is inherently corrupt. It is most dramatically illustrated by the famous comparison of the state to a band of robbers and the anecdote of Alexander the Great in Book Four of *De Civitatae Dei*:[41]

> "Remove justice and what are kingdoms but gangs of criminals on a large scale? What are criminal gangs but petty kingdoms? A gang is a group of men under the command of a leader, bound by a compact of association, in which the plunder is divided according to an agreed convention . . .
>
> For it was a witty and truthful rejoinder which was given by a captured pirate to Alexander the Great. The King asked the fellow, 'What is your idea, in infesting the sea?' And the pirate answered, with uninhibited insolence, 'The same as yours, in infesting the earth! But because I do it with a tiny craft, I'm called a pirate: because you have a mighty navy, you're called an emperor.' "

---

[36] In Arendt, *supra* n.3, there is a variation on this problem, which recalls the tension between the responsibility to God as other and to all others outlined by Derrida in *The Gift of Death*. Arendt argues that for Augustine the law is, at root, the law of *caritas*. *Caritas* can be summed up in the commandment to love your neighbour as yourself. The love spoken of here must be love that denies the self and the world if it is not to fall into the snares of *cupiditas* and become a love of the world. *Caritas* is love as God (*ibid.*, 93). Loving in this way makes the neighbour into an example of God's creation; it is a love directed towards a specific manifestation of a universal project. Arendt is concerned that the idea of the neighbour will lose a concrete sense of its rootedness in the affairs of the world. *Caritas* means that the neighbour is "loved neither for his sake" nor the lover's sake. Love as *caritas* risks "destroy[ing] every human standard and separat[ing] love of [the]neighbour from any carnal love" (*ibid.*, 94).

[37] See Gilson, *supra* n. 3: "In his [Augustine's] eyes the individual is never separated from the city. To find the basic reason . . . [is] to return to the root of moral life, to love and therefore to the will." (*Ibid.*, 236.)

[38] St. Augustine, *supra* n. 1, XII, 22. For a most inventive engagement with *De Civitate Dei* in modern critical legal thought, see P. Fitzpatrick, *The Mythology of Modern Law* (London, Routledge, 1992).

[39] *Supra* n. 1, XII, 24.

[40] *Ibid.*, XII, 28.

[41] *Ibid.*, IV, 139.

What are the implications of this potentially radical passage? There is a scholarly debate on its relevance for a theory of resistance to the law's disorder.[42] The conventional reading would stress that Augustine is describing the need for a constituted order to discipline and control corrupt humanity. Although this is an entirely justifiable interpretation, the inherent corruption of humanity suggests that there can never be a ruler or a government that can claim absolute legitimacy. Rather than found secular power, Augustine makes the legitimacy of government questionable. The contradictions in this theory of human nature thus assume strange proportions in Augustine's political theory, stressing simultaneously both human potential and failure in the absence of God.

To realise the radical implications of the anecdote of Alexander the Great and the pirate for a theory of the relation between positive law and the law of love, it is necessary to reconsider Augustine's disagreement with the Ciceronian definition of the commonwealth as an "association of men united by a common sense of right or of justice".[43] For Augustine, this cannot be an acceptable definition. If justice, in an Aristotelian sense, is to assign to every one their due, then any just state must have at the centre of its polity a respect of the general due to the one true God. Augustine proposes a second definition: "a people is the association of a multitude of rational beings united by a common agreement on the objects of their love". There is something very interesting here. Augustine is, at one level, returning to the classical idea of justice as proportion, as equality of shares. At the same time, there is something excessive about love that cannot be reduced to a felicific calculus. Justice to Augustine is linked to *caritas* and to love: "*caritas magna, magna justia est; carita perfecta, perfecta justia est*".[44]

Although it is necessary to continue to have recourse to the classical Aristotelian notions, justice will always be in excess of any human or positive manifestation. Justice as excess, however, cannot be co-ordinated with either revealed law or the law of human institutions as it is linked to the coming of The City of God.

What does this mean? It is necessary to return to the original contradiction of love. It has been argued that love is essentially double in Augustine; that love of God and love of the world are inseparable. This would be the problematisation of the distinction that founds The City of God; a disturbance that is not the rejection of the City of God, but the articulation of a new theory of its coming and its deferral.

The City of God is predicated on an essential separation between the two loves, *caritas* and *cupiditas*. The Earthly City is associated with *cupiditas*. It is

---

[42] See H.A. Deane, *The Political and Social Ideas of St. Augustine* (New York, Columbia University Press, 1963) 78. For further consideration see N. Figgis, *The Political Aspects of Saint Augustine's City of God* (London, Longmans, 1921) 51.

[43] *Supra* n. 1, XIX, 21.

[44] *De Natura et Gratia*, quoted in Deane, *supra* n. 42: "[w]here love is great, justice is great; where love is perfect, justice is perfect". As there is no English word for the Latin *caritas*, any translation of this passage is tentative.

based on love of the self and contempt of God.[45] The love of The Earthly City takes the self's need for aggrandisement as its source. It is the site of reason's sovereignty in the absence of God: "the wise men and philosophers of the one city live by the standards of men; they either pursued the goods of their bodies or of their minds or the goods of both".[46] The Heavenly City, on the other hand, is built on the contempt of the self and the love of God. It would be impossible to co-ordinate the justice of The Heavenly City with any object or institution. Essential to its quality is its advent:[47] The Heavenly City is anticipated, and yet to be realised in the affairs of men.

Although this passage might read as a combative statement of a belief system trying to define itself against a paganism that it associated with a fallen world, it can be opened to a different perspective informed by an atheology that persists in absurd and impossible beliefs. A consequence of the aporia of *caritas* and *cupiditas* would be the inseparability of the two cities. Deployed in this context, the aporia suggests that although love founds government in human sociability, in the bond between men, this foundation is always inadequate. However, the aporia cannot be resolved by trusting to a transcendental deity. Although love gestures to a beyond, it does so within the essential context of the world: a location that cannot be erased or cancelled out in a triumph of *agape*. The commonwealth or the state sits at the centre of this tension. It is both legitimate and illegitimate: a consequence of the fall and the need to restrain sin, but itself a great sinner. The state must be judged in the spirit of a love that is still to come; a love that is identified with the impossible arrival of The Heavenly City on earth.

There is a further development of this aporia that returns to the question of faith.[48] The Heavenly City has to be imagined through a faith in futurity. However, returning to the previous argument where faith was seen to describe the fall of divinity into the world of finitude, it could be said that one effect of the aporia is to locate The Heavenly City in the now, in the present. This would not resolve the aporia of faith, because it would return to the unfulfilled desire of the subject of *cupiditas* and the longing for the love to come. Love and faith both celebrate the here and now and anticipate the advent of The Heavenly City.

---

[45] *Supra* n. 1, XIV, 1.

[46] *Ibid.*, XIV, 28.

[47] See Alliez, *supra* n. 7. Alliez argues that Augustine's philosophy works against itself; rather than delivering "transcendence", a "break between what is beyond and what is here below", his thought delivers the "autonomy of the temporal" (*ibid.*, 83). The argument of this paper resists this reading; *Civitas Dei* is an articulation of the aporia between the transcendental and the world of time.

[48] There are resonances here with what Derrida has described as a messianism: see *Spectres of Marx* (London, Routledge, 1994). This is, at once, both a religious messianism and a revolutionary messianism of the radical socialist tradition. Within both traditions it is necessary to disassociate a messianism that imposes a universal structure of communism or a dictatorship of saints from a messianism that remains open to a future that will not be a duplication of the past, to an event of rupture: the rupture has to be expressed in a language that is paradoxical. This "revolutionary" paradox is a deconstructive thinking of justice that reinvents present systems of justice.

These tensions run through one possible manifestation of The Heavenly City, the vision of the City of Jerusalem that appears in the *Book of Revelation*:[49]

"Then I saw the great City, the new Jerusalem, coming down out of heaven from God . . . And I heard a great voice from the throne, saying; "See the dwelling of God with men; and he will dwell among them, and they will be his people, and God himself will be with them.' "

What is this dwelling in the world of God and man? The Hebrew etymology[50] of the word "faith" suggests that it might provide a clue. In *The Old Testament*, the root of the Hebrew word for faith has the meaning of refuge, of making one-self safe, and can be contrasted with a similar root that means self-reliance. Related to the stem for faith is a root that carries the sense of anticipation, of awaiting a future. Perhaps the infinite separation and presence of God in man-womankind is the site where the aporia of the law is founded in love for what is, and faith for what is to come.

---

[49] *Revelations* 20, 2–5; *De Civitate, supra* n. 1, XX, 17.

[50] For the etymology of the word, see R. Bultmann and A. Weiser, *Faith* (Edinburgh, Adam and Charles Black, 1961) 1. Relly Bauman, of the University of Canterbury, was also of great assistance in the translation of the Hebrew words for faith. The Hebrew root of the word *hsh* has the meaning of seeking or finding refuge, making oneself safe (*ibid.*, 23); it can be contrasted with *bth*, which can mean self-reliance, or self-protection through one's own strength, to suggest that *hsh* describes a relationship of profound dependence, of a seeking for something that is outside the control of the individual. Tracing the Hebrew etymology of faith further reveals that it is connected to another set of verb stems *qwh*, *yhl* and *hkh*, which, as a group, describe the action of anticipation, of waiting for a future. *Qwh*, carries into *qaw*, a twisted rope measuring line; *yhl*, the action of giving birth to, with an associated sense of painful labour (*ibid.*, 26). In a more sacred register, these verbs describe a hope for salvation, especially in the sense of the anticipation of the godly for coming revelation. Later in the Old Testament these stems became assimilated to the stem *mn* (*ibid.*, 31), a term which added another series of meanings which covered the sense of the "comprehensive, elusive and personal reciprocal relationship between God and man" (*ibid.*, 32). There is a strong relationship between the Greek term *pstis* in the New Testament and the range of meanings covered by the Hebrew stems; faith is, now, however, linked to the words of Christ, to the *Kerygma*, to a heeding of the Gospel.

4

Reason and Religion

TIMOTHY MACKLEM

INTRODUCTION

Whether secured by law, by tradition, or both, the basic political freedoms, such as freedom of religion, matter to us for reasons, reasons that have to do with the value that the exercise of those freedoms is thought to contribute to the lives of those who enjoy them, and, indeed, to the community at large. To put it simply, we insist upon those freedoms because we believe that their continued existence is essential to our ability to pursue worthy lives. At the same time, however, we have very different understandings of what it is that makes a life worthy. By this I do not simply mean that we have different goals in life and so have different projects to pursue, different beliefs to maintain. Rather I mean that we have different understandings of the nature of value itself, different notions of how to assess what makes a life worth living, and so have different perceptions of the role that the basic political freedoms, such as freedom of religion, might possibly play in the construction and pursuit of a worthy life.

These differences in perception are of more than theoretical concern; they have real practical significance. Since our different understandings of the nature of value offer different reasons to secure freedom of religion, they lead to rather different descriptions of the beliefs and practices that should be entitled to the protection of freedom of religion. It follows that the success of a claim to freedom of religion may well turn on the answer to a dispute not only about the particular values that are said to justify the freedom, but also about the way in which those values are to be understood. When we disagree with one another, as we frequently do, over such questions as whether pacifism is a religious belief, and if so whether conscientious objection to military service is entitled to the protection of freedom of religion, our disagreements often, perhaps typically, stem from deeper disagreements about the nature of value. In other words, our practical disagreements here have their roots in theoretical disagreements about value and how to understand it.

In what follows I would like to explore the implications of disagreements about value in this setting by examining two of the most prominent justifications for freedom of religion, justifications that suggest rather different reasons for securing the freedom and so offer rather different accounts of its scope. In my view both of these justifications exhibit serious weaknesses, weaknesses that can be traced to weaknesses in the understandings of value on which they are based. I want to do more than merely criticise, however, and so I will conclude by offering what seems to me a better justification for freedom of religion, one that is based on a better understanding of the nature of value.

CONVENTIONAL APPROACHES TO FREEDOM OF RELIGION

Conventional accounts of freedom of religion, particularly those developed in the context of the First Amendment to the United States Constitution, have tended to address themselves to the question of the proper meaning of the term religion. When claims to religious freedom have been advanced by bodies not traditionally recognised as religious, such as Scientologists,[1] or in support of the exercise of personal convictions not necessarily regarded as religious, such as a conscientious objection to armed conflict,[2] or in support of activities that have not conventionally formed part of religious ceremony, such as the use of moose meat for a funeral potlatch,[3] those claims have been assessed by drawing analogies between the social practices underlying the claims and the practices of well recognised religions, so as to determine whether the beliefs and rituals for which freedom is claimed have parallels in religions to which freedom is clearly due.[4] For example, Kent Greenawalt begins his analysis of religion as a concept in constitutional law by observing, with approval:[5]

> "no-one doubts that Roman Catholicism, Greek Orthodoxy, Lutheranism, Methodism, and Orthodox Judaism are religions. Our society identifies what is indubitably religious largely by reference to their beliefs, practices, and organizations."

There is an obvious ambiguity in such accounts of freedom of religion, an ambiguity that arises from the fact that they offer a semantic response to what is apparently a moral question. We are concerned here, not to know how the term religion *is* used, whether in the world at large or in the legal community, but to know how the term religion *should* be used, in the interpretation, the application and the justification of a fundamental freedom. That is to all intents and purposes a moral question. It follows that if a semantic answer is given to that

---

* I would like to thank John Gardner and Peter Oliver for their comments on this piece.

[1] *Founding Church of Scientology* v. *United States*, 409 F 2d 1146 (D.C. Cir. 1969).

[2] See *United States* v. *Seeger*, 380 US 163, 166 (1965): the interpretation of a statute requiring belief in relation to a Supreme Being was held to include a belief that occupies "a place in the life of its possessor parallel to that filled by the orthodox belief in God of one who clearly qualifies for the exemption".

[3] See *Frank* v. *State*, 604 P 2d 1068 (Al. 1979).

[4] For a prominent and relatively liberal version of this approach see J.H. Choper, "Defining 'Religion' in the First Amendment" [1982] *Univ. of Ill. L. Rev.* 579.

[5] K. Greenawalt, "Religion as a Concept in Constitutional Law" (1984) 72 *Cal. L. Rev.* 753, at 767. For an argument along similar lines see G.C. Freeman III, "The Misguided Search for the Constitutional Definition of 'Religion' " (1983) 71 *Georgetown Law Jo.* 1519.

apparently moral question, then either the answer must be taken at face value, in which case it is to be understood as implying that the question is, despite appearances, a semantic one, or it must be treated as a moral answer to a moral question, albeit in semantic disguise. Otherwise the answer would be simply incoherent. In fact, I believe that the answer must be treated as a moral answer in semantic disguise, for in my view the question of the meaning of religion here cannot be understood other than as a moral question. Let me explain by exploring the alternative.

Semantic accounts of freedom of religion do not tell us, other than in semantic terms, why one understanding of religion should be preferred to another in the application of a fundamental freedom. Yet our reason for wanting to know which understanding should be preferred is not semantic but moral, not descriptive but normative. Our concern is not with linguistics but with justice. In the setting of a fundamental freedom what matters is not how the word religion is correctly used, whether generally or as a term of art, but how it should be used in order to arrive at a just outcome in balancing the requirements of personal autonomy against those of the public good.[6] It follows that a semantic approach to freedom of religion is necessarily dependent upon some prior moral justification which, if not explicitly stated on the face of a given account of freedom of religion, must be treated as implicit in it. In short, the meaning of religion in this setting is a moral, not a semantic, question and so requires a moral, not a semantic, answer. Are there any circumstances, however, in which a semantic answer to that question could imply the moral justification that is needed to save the answer from incoherence?

There is one obvious setting in which that kind of implicit justification might be thought to be available. A number of countries, of which the United States is the most prominent example, have made freedom of religion part of their law, by entrenching that freedom in a written constitution. Accounts of freedom of religion that take such countries as their frame of reference might be understood as implying that the proper justification for the freedom is the fact that its entrenchment was the product of a democratic decision (or some other authoritative pronouncement), whether of a constitutional convention or some other body. In other words, according to such accounts freedom of religion is implicitly taken to be justified by the just character of its source. Whatever reasons may support the exercise of democratic authority necessarily support actions taken by that authority. Having settled the problem of justification in this way, conventional accounts of freedom of religion can then plausibly address the proper application of the freedom by interpreting the concept of religion in exclusively linguistic terms. That is to say, they are able to take the view that in

---

[6] I am not suggesting here that there is any inherent conflict between the requirements of personal autonomy and those of the public good: see J. Raz, *The Morality of Freedom* (Oxford, OUP, 1986) at 213ff. I am assuming, however, that incidental conflicts between the claims of autonomy and the public good clearly do arise, and that the proper interpretation and application of a fundamental freedom involve the resolution of such conflicts.

order to understand the concept of freedom of religion and its proper application we should simply ask ourselves what the word religion means, for that is the word that the democratic authority used when entrenching the freedom. Once we have discovered the proper answer to that question we will be able to apply the concept in a manner that is justified.

There are ready objections, however, to a reference to democratic antecedents as an answer to the problem of determining the legitimate scope of freedom of religion. Notice, for a start, the conditions that would have to be met before such a line of reasoning could be even entertained. First, and as I have already indicated, freedom of religion would have to be understood as a purely legal right, the moral justification for which lies in the justice of the procedure by which it was enacted into law. Second, the application of that legal right would have to be governed by a recognised, presumably democratically authorised rule of interpretation, one that required the right to be understood in semantic terms. In other words, there would have to be a double authorisation by some democratic body, an authorisation not merely of the guarantee but of its interpretive principle, an authorisation that granted one understanding of the word religion (be it a dictionary definition, or the reading said to be intended by the framers of the constitution) the authority of law. Finally, the application of that authorised rule of interpretation to the legal right would have to exhaust the judicial obligation to secure freedom of religion. For that to be true there would have to be a recognised, presumably democratically authorised theory of the judicial role, one that required the judiciary to do no more than apply the authorised rule of interpretation to the legal right, even when to do so would be to fail their moral obligation to give effect to the freedom, as when, for example, certain practices that would be protected by a moral principle justifying freedom of religion would not be protected by the application of the authorised rule of interpretation to the legal right.

It goes without saying that nowhere are all three of these conditions met. In many, perhaps most, parts of the world freedom of religion has yet to be guaranteed in law. Where it is guaranteed in law, the proper approach to its interpretation remains a matter of great dispute. That dispute is a product of the fact that no democratically authorised rule of interpretation of freedom of religion (or any other freedom) exists, let alone a rule requiring the freedom to be understood in semantic terms. Finally, even where freedom of religion has been guaranteed in law, and even where an approach to its interpretation might at least be alleged to have been agreed upon, it is simply not the case that there is any democratically authorised account of the judicial role that would regard a judge's moral obligation to secure that freedom as exhausted by his or her interpretation of the legal right to it.

What is more to the point here, even if all those conditions were or could be met, the problem of justification would be merely postponed, not resolved, for the simple reason that there is a difference between justifying a certain form of authority and justifying what that authority has done. It is right, and so justifiable, that most political decisions, including a decision to secure freedom of religion, be taken by a democratic body, but it does not follow from this that any of the decisions taken by that body are themselves justifiable, other than in procedural terms. Just procedures do not necessarily produce just outcomes, not, that is, all things considered and having taken the justice of those procedures into account. Yet, and as I have already indicated, a just outcome in balancing the requirements of personal autonomy against those of the public good is precisely what is sought here.[7]

It follows that if conventional accounts of freedom of religion are to be understood as offering a semantic response to what is inherently a moral question, those accounts must be regarded as inadequate. But surely, for that very reason, this cannot be the best way to understand them. It seems quite implausible to me that the considerations that I have just drawn attention to could have escaped the notice of the proponents of conventional accounts of freedom of religion. If I am right in this then it must be unwise to understand those accounts in semantic terms, whatever their appearance. Surely the better interpretation of them must be that they offer a moral answer to what they recognise to be a moral question, albeit a moral answer that is in semantic disguise. On that interpretation, conventional accounts of freedom of religion offer protection to those systems of belief that have features in common with traditional religions because they take traditional religions to be morally superior to their rivals. It would follow that the apparently semantically based comparison of features between well recognised religions and beliefs not traditionally recognised as religious implicitly recognises value in, and so offers protection to, those features of belief that can be matched to features of belief that have long been acknowledged to be a source of value.[8]

Once again, there are two ways to understand such a claim, one of which is rather more plausible than the other. First, the claim might be understood as a

[7] This is a matter that deserves greater consideration than I have space to give it here. I must admit at once that the rather summary expression of it in the text runs two points together. However, since I believe that both points are true their conflation should not serve to undermine the argument that I am trying to make. The first point is that a semantic inquiry into the meaning of religion cannot yield a single right answer without the assistance of moral argument, for a concept such as religion has many meanings and can be put to many purposes, each of which may make a different meaning central to the concept. It follows that a semantic inquiry into the meaning of religion in a guarantee of freedom of religion, even if democratically authorised, would simply beg the moral question of what religion should mean there. The second point is that, even if and to the extent that such an inquiry could be said to yield a definitive answer, that answer would give rise to only a *prima facie* obligation on the part of those who are bound to respect a guarantee of freedom of religion to treat that answer as definitive of the guarantee and thus of their obligation. It would not be possible for them to know whether that answer was morally conclusive without further, moral inquiry into the proper scope of the freedom.

[8] I should note here, lest I give the appearance of being unfair, that conventional accounts of freedom of religion typically refer to well recognised religions rather than to traditional religions. However it seems right to equate the two descriptions, since by well recognised the proponents of conventional accounts appear to mean well recognised in their particular cultural tradition. That would explain why, in the passage quoted above, Kent Greenawalt describes what he calls the indubitably religious in exclusively Judaeo-Christian terms.

claim that the only valuable religious beliefs are those beliefs that share the features of traditional religions. It would follow, however, that traditional religious beliefs are the exclusive sources of value in this setting and that all other religious beliefs are entirely without value. Not only is this untrue; it is very unlikely that the proponents of conventional accounts of freedom of religion believe it. It would require, for example, that Buddhism be regarded as being without value, since Buddhism is not well recognised in the Western traditions to which conventional accounts of freedom of religion refer.

The second and more plausible way of understanding such a claim, then, is as a claim that traditional religious beliefs, and those beliefs that share their features, are more valuable than other religious beliefs. On this reading, traditional religious beliefs are the pre-eminent, albeit not the exclusive, sources of value in this setting, and it is their eminence that warrants the extension to them of a degree of protection that is denied to other beliefs. In other words, the claim here is that while many religious beliefs are valuable, only a few religious beliefs, well recognised by all of us, have such a capacity to generate value that their continued existence in our culture is essential to our capacity to pursue worthy lives. It will be noticed that underlying such a claim is a particular understanding of the nature of value, commonly described as value monism, coupled with a belief that human well-being consists in maximising the presence of value in human lives. By value monism I mean an account of value that treats the various sources of value in life as no more than means to the realisation of a single, more profound value, such as happiness perhaps, or dignity, or honour, or redemption, a value to which any successful human life must be dedicated and to which all other values can be reduced.

Now of course value monism need not be conventional in its account of the sources of value. There is no necessary connection between a monistic approach to value and the view that traditional sources of value, in this case traditional religions, are the exclusive or even the pre-eminent source of value in human life. On the contrary, part of the point of value monism is that it is capable of recognising and assimilating any number of different sources of value. Nor does value monism need to be coupled with a commitment to the maximisation of value. On the contrary, it is entirely possible to believe that there is ultimately only one value to which any successful human life must be dedicated and yet also to believe that that value is not most fully realised by being maximised. In practice, however, and as its application to the question of religious freedom confirms, value monism tends to be both maximising and conventional, for the following reasons.

First, while it is possible for proponents of value monism to distance themselves from a commitment to the maximisation of value, it is only natural to be interested in degrees of value once one has rejected the significance of kind. After all, if there is only one value to which any successful human life must be dedicated, and yet if in practice human beings commit themselves to the pursuit of values of many different kinds, as they do, the variety of human pursuits, if not simply the product of moral ignorance, is most naturally explained by a desire to accumulate the value, be it happiness or some other, to which all human beings are and must be committed. In other words, the reason that human beings pursue a variety of values that do not ultimately differ from one another is that human beings are engaged in a search for those sources of value that have the greatest capacity to generate the ultimate value that makes life worth living, a value that they hope to maximise in their own lives.[9] If, then, human beings commit themselves to a variety of religious beliefs, it is because they are engaged in a search for the belief or beliefs with the greatest capacity to promote human happiness, or to secure human salvation, or whatever it is that they take to be the ultimate good.

Second, as I have just suggested, on a monistic account of value, sources of value differ from one another, not in their capacity to generate different kinds of value, but in their capacity to generate the same value for the same or different kinds of people. While some sources of value, by which I mean some sources of the ultimate value to which all successful human lives must be dedicated, may be equal in their capacity to generate value, other sources of value are clearly superior in that respect. If human beings are committed to the maximisation of value in their lives, for the reasons just given, they must be correspondingly committed to the preservation and promotion of those sources of value that have the greatest capacity to generate value. While such sources of value might in theory be found anywhere, they rather naturally tend to be looked for in those sources of value that have been shown over time to yield the most value for the most people, namely, traditional or conventional sources of value, or in this setting, traditional or conventional religious beliefs.

Of course it may be the case that a society has failed to recognise that certain sources of value possess a high capacity to generate the value to which all human beings must be committed. It may also be the case that a society has failed to recognise that certain sources of value that have a weak capacity to generate value for most people have a great capacity to generate value for a few. If and to the extent that this can be proven, novel or marginal sources of value may be fostered and protected in the same way as traditional or conventional sources of

---

[9] It is commonly assumed that human beings seek sources of value that suit them. The question is what this means. First, it must mean that the ultimate good is affected by suitability, as it would not be, for example, if it consisted of preserving honour or integrity. Secondly, suitability must mean something more than aptness. Certain activities are not sources of value for anyone. No-one seeks them, though many find them. Other activities are sources of value for some but not others, for they are such as to yield their value only to those with the appropriate capacity. Since people differ from one another, and since they are bound to seek value in activities that will yield value to them as they are, it is possible to explain a certain range in the sources of value pursued by human beings as a product of the differences between those human beings. Yet people pursue a wider range of values than this, for they pursue a number of apparently different values at once. Why do they do this? It cannot be because their well-being depends on the pursuit of different values, for on a monistic account values are not ultimately different. Two other explanations seem possible, both of which involve the maximisation of value. People might be looking for the source of value with the highest yield or they might be confronting a problem of diminishing returns in one source of value and be seeking alternatives to it.

value. Indeed, novel or marginal religious beliefs are sometimes granted the benefit of freedom of religion on this basis. However, and again rather naturally, the most widely recognised method of securing the benefit of freedom of religion is to show that the features of a novel or marginal religious belief correspond to the features of traditional or conventional religious belief, and so can be assumed to have a corresponding capacity to generate value. More commonly, however, novel or marginal sources of value are regarded as having a relatively weak capacity to generate value, so that commitments to them, while not prohibited, are not especially protected, for to do so would be to foster and promote commitments that diminish rather than enhance the prospects for the realisation of value in human life. In this way the conventional bias of value monism remains intact.

When understood in moral rather than semantic terms, then, conventional accounts of freedom of religion exhibit an overly restrictive view of the kinds of belief that may underpin or at least nourish the pursuit of a successful human life, a view that is a product of the monistic understanding of value that informs those accounts. Such accounts fail to recognise that sources of value, here religious faiths, differ from one another not so much in their capacity to generate the same value for the same or different kinds of people, but in their capacity to generate different kinds of value for the same or different kinds of people. In other words, an unconventional source of value may indeed generate less of the value that the conventionalist notices, but it does so because it is primarily directed to the generation of a different value, one that has a different but no less important role to play in the pursuit of a successful life, at least for all those people who for reasons of character or choice have committed themselves to life projects that depend upon that source of value for some portion of their worth.[10]

PSYCHOLOGICAL APPROACHES TO FREEDOM OF RELIGION

For the purpose of exploring religion as a psychological phenomenon, in his *The Varieties of Religious Experience: A Study in Human Nature*,[11] William James adopted what he described as an arbitrary definition of religion, as "the feelings, acts and experiences of individual men in their solitude, so far as they apprehend themselves to stand in relation to whatever they may consider the divine",[12] where experience of the divine is understood to mean a personal emotional experience centred upon happy acceptance of the universe and what it requires

---

[10] I expand upon this in the opening paragraphs of the section entitled *Faith as a Basis for Freedom of Religion*, Religious and Secular Justifications, *infra*.

[11] W. James, *Writings 1902–1910* (New York, Library of America, 1987) 1. *The Varieties of Religious Experience* was originally delivered as a series of lectures at the University of Edinburgh in 1901–2.

[12] *Ibid.*, 36.

of each of us.[13] James intended this definition to be flexible enough to include those spiritual beliefs, such as transcendentalism, that involve an acceptance of "the spiritual structure of the universe" but do not refer to a particular deity.[14] According to James, "from the experiential point of view" beliefs of that kind are as much religions as are Christianity or Buddhism (itself without a deity after all).[15]

This distinctive focus on the internal attitude of religious believers has made James' psychological understanding of religion, and others like it that have followed in its wake, appealing to those courts and commentators who have been reluctant to interpret freedom of religion by reference to the external features of religious belief, lest by doing so they enshrine religious orthodoxy. A psychological understanding of religion appears to offer an answer to the concerns about conventionalism and value monism set out above, for it appears to offer the degree of flexibility necessary to permit the recognition and protection of the very different beliefs that people may reasonably commit themselves to in the course of developing and pursuing a worthy life.

According to the most highly developed and most influential psychological account of freedom of religion, every person has a religion, and that religion is composed of that person's deepest commitments or ultimate concerns.[16] However secular those commitments or concerns may seem to others they nevertheless merit protection as a religion, "for autonomy of belief can be safeguarded only if the believer is entrusted with the task of articulating and ranking his own concerns".[17] In other words, the test of what constitutes a religion here is purely subjective.[18] Society can require that a belief or activity be a matter of ultimate concern in order to obtain the protection of freedom of religion, but only the individual can determine what is of ultimate concern to him or her.

It must be said that there are some startling consequences of this point of view. To take the most obvious, this account of religion makes it impossible for anyone to lead a secular life, unless of course his or her life is utterly shallow and inconstant, devoid of anything that he or she could regard as an ultimate concern. Just as surprisingly perhaps, this account of religion makes it impossible to lead a religious life, and to claim the freedom to do so, unless religion is at least part of one's ultimate concern.[19] A Catholic, for example, could not obtain the protection of freedom of religion in support of the practice of some tenet of

---

[13] *Ibid.*, 36, 42, 44, 50.

[14] *Ibid.*, 36.

[15] *Ibid.*, 38.

[16] Note, "Towards a Constitutional Definition of Religion" (1978) 91 *Harv. L. Rev.* 1056.

[17] *Ibid.*, 1076.

[18] The claim that religion is equivalent to ultimate concern, while giving the appearance of objectivity, is in truth just another way of expressing the view that the meaning of religion is a subjective question, for the function of the claim is to transform an objective inquiry into the meaning of religion into a subjective inquiry into the content of an individual's ultimate concern.

[19] Moreover, ultimate concern is "an act of the total personality, not a movement of a special and discrete part of the total being". It follows that to qualify as an ultimate concern a commitment must be "unconditional, made without qualification or reservation": *supra* n. 16 at 1076, n. 110.

the Catholic religion unless Catholicism in general and that tenet in particular formed part of his or her ultimate concern, and this no matter what view the doctrines of the Catholic religion itself might take on the proper role of religion in individual life.

Of course, to say that consequences are startling is not to say that they are morally unjustified. Is there a way, then, to make moral sense of the claim that freedom of religion should protect what each person takes to be his or her ultimate concern? As I have said, the protection of ultimate concerns appears to offer freedom of religion an attractive degree of flexibility, the very flexibility that is denied by conventional accounts of the freedom's scope. Does the protection of ultimate concerns, in the very act of doing this, rob freedom of religion of its moral authority? In order to address that question it is necessary to be somewhat more precise about what is meant by the protection of ultimate concerns.

There are two possible ways to understand the claim that religion should be equated with ultimate concern, one of which is rather more plausible than the other. First, the claim might be understood as a claim that individual people are in the best position to know what is good for them, and so are in the best position to decide whether a set of beliefs to which they have committed themselves or would like to commit themselves is capable of sustaining their well-being, either comprehensively or in some critical respect. So understood the claim would be a claim about knowledge of the good, rather than a claim about the content of the good. Some support for this reading can be found in the language in which the claim has been justified. As indicated above, the leading exponent of the identification of freedom of religion with the protection of ultimate concerns has contended that "autonomy of belief can be safeguarded only if the believer is entrusted with the task of articulating and ranking his own concerns".[20] To articulate and to rank one's own concerns might mean to know one's own concerns and thereby to commit oneself to some portion of that which is otherwise recognised to be good, that is, to that which is good other than by virtue of one's commitment to it. To be entrusted with that task is to be entrusted with the task of identifying and selecting the beliefs and practices that one's life is to be committed to.

Understood in that way the protection of ultimate concerns is of course perfectly sensible, although it would seem to have more to do with liberty than with religion. People are often, perhaps typically, in the best position to know what is good for them, in this case to know whether a religious belief is capable of sustaining their well-being. They may be mistaken in their assessment of this, but they are less likely to be mistaken than are others. What is more, their opportunity to exploit their knowledge of what is good for them, by acting on their best sense of what is good for them, is a fundamental part of what it means for them to be authors of their own lives, a role that I take to be central to the well-being

---

[20] *Supra*, n. 16.

of every person. This is so even when they are mistaken in their assessment of what is good for them, as they often are.

It seems to me, however, that in fact it is not possible to understand the claim that freedom of religion should be identified with the protection of ultimate concerns as a claim that individual people are in the best position to know what is good for them, for to read the claim in that way would not begin to explain its scope. The fact that a believer is in the best position to know what is good for him or her would suggest that any belief must be freely chosen if it is to warrant the protection of freedom of religion, but it would not and could not be taken to suggest that any belief that is freely chosen should be protected as a religion. Yet that is precisely what the protection of ultimate concerns would require.

The second and more plausible way to understand the claim is as a claim that people must determine for themselves what is good and what is not, and so must determine for themselves whether a set of beliefs is worthy of the kind of fundamental commitment that can be called religious because, like traditional religious commitment, it is a matter of ultimate concern for them. So understood the claim is a claim about the content of the good, rather than a claim about knowledge of the good. On this reading, personal commitment is the exclusive source of value in the life of any human being. A belief or practice becomes valuable and so worthy of being protected as religious just because one is committed to it. In other words, the claim here is that any belief is capable of being valued. Consequently, a belief becomes valuable for any particular person when it becomes the object of the appropriate kind of commitment on the part of that person, the kind of commitment that treats that belief as valuable. It will be noticed that underlying such a claim is a particular understanding of the nature of value, commonly described as subjectivism. By subjectivism I mean an account of value that treats value, not as a property of the object that is valued, but as a property of the person who finds that object valuable. Such accounts by their very definition deny the possibility of objective value. They deny that value is a property that is possessed by an object, an object such as a religious belief or a religious practice, and insist instead that beliefs and practices are only valuable if and to the extent that somebody finds them so.

Subjective accounts of value raise concerns of two kinds, one of them entirely familiar, the other perhaps less so. The first concern is that they offer people other than the subject no reason to regard an object, in this case a belief or practice, as valuable and so worthy of respect. If freedom of religion embraces whatever is of ultimate concern to any person, then it must embrace beliefs and practices of all kinds, or at least of all kinds that any person is ultimately concerned with. People are in fact ultimately concerned with beliefs and practices that range from feminism to girl power, from Jesus to Elvis, from loving one's neighbour to participating in key parties. Some of those beliefs and practices can be recognised as valuable, although it might be difficult to recognise them as religions. Others, however, are mere obsessions, devoid of value as far as anyone but those committed to them can tell. The bare fact that a belief or practice is of ultimate concern to someone is no reason for any other person to regard that belief or practice as valuable and, more pertinently, no reason for any other person to respect it. That being the case the protection of ultimate concerns cannot be the basis for freedom of religion if the foundation for that freedom lies, as it must, in the respect that is owed to it by all members of the community.

The second concern is that subjective accounts of value are incapable of offering subjects themselves any reason to regard an object, in this case a belief or practice, as valuable and so worthy of respect. It is surely significant that subjective accounts of value always maintain an objective aspect, in that they always describe value as an attribute of an object. We say, in apparent subjective mode, and of one person's appreciation of another, that she is beautiful for him, or that he thinks she is beautiful, or that he finds her beautiful. When we do so, however, we preserve a link between beauty and its object. According to subjective accounts of value, of course, this degree of objectivity is merely nominal, for the logic of those accounts is to locate value wholly within the subject, to insist that in the descriptions of beauty just given beauty flows entirely from the perception of the beholder, so that the beauty there identified is not a property of the woman who is said to be beautiful but of the man who says she is so. Yet in fact it is the objective aspect of such descriptions, the allegedly nominal link that they preserve between beauty and its object, that is entirely responsible for the persuasiveness of those descriptions as accounts of value. Without that aspect they could not be said to identify value, even in the life of the beholder. Rather what they would identify is a fixation, be that fixation obsessive, so as to amount to an ultimate concern, or be it merely tentative.

When we say of one person's appreciation of another that she is beautiful for him we imply privacy and what it may reveal; when we say that he thinks she is beautiful we imply lack of knowledge and what it may conceal; when we say that he finds her beautiful we imply discovery and what it may yield.[21] Each of those implications is an implication of objective value. Without them, or without some similar attribution of objective value, there would be no beauty to behold. On the contrary, descriptions of beauty would have to be understood as no more than descriptions of the beholder and his idiosyncrasies, and their externality would have to be recognised as the product of a projection upon the mirror of the world of a beauty that the beholder finds only in himself. Yet in fact the reason people interact with the world, quite apart from the difficulty of doing anything else, is that there is value in doing so, a value that is not simply the projection of something that those people already possess. In other words, the progress of a life is not merely narcissistic; it is a matter of realising, in the most creative sense of that word, the beauty that life has to offer. Subjective accounts of value suppress this fact, or refer to it in ways that they set aside as nominal, and in doing so offer no reason for the subject, himself or herself, to

---

[21] Of course we also imply the perspective of a third party, but that is another matter, the subject of the first concern. The issue that I am seeking to explore here is the second concern, namely, the capacity of subjectivism to explain value as it is experienced by the valuer.

find value in the world or, in the context that concerns us here, to regard anything outside themselves as a matter of ultimate concern.

When understood in subjective terms then, and in my view that is the only way to understand them, psychological approaches to freedom of religion offer an undernourished account of the value of religious freedom, one that cannot explain the hold of that freedom upon society at large or even upon the life of the believer. Psychological approaches to freedom of religion obtain their flexibility at the cost of their substance, develop their attraction at the cost of their meaning. The task, therefore, must be to arrive at an account of freedom of religion that is simultaneously flexible and substantial.

FAITH AS A BASIS FOR FREEDOM OF RELIGION

If the nature of value is neither singular nor subjective, as these accounts of the weaknesses in conventional and psychological justifications of freedom of religion tend to suggest, then the logical conclusion must be that value is both plural and objective. By plural here I mean an understanding of value that regards many, perhaps most, sources of value in life as irreducible to any one, more profound, source of value. By objective I mean an understanding of value that regards value as a property of the object that is valued, rather than as a property of the person who finds that object valuable. Is it possible to develop a persuasive account of freedom of religion on the basis of value pluralism? If so, then the persuasiveness of that account may reinforce the persuasiveness of value pluralism, and vice versa.

What in religion might a value pluralist value? Assume for the moment that the term religion refers to collective participation in institutions and practices that manifest a set of beliefs that is not based on reason alone but is held, at least in part, on the basis of faith. The key elements in this definition are a set of beliefs, of whatever kind, and the manner in which they are subscribed to, namely as a matter of faith. The definition deliberately eschews any reference to the content of religious doctrine, for in my view it follows from the rejection of conventional accounts of freedom of religion that the justification for the freedom cannot be found in religious doctrine.

Religious and Secular Justifications

I have noted above that conventional accounts of freedom of religion see in the doctrines of traditional religions, and in the institutions and practices that those doctrines inspire, a capacity to generate value that is sufficiently special to warrant fundamental protection. I have argued that in doing so conventional accounts exhibit an overly restrictive view of the kinds of religious beliefs that may underpin or at least nourish the pursuit of a successful human life, for they fail to recognise that sources of value differ in kind as well as in degree. My claim here is that even an inclusive view of religious doctrine cannot serve as the basis for freedom of religion. Let me explain that claim by expanding briefly upon my previous objection to conventional accounts of freedom of religion.

What needs to be shown in order to supply a moral reason for restricting freedom of religion to conventional religious beliefs, say to the Catholic, the Buddhist, or the Puritan, is that the beneficiaries of the restriction make a contribution to human well-being that is not merely different from the contribution made by the victims of the restriction, but different in what makes it worthy of fundamental protection. In other words, it must be shown *both* that some beliefs, and the conduct that they inspire, deserve protection and others do not, and that the distinction between the deserving and the undeserving is the distinction between the religious and the secular or, more narrowly, between conventional religious beliefs and other beliefs.

In my view, the first of these propositions is true and the second is false. Not every religious belief deserves fundamental protection, but those beliefs that deserve protection are not exclusively conventional, while those beliefs that do not deserve protection are not exclusively unconventional. Conventional religious beliefs, and the institutions and practices that they inspire and sustain, are not inherently more valuable than unconventional beliefs, nor more vulnerable. There is no moral reason, therefore, to restrict the benefit of freedom of religion on the basis of a doctrinal distinction between what has conventionally been regarded as religious and what has not.

There is a deeper point here, however, and that is that any reliance upon religious doctrine, conventional or unconventional, as the source of the justification of religious freedom is misguided, for religious doctrine cannot be made to yield a commitment to religious freedom that is at once recognisable and acceptable as the basis for a fundamental political guarantee. The reason is a value pluralist one. The account of morality that is embodied in religious doctrine is necessarily partial and incomplete, rather than plural and comprehensive, for even the most tolerant of religions does not and cannot take other accounts of morality to be as true as its own. In itself, of course, there is nothing wrong with this. On the contrary, much individual and group morality displays this form of partiality and is not necessarily wrong to do so, for the account of morality that each of us gives, whether as an individual or as a group, need only be as comprehensive as is required to accommodate the well-being of those to whom we are responsible.[22] But it follows that a partial and incomplete account of morality is inappropriate for adoption by the state, whose policies and institutions must reflect a comprehensive, value-pluralist account of morality if they are not to exclude the recognition of values upon which the well-being of certain human beings depends, human beings who necessarily fall within the ambit of the

---

[22] Partial and incomplete accounts of morality are of course inaccurate. My point is simply that they are not necessarily harmful.

state's responsibility. It follows further that the freedom of religion whose guarantee lies at the foundation of the state must be based upon, and assessed against, a view of morality that is capable of embracing all those for whom the state is responsible. Religious morality, which is accountable only to those who have freely embraced its tenets, does not and cannot meet this requirement.

What this reveals, then, is that the morality justifying freedom of religion must be secular, not religious. It follows that religious doctrine cannot serve as the moral inspiration for a guarantee of freedom of religion, and that doctrinal accounts of that guarantee, those accounts that assess the meaning and scope of freedom by reference to the content of religious doctrine, are simply misguided. This is not to assume one's conclusions, to say that the morality justifying a fundamental freedom must be secular because the morality justifying any fundamental freedom must be secular. Rather it is to say that only a secular morality is capable of providing the connection to human well-being that is necessary to justify a fundamental freedom.

Faith and its Value

If reference to doctrine is to be ruled out, at least initially, the possibility remains that faith itself provides the moral basis for freedom of religion. In order to explore that possibility it is necessary to explore the meaning and value of faith. At its most basic level, the concept of faith describes the manner in which a particular belief or set of beliefs may be subscribed to by human beings. In that sense of the word, faith exists as a form of rival to reason. When we say that we believe in something as a matter of faith or, to put it the other way round, when we say that we have faith in certain beliefs, we express a commitment to that which cannot be established by reason, or to that which can be established by reason but not for that reason. The rivalry between the two concepts is real but not complete therefore. Faith and reason are modes of belief with different sources and different characters, but not necessarily different consequences. The particular consequences of faith may defy reason, as when faith prompts us to believe or do what we would otherwise have no reason to believe or do, but they may also be consistent with reason, as when faith prompts us to believe or do what we otherwise have reason to believe or do. Christian faith, for example, asks us to believe in the possibility of a life beyond material existence, with all that that implies, a possibility that rational thought would regard as not merely unverifiable but unknowable, perhaps unintelligible, given the intimate connection between the nature of life and the fact of death, between the evanescence of the human spirit and the materiality of the human body. Yet Christian faith also asks us to believe in the redemptive power of love, a power that rational thought might well endorse. What is important is that in either case faith treats itself as a reason to believe, and to act in accordance with belief, without submitting to the conditions of reason.

This gives rise to an obvious problem. The assessment of value, and thus the assessment of devices such as fundamental freedoms that are designed to yield value, is necessarily rational. Yet faith is not based on reasons. How can an irrational attachment be rationally determined to be valuable? Are we driven to the conclusion that faith is incapable of yielding value other than accidentally, as when it calls upon us to endorse what we have independent reason to endorse? The answer is negative in form. One of the things that we have to deal with in life, and one of the things that can affect our well-being, is the unavailability of reasons. The quest for reasons in life is sometimes troublesome and difficult, but at other times impossible. Where the quest for reasons is impossible, but commitment is potentially valuable, faith can come into play. It follows that there is reason to seek, and value in finding, a way to come to terms with the unknowable where to do so is necessary to human well-being.

It is often the case in life that one cannot know in advance that something is worth doing, because it is in the nature of the project or activity that one can only know whether it is worth doing by doing it. This is not simply a matter of lack of information. Rather it is a question of activities the value of which derives in part from the very fact of commitment to that activity, so that the value of the activity is unknowable in advance of commitment to the activity. When we decide to move from one city to another, or to exchange one job for another, or to start living as the partner of one person rather than another, we necessarily commit ourselves, to a neighbourhood, to a workplace, to a man or woman, without full reasons to do so, for one can only know fully whether a neighbourhood is worth living in by living in it, whether a place is worth working in by working in it, whether someone is worth living with by living with them. In each of these settings an act of commitment has to be made in advance of the existence of the value that might justify the commitment, and that act of commitment cannot be based upon reason, therefore, but must be based on faith.

All ventures into the unknowable, then, all leaps into the dark, depend on faith. Or, to put it somewhat differently, faith is required in order to make any commitment that involves a projection into the future where one's ability to realise the value that arises from the commitment is incompatible with the existence of sufficient reasons for making the commitment in the first place. It follows that faith is facilitative of those activities that depend on the connection between oneself and others, or between oneself and certain sets of circumstances, when a search for reasons to commit oneself to those activities would be inconclusive. Activities of that kind often constitute valuable options in life. In such settings faith provides a basis for action in the absence of any possibility of adequate reasons for action.

This does not mean that all ways of coming to terms with the unknowable are valuable. It may well be that some questions that confront us should simply be left unanswered, that some commitments that are offered to us should be left ungrasped, that we should be prepared to acknowledge the mysteries of life and to accept the limits of our condition. It is certainly the case that some purported responses to such questions and commitments are dangerous or worse. It follows that the role of faith in enabling us to make leaps into the dark is a necessary but not a sufficient condition for regarding the exercise of faith as valuable, and hence for protecting the institutions and practices that make faith possible.

Religion and its Value

Faith, as I have so far considered it, involves commitments that there can be no prior adequate reason to make, because the nature of the commitment is such that the value of the commitment is unknowable until the commitment is made. Religious faith, however, is typically attached to beliefs in and commitments to matters which, from the perspective of rational believers, are far from unknowable and which there may well be reason to make or not to make. Assume that the elements of religion are as I described them above but with a doctrinal qualification. Religious doctrine, it seems fair to say, has been traditionally and typically based upon a set of beliefs, first, about the nature and purpose of human life and in particular, about the possibility of a life other than material existence and, second, about the nature of the good and, in particular, about the possibility of moral grounds that lie beyond human life and beyond human reason. The question is whether faith in such matters is justified and, if so, when and under what circumstances it is justified.

Are the topics of religious belief truly unknowable and, if so, must they be addressed on the basis of faith in order to enable human beings to make commitments that are essential to their well-being? From a fully rational point of view, the view that most human beings adopt, the answer must be no. A commitment to life itself, and to the various projects that constitute the particular life of any person, does not involve a venture into the unknowable, and indeed could not be thought to do so unless one regarded life as being so bound up with death as to make the fact of life as unknowable as the fact of death sometimes appears to be. Even from that point of view, however, life could not be said to amount to a venture into the unknowable, for from a rational perspective death is no mystery, however upsetting it may be.

By the same token, a commitment to the good and all that it requires of us does not involve a venture into the unknowable either, for moral grounds do not lie beyond human life and are not inaccessible to human beings on the basis of reason. On the contrary, it is a necessary feature of morality that any account of it must be fit for human beings and the lives that they are bound to lead,[23] and it is one of the principal functions of human reason, a function that reason has long and successfully discharged, to offer us a rich and complex account of the content of that morality. It follows that human well-being, which clearly

---

[23] See J. Raz, "A Morality Fit For Humans" (1993) 91 *Mich. L. Rev.* 1297.

depends upon a complete commitment to life and a full understanding of morality, is not necessarily dependent upon an act of religious faith.

But is this true for all human beings? Is it the case that we are all capable of adopting a fully rational point of view in response to all issues that confront us, or should be? If what is required here is an approach to well-being that is capable of accommodating the character and commitments of very different people, and if the guarantee of certain rights and freedoms is one way of ensuring that the well-being of every person, however idiosyncratic, is capable of being realised, is it not essential that the guarantee take into account the fact that for some people the nature of life and the content of morality are unknowable on the basis of reason alone? For such people faith in the beliefs that form the content of religious doctrine is critical to the achievement of well-being, for their character is such that their well-being requires them to commit themselves to what, again for them, is and must remain unknowable. The question is whether they are to be condemned for this, or whether our account of morality and the institutions and practices that serve to implement that morality must be such as to serve them as they are. The answer clearly depends on the nature of the beliefs to which they have committed themselves.

There is an important difference between religious faith and the individual and local acts of faith that are often involved in commitments to new neighbourhoods, new jobs or new relationships, and the difference is that religious faith is not faith in the value of a particular commitment, but faith in the value of a belief that is designed to sustain all or at least most of one's commitments in life. Following the line of argument sketched earlier, faith is valuable where the inability to make the commitments that faith makes possible would have a negative impact on well-being, both because the commitments in question are potentially valuable and because failure to make them would be harmful. The challenge of religious faith, then, is that it does not merely function as the trigger for the making of a commitment, like faith in a new neighbourhood, a new job or a new partner, but, just because it is faith in a certain set of beliefs, governs the character of any consequent commitment and so governs the value of that commitment. It follows that religious faith serves the well-being of religious believers if and to the extent that religious beliefs have the capacity to inspire commitments that are capable of contributing to well-being. In such circumstances religion may be critical to well-being and so worthy of fundamental protection. Otherwise there is simply no value in religious faith.

Clearly much more needs to be said in order to complete the picture of a value-pluralist account of freedom of religion. At a minimum some explanation needs to be given of the kinds of belief that can sustain well-being and those that are likely to sap it. That distinction needs to be compared to the distinction between traditional and non-traditional religions, so as to determine to what extent there is merit in our habit of granting special protection to traditional beliefs. While the concept of religion cannot be relied upon as a means of determining the scope of freedom of religion, the concept must bear some weight if the freedom is to be recognisably religious, so that further explanation needs to be given of the relationship between the concept of religion and the moral purpose that underlies the protection of beliefs and practices that fall within that concept. I cannot go into these questions here. My purpose in this paper has simply been to describe the contours of a value-pluralist account of religion, and to suggest that, unlike the conventional and psychological approaches to freedom of religion, a faith-based approach to the freedom, like value-pluralism itself, is at once sufficiently flexible to accommodate the well-being of every human being and what that requires, and sufficiently substantial to offer other human beings reason to respect and to sustain the quest for well-being on the part of each of their fellows.[24]

---

[24] For a more extended examination of the issues raised here see T. Macklem, "Faith as a Secular Value" (2000) 45 *McGill Law Journal* (forthcoming).

5

Faced by Faith

ANTHONY BRADNEY

INTRODUCTION

WITHIN Great Britain religion is now largely a private matter. Rates of religious observance are low.[1] The fact of an individual's observance or non-observance is seen as having little significance for their public life.[2] In the British legal systems this retreat by religion into the realm of the private has combined with a constitutional and legal history which has increasingly discouraged religion from being either the ground to a legal claim or an argument within a claim. A British legal tradition, which is said to be one of neutrality and tolerance towards religion, has translated into a legal system which is often deaf to religion.

Religious belief has usually received no positive protection under British law. Neutrality towards religion in the courts, it is commonly said, has meant a lack of interest in the religious beliefs of those who have appeared before the courts.[3] Tolerance has meant allowing all individuals equal access to civil life by removing restrictions on religious groups previously imposed by the law.[4] The result is a separation of church and state, religion and law, which some have seen as "a crucial development in Western Christian culture", allowing a multi-religious country to maintain social stability.[5] Detailed enquiry suggests that this separation is in fact far from complete. Religions are not treated equally by the law; religion is not absent from the substance of the law.[6] This essay is not,

[1] I use the term "Great Britain" deliberately, referring to England, Wales and Scotland but excluding Northern Ireland. Rates of religious observance are different as between all these areas. Northern Ireland has much higher rates of observance and, for obvious reasons, religion is a matter of more pressing significance than is generally the case in Great Britain. (For rates of observance see P. Brierly and H. Wraight (eds.), *UK Christian Handbook 1996/97* (London, Christian Research, 1995) 241).

[2] Thus, for example, religion is not seen as being important in analysing voting patterns. (P. Norton, *The British Polity* (3rd edn., London, Longman, 1994) 93.

[3] *Re Carroll* [1931] 1 KB 317 at 336; *Versani* v. *Jesani* [1998] 3 All ER 273 at 285.

[4] See, for example, the Roman Catholic Relief Act 1829. The Human Rights Act 1998 changes this picture to some extent, though even here there are limitations to the positive protection afforded to religious belief. The Act applies only to the actions of public authorities (s. 6(1)) and to the interpretation of primary and secondary legislation (s. 3(1)).

[5] D. Saunders, *Antilawyers: Religion and the Critics of Law and State* (London, Routledge, 1997) 3.

[6] A. Bradney, *Religion, Rights and Laws* (Leicester, Leicester University Press, 1993).

however, concerned with this broad issue of the relationship between religion and law in a largely secular modern state. Instead it focuses attention on the legal system's treatment of those comparatively rare individuals who do not see their religion as being private or peripheral.

There are people in Great Britain whose religion is the key to their own sense of their self-identity.[7] For such individuals their religion is central to their lives, determining their behaviour in most or all respects.[8] Not all religions in Great Britain are equally likely to produce such obdurate adherents. Indeed, religious traditions which are comparatively new to Great Britain often contain a greater proportion of obdurate believers than do traditions which have extensive historical roots in Great Britain. One recent survey found that "[a]round nine in ten Sikhs, Hindus and Muslims said that religion was important to the way they led their lives, compared with only six in ten Christians".[9] In some cases the religious tradition that obdurate believers follow will not only be new to Great Britain but will also be very different from the cultural traditions that are central to the history of Great Britain. In such cases a difference both in religious and cultural tradition may separate the obdurate believer from their fellow citizens. In itself the difference in cultural tradition may lead to believers being treated differently from other citizens and, arguably, not equally with other citizens.[10] However, the unyielding nature of their faith is also, in itself, something that separates the obdurate believer from the rest of the community; in this separation the believer may be Anglican or Quaker as much as Muslim or Buddhist. This also will lead to obdurate believers being treated differently and, arguably, not equally with other citizens.

The phenomenon of obdurate religious belief is widely misunderstood within British society. In looking at the way in which religious belief is commonly regarded in British society "one sometimes gets the feeling that religion is like stamp-collecting or playing squash, a minor hobby".[11] This, perhaps, is not surprising. The comparatively low level of religious belief has already been noted above. Even those people in Great Britain who are believers usually hold to their religion fairly lightly. In one survey 40 per cent of religious believers questioned felt that their religion made no difference to their day-to-day lives.[12] In this context a general failure to understand, let alone empathise with, the obdurate believer is understandable. Primacy of faith, indeed primacy of any clear and

---

[7] See, for example, T. Modood, "Culture and Identity" in T. Modood *et al.*, *Ethnic Minorities in Britain* (London, Policy Studies Institute, 1997) 297.

[8] B. Parekh, "Religion and Public life" in T. Modood (ed.), *Church, State and Religious Minorities* (London, Policy Studies Institute, 1997) 21.

[9] *Social Focus on Ethnic Minorities* (London, HMSO, 1996) 14–15. See also Modood, *supra* n. 7.

[10] Such unequal treatment involves not only simple racist behaviour but also the more complex phenomenon, first discussed by Said, of the denigration by occidental society of oriental culture. (See E. Said, *Orientalism* (Harmondsworth. Penguin Books, 1985).)

[11] K. Knott, *Religion and Identity, and the Study of Ethnic Minority Religions in Britain* (Leeds. University of Leeds Community Religions Project, 1986) 4.

[12] *Social Trends*, Vol. 26 (London, The Stationery Office, 1996) 225.

extensive philosophical viewpoint, is inimical to the way in which British society now functions. The obdurate believer's faith in the timeless and boundless significance of their religious system stands in stark contrast to modernity's "reflexivity . . . [which involves] the susceptibility of most aspects of social activity, and material relations with nature, to chronic revision in the light of new information or knowledge".[13] The difference between the committed worldview of the obdurate believer and the pragmatic attitude of the average modern British citizen is difficult to exaggerate. Giddens argues:[14]

> "[T]o live in the universe of high modernity is to live in an environment of chance and risk, the inevitable concomitants of a system geared to the domination of nature and the reflexive making of history. Fate and destiny have no formal part to play in such a system, which operates (as a matter of principle) via what I shall call open human control of the natural and social worlds."

Obdurate believers do not, cannot, experience this "high modernity" because their identity and thus their actions are tied to what is, for them, a pre-ordained system of values and commitments. Modernity in modern Britain and obdurate religious belief are polar opposites as forms of consciousness.

Analysing the treatment of this unusual group of obdurate believers in court is important for two reasons. First, this group of people represents a significant section of the population. The level and strength of religious belief in Great Britain can be underestimated. Ten per cent of the population of the United Kingdom attends a religious service at least once a month.[15] Whilst this level of attendance is low when compared with that in many other countries it still represents several million people.[16] Not all of these people will be obdurate believers but the number taken from this group that will be unyielding in their faith is still likely to be sizeable. Moreover, as seen above, it is a section of the population which is likely to have disproportionate representation amongst ethnic minorities communities within Great Britain. Secondly, the analysis of this interaction between court and believer provides a paradigmatic account of the relationship between religion and law, highlighting differences and difficulties that are likely to occur in a less sharp form, even when the encounter is between the law and those who are more restrained in their faith.

The argument in this essay is based on an analysis of three cases. To move from judgments in just three cases to arguments about the relationship between religion and law or even the attitude of British judges might at first sight seem to be a large and unjustifiable leap. It is important, therefore, to note that these cases are presented as simply as illustrations of strains that can arise when

[13] A. Giddens, *Modernity and Self-Identity* (London. Polity Press, 1991) 20.
[14] *Ibid.*, 109.
[15] *Supra* n. 12.
[16] The United Kingdom has the lowest rate of active church membership (15 per cent) of countries surveyed in Europe (*Social Trends*, Vol. 24 (London. The Stationery Office, 1994) 145). The total population of the United Kingdom in 1994 was 58.4 million (*Social Trends*, Vol. 27 (London. The Stationery Office, 1997) 16). 15 per cent of 58.6 million is 8.76 million.

British courts judge obdurate believers. This essay is not an exercise in empirical sociology. We know too little about the actual behaviour of the British judiciary.[17] This essay, however, does not attempt to add to such knowledge as we
have about the generality of judicial behaviour. It is about what British judges
sometimes do when confronted with obdurate believers. Whether the cases are
typical or untypical is not the point; whether the issues discussed reflect what
judges regularly do and whether the behaviour of judges in the lower courts is
similar to the behaviour of judges in the higher courts is not the subject matter
here. The contention of the essay is simply that the cases discussed show problems that have occurred in the interaction between judges and believers, that
these problems are likely to recur, and that these problems are important.

THE HERMIT IN THE FOREST

In 1984 the Employment Appeal Tribunal heard the case of *Chauhan* v. *Ford
Motor Company*.[18] Chauhan claimed exemption, under section 58(4) of the
Employment Protection (Consolidation) Act 1978, from a union maintenance
agreement providing for compulsory trade union membership for Ford employees, on grounds of his religious beliefs. Chauhan had at one time been a union
member but that membership had lapsed. He had never previously referred to
his religious beliefs during the course of his employment. It was only when the
matter of his lapsed membership was raised with him that he revealed his religious beliefs. In evidence in support of his claim Chauhan cited Lecture IV in the
Laws of Manu which describes the need for male Hindus to retire to the forest
after they have discharged their family responsibilities as part of the process of
spiritual growth which should occur during each individual's life. He had, he
asserted, reached a stage in his life when trade union membership was no longer
appropriate because he should withdraw from worldly pursuits. He offered to
pay a sum to charity which was the equivalent of the trade union membership
dues.

In rejecting Chauhan's application the Industrial Tribunal, in a passage later
explicitly approved by the Employment Appeal Tribunal, argued that:

> "In order to make a judgement on a man's beliefs and motivations it is necessary to take
> account of his actions as well as his words. For our own part, we find it extremely hard
> to reconcile the applicant's three-year silence with his protestations of conscience."

[17] There has been a lot of valuable work in this area. It has covered many different areas of law.
What unites all the studies is the conclusion that, notwithstanding doctrinal theory, the behaviour
of lower, unreported courts does not, in any straight forward way, simply reflect the rules and principles laid down for these courts in the reported precedents of the higher courts. See, for example,
Custody After Divorce (Oxford, Oxford Centre for Socio-Legal Studies, 1977).

[18] An abbreviated version of the judgment is to be found at (1985) 280 *Industrial Relations Legal
Information Bulletin* 11. However the comments in this essay are based upon the full transcript of
the judgment which is found on the LEXIS database.

Implicitly they held that Chauhan's continued employment with Ford, and his failure to raise his beliefs with the company or the union until questioned, contradicted the religious motivation for failing to join a trade union, the need to withdraw from the world, that he claimed. Chauhan lost his claim for unfair dismissal.

On superficial analysis the tribunal's attitude seems unremarkable. *The Laws of Manu* can be used to justify Chauhan's claim for the necessity of withdrawal from the world. Verse 42 of the fourth lecture says:[19]

"Let him always wander alone, without any companion, in order to attain (final liberation), fully understanding that the solitary [man, who] neither forsakes nor is forsaken, gains his end."

However, the lecture seems to demand far more than a refusal to join a trade union. The next verse runs:[20]

"He shall neither possess a fire, nor a dwelling, he may go to a village for his food, [he shall be] indifferent to everything, firm of purpose, meditating [and] concentrating his mind on Brahman."

The message of the chapter is a call for a withdrawal from the ordinary material world, which seems to sit uneasily with Chauhan's wish to retain employment with the Ford Motor Company. As the tribunal judgment suggests, his actions appear to be at odds with his religious claims. Yet, contrary to the tribunal's analysis, if Chauhan's religious claims were not genuine, why did he refuse to join a trade union and, at the same time, offer to pay a sum equivalent to trade union dues to charity thus removing any financial advantage from his refusal?

In order to understand the apparent paradox of Chauhan's position, and in order to assess the validity of the tribunal's approach to the case, we need to look at the position of a Hindu litigant in a secular court of a country with a Christian tradition. First it is necessary to note that within Hindu theology and practice there is nothing unusual in Chauhan's wish to withdraw from the world. Carey, amongst others, has described:[21]

"the classic Hindu ideal whereby the individual renounces his householder status and becomes a monk towards the end of his life, after discharging his family duties . . . [and] the alternative ideal whereby an individual renounces the world whenever he realises the futility of worldly pleasure."

[19] *The Laws of Manu* (G. Buhler, trans., Delhi, Motil Banarsidass, 1964) 206 (translator's parentheses).
[20] *Ibid.,* 206.
[21] S. Carey, "Initiation into Monkhood in the Ramakrishne Mission" in R. Burghart (ed.), *Hinduism in Great Britain* (London, Tavistock Publications, 1987) 135. See also D. Funk, "Traditional Orthodox Hindu Jurisprudence: Justifying Dharma and Danda" in V. Nanda and S. Sinha (eds.), *Hindu Law and Legal Theory* (Aldershot, Dartmouth, 1996) 28.

As Raja Rao writes in his novel, *The Chessmaster and His Moves*:

> "once you have had twenty or thirty years of this householder's life, you go to the forest and become a thinker, a man in meditation, and meditation is best in the forest—much of indian wisdom was born in the forest . . .
> . . . All indians know of the forest." [22]

These ideals, like other Hindu ideals, must be translated into actual practices which are affected by the geographical and social location which the believer finds himself in. In India the believer may withdraw and find "[a] tremendous reverence . . . shown" by the population at large.[23] Food can be obtained from a willing population through begging. There is a forest to withdraw into. Chauhan would have been unlikely to obtain the same treatment from the general population of London, nor was there the same possibility of physically being a hermit. Knott has shown how traditional Hindu temple practices in Leeds have to accommodate themselves to the particular local circumstances of their setting.[24] That one should find a process of local adaptation in the attempt at asceticism is, in this context, unremarkable. A partial withdrawal from the material world, such as Chauhan attempted, may be all that most male Hindus can manage in modern Britain.

According to what standard did the tribunal find Chauhan's behaviour so unreasonable as to lead it to doubt that he was genuine? Chauhan sought to do what many, probably most, Hindus believe ought to be done. His attempt was imperfect. In most theologies failure is seen as part of the nature of the religious life, where frail humanity seeks to live according to divine standards. Did a secular tribunal, operating in the context of a Christian social tradition, understand the theological, social and psychological subtleties and complexities of someone who was part of the Hindu diaspora? It may be legally right to hold, in the tribunal's words, that to "make a judgement on a man's beliefs and motivations it is necessary to take account of his actions as well as his words", but in applying that test it is necessary to remember that actions are frequently culturally contingent. A failure by the tribunal to take this into account explains why a man who, in the tribunal's view, was not genuine in his religious motivation was willing to hand over a sum equivalent to his membership dues to charity, thus removing any financial advantage to non-membership.

THE RECEPTIONIST'S TALE

In June 1985 Barbara Janaway sought an order of certiorari to quash a decision by Salford Area Health Authority to uphold her dismissal as a medical recep-

---

[22] R. Rao, *The Chessmaster and His Moves* (New Delhi, Vision Books, 1988) 43–4.

[23] Carey, *supra* n. 21 at 155.

[24] K. Knott, "Hindu Temple Rituals in Britain: The Reinterpretation of Tradition" in Burghart (ed.), *supra* n. 21. See also K. Knott, *Hinduism in Leeds* (Leeds, Community Religions Project, University of Leeds, 1986) ch. 3.

tionist. The case was successively heard by the High Court, the Court of Appeal and, finally, the House of Lords.[25]

Janaway was a medical receptionist and had been asked to type a letter which she understood to be a letter of referral to make an appointment for a patient to undergo an abortion.[26] Before taking up her job she had not been told that she would have to type correspondence which related to abortions. Janaway was a Catholic and held to the traditional Catholic position that abortions were morally wrong. She therefore refused to type the letter.[27] Janaway argued that she was entitled to the protection of section 4(1) of the Abortion Act 1967 which allows anybody who would otherwise be required "to participate" in abortions to refuse that participation on grounds of conscience.

In a series of judgments all three courts rejected her claim. Janaway was wrong, the courts said, in claiming that she was participating in abortion if she typed the letter as requested. The nine judges who gave judgment in this case were divided about why Janaway was wrong. Some judges turned to the criminal law's concept of participation for assistance; others sought a "plain English" interpretation of the idea.[28] All nine judges agreed that, whatever "participate" meant, it did not mean what Janaway thought it meant. All nine agreed that typing a letter which related to an abortion could not be said to be participating in that abortion. Janaway therefore could not have the protection of section 4.

As in the case of *Chauhan* the court's attitude in *Janaway* seems unremarkable on first analysis. Using traditional and familiar legal tests the courts simply found that the litigant did not meet the criteria for protection set out in the Abortion Act. Yet deeper analysis, once again, shows a more complex picture which is closely analogous to the position in *Chauhan*. Janaway, like Chauhan, sought the protection of a statutory regime designed to protect the individual conscience. *Prima facie* such regimes appear to be of great assistance to obdurate believers. However, both Janaway and Chauhan found that the statute whose assistance they sought did not in fact protect them. Chauhan was told that his actions showed that he was not genuine in his religious beliefs. Janaway was told that, notwithstanding her own belief, in typing letters she would not be participating in a matter forbidden to her by her religion. As Nolan J put it at first instance, "[a]s a matter of plain English" what Janaway had been asked to do could not amount to participation in an abortion.[29] In both *Chauhan* and *Janaway* it was held that actions, in Janaway's case proposed actions, did not

[25] R. v. *Salford Area Health Authority*, (*The Times*, 13 Feb. 1987); R v. *Salford Area Health Authority, Janaway* v. *Salford Area Health Authority* [1989] AC 537.
[26] The letter was in fact a letter to make an appointment with a consultant to see whether or not an abortion was appropriate (R v. *Salford Area Health Authority* [1989] AC 537 at 544).
[27] R. v. *Salford Area Health Authority* [1989] AC 537 at 545.
[28] For an examination of the various nuances of these judgments see A. Bradney, "Making Cowards" [1990] *Juridical Review* 129.
[29] This ordinary language approach to the interpretation of the statute was later approved in Lord Keith's single substantive judgment in the House of Lords: *Janaway* v. *Salford Area Health Authority* [1989] AC 537 at 570.

match the religious beliefs claimed by the litigant in the court. In Janaway's case the courts did not refuse to accept that her religious beliefs were genuine. However, since the majority of judgments turned not on a technical interpretation of the law but on an ordinary language construction, the courts implicitly held that Janaway's view of the actions required of her by her employers was either irrational or unreasonable.

The decision in *Chauhan* stems from a failure fully to comprehend the religious world-view of the litigant. In *Janaway* the courts chose to deny the legitimacy of the religious world-view of the litigant. In doing so the judgments in *Janaway* deprive section 4(1) of much of its potential effect by substantially limiting those who come under its ægis. A different approach to the interpretation of the section is not hard to envisage. Section 4 was not a part of the original Bill permitting abortions first put forward by David Steele. It was added to the Bill during its passage through the House of Commons in response to those who argued that Roman Catholics would have to leave the health service if the Bill was passed into law without a conscience clause.[30] Thus this section is primarily concerned with the protection of the consciences of those who work in the health service and the potential mischief involved in a failure to so protect. The mischief approach to statutory interpretation would have us ask what potential mischief the statutory provision in question was trying to remedy and then give the provision such interpretation as will allow the provision to fulfil its purpose.[31] On occasion, in following this approach, the court may need to demonstrate considerable creativity in order to arrive at an appropriate result.[32] Using this approach to statutory interpretation it therefore seems appropriate to begin an enquiry into the possible application of the section with the questions whether the litigant genuinely believed that they would be participating in an abortion and whether such a belief was reasonably held in the light of their religious convictions. Such an approach would have served both to protect the consciences of those who find themselves in Janaway's position and to prevent the possibility of health service employees illicitly using the conscience clause as a way of avoiding what would otherwise be their contractual duties.

THE LAW OF LOVE

In 1995, Ward LJ gave judgment in the case of *Re ST (A Minor)*.[33] This wardship case concerned an attempt by a grandmother to have the care and control

---

[30] See, for example, Bernard Braine, H of C Standing Committee Reports 1966/67, Vol. X, col. 551 and Norman St John Stevas, col. 561. Specific reference was made to nurses, doctors and midwives but there was also a more general reference to members of the medical professions.

[31] *Heydon's Case* (1584) 3 Co.Rep. 7a.

[32] See, for example, *Davies* v. *Johnson* [1978] 1 All ER 841.

[33] This case is unreported and there is no record of it on the LEXIS database. There is a news report of the case in the *Guardian*, 25 Nov. 1995. My comments are based upon a transcript of the judgment supplied to me by The Family.

of her grandson, S, transferred from her daughter, NT, to herself. The sole ground for the grandmother's action was the fact that her daughter and grandson were living communally in a group which was part of the new religious movement now known as The Family.[34] The Family has acquired a degree of public infamy as a result of allegations which surround its attitude to sexuality, and in particular its attitude to child sexuality.[35] In cases prior to *Re ST*, most notably in *Re B and G*, members of new religious movements, particularly those which had achieved public notoriety, had lost custody battles because of the court's view of the effect their religious behaviour would have on their children.[36]

In his judgment Ward LJ rejected the grandmother's application. Ward LJ said, however, there was much in the mother's attitude that troubled him. Early in his judgment he noted that:

"The mother claims the inalienable right to love her God as she chooses, which is a love she submits brooks no interference from a Court of Law because she is entitled to the fundamental freedom of thought, conscience, and religion."

When he looked at the mother's evidence he observed:

"NT's closing words to me were to plead with me not to denigrate the Law of Love [The Family's central doctrine]. It was an extraordinary observation from her. I would have expected her to plead with me not to remove her son. Many mothers, often totally hopeless mothers, have begged for that mercy. But NT did not. It was if the integrity of the Law of Love was more important to her than S. Where is her sense of priorities?"

Finally, he devoted a section of his concluding appendix to the question, "[d]oes NT place S's interests first and will she continue to do so?".

Unlike *Chauhan*, *Re ST* does not involve the court claiming that there is a mismatch between a litigant's claimed religious beliefs and the objective actions found in the case. However, in a similar fashion, it does involve the court questioning whether the religiosity put forward by the litigant matches any acceptable view of the world. Ward LJ notes with concern that :

"The fact is that most of those within The Family remain there because of their faith in what it offers. *For most it is blind faith* [emphasis added]."

Elsewhere in his judgment Ward LJ said that he was "disturbed" by the "fervour" with which members of The Family held their convictions and noted that they could not be swayed by "common-sense". By contrast, at several points in

---

[34] The group was previously known as the Children of God.

[35] For an essay on the academic literature on The Family see J. Saliba, 'Scholarly Studies on The Family/the Children of God: A Comprehensive Survey" in J. Lewis and J. Gordon Melton, *Sex, Slander, and Salvation* (Stanford, Cal., Center for Academic Publication, 1994).

[36] In *Re B and G*, in removing custody of two children from a Scientologist father who had had the children living with him for five years, Latey J described Scientology as both "immoral and socially obnoxious" and "corrupt, sinister and dangerous": *Re B and G* [1985] FLR 134 at 159.

his judgment The Family were commended when they adhered to what Ward LJ believed to be mainstream Christian beliefs. Thus, for example, he said:

> "The Family do not deny their belief in healing by faith. They assert it. *They are fully justified in doing so. It is an established tenet of Christian belief.* [emphasis added]."

Elsewhere he commented that:

> "[NT] had undergone a remarkable change [when she joined The Family] but it is no more than one would expect from the cataclysmic religious conversion which she and many others have experienced. *Being 'reborn' is a phenomenon which happens to some members of established churches. It does not only affect those at the loony extremes of Christianity* [emphasis added]."

In his description of The Family Ward LJ created a contrast between a religiosity which is dominated by a simple, overwhelming faith which ignores the "common-sense" beliefs of society and one which is milder, more uncertain of itself and which accords more closely to the mainstream of Christianity. The latter is acceptable; the former is not. Towards the end of his judgment Ward LJ observed

> "My concern for NT is that she fails to put S first. The Family comes first. Her devotion to Berg [the founder of The Family] is so total that it has drained her intellectual reserves and she, like most of those about her, and like Portia, is blinded by love for him and 'cannot see the pretty follies that they themselves commit'."

Before rejecting the grandmother's application for care and control of S, Ward LJ required both NT and leading members of The Family to accept a large number of conditions. Some of these conditions, for example regarding his future education, related directly to the treatment of S. Others, however, concerned the way in which both NT and other members of The Family should view their religion. NT, for example, was required to say that she put the welfare of S before her commitment to The Family. Leading members of The Family were obliged to accept their founder's responsibility for some past instances of child sex abuse within The Family. NT was permitted to retain care and control of her son only when Ward LJ became convinced of the mother's "maturity" as evidenced by what he took to be greater moderation in her religious beliefs.

In *Chauhan* the law denies the claim of religiosity. In *Janaway* the law tells religiosity that its view of the world is not acceptable in court. The law repeats this view in *Re ST* and goes on to demand a change in the way in which both the religion and the believer behave.[37]

---

[37] This is not to say that Ward LJ's decision was necessarily incorrect. Ward LJ was bound in law to attend only to the best interests of the child in the case, not the religious needs of the parent or the theological position of the religion involved. Moreover his judgment was based on a full examination of expert evidence and contains a balanced account of The Family which is in marked contrast to some earlier judicial comment on new religious movements. For a more detailed consideration of this case in the context of the law relating to child custody see A. Bradney, "Children of a Newer God" in S. Palmer and C. Hardman (eds.), *Children in New Religious Movements* (New Brunswick, N.J., Rutgers University Press, 1999) 210 .

EDUCATION, RELIGION AND THE JUDICIARY

The conflict between religion and law in British courts revealed in the three cases above is structural. What is important is not the fact that all three believers lost, either in the sense that their claim was rejected or in that they were required substantially to modify their religious behaviour. Cases where obdurate believers won could be adduced.[38] What is important is why the believers lost in these cases.

One matter that divides the three cases above is the level of information about the religious beliefs that the litigants professed that was available to the courts concerned. In *Re ST*, the one case where the believer succeeded in the litigation, Ward LJ heard evidence from seven expert witnesses. Four gave evidence about the beliefs and practices of The Family and three gave evidence about the effect of living in a Family commune on S. Seventy-nine A4 pages of Ward LJ's judgment are devoted to discussion of this evidence. In addition Ward LJ also heard evidence about The Family from members of The Family, including the mother, NT, and large parts of his judgment are concerned with this evidence. By contrast in *Janaway* the religious beliefs of the litigant are never discussed and in *Chauhan* the only evidence about the litigant's religious beliefs is given by the litigant himself. Chauhan, it might be argued, lost his case because the members of the tribunal knew too little about the practice of Hinduism in the context of a modern industrial society. Janaway's views are said by the courts to be outside the realms of ordinary linguistic usage yet the court does not investigate how widely people adhere to her views and thus her linguistic usage. By contrast NT lost less heavily than might have been forecast because of what the court learned about the reality of her faith and practice.

Ignorance about the *mores* of others often manifests itself as hostility or, at best, indifference. Given the general level of ignorance about, and apathy towards, religion obdurate believers may in general benefit from an attempt to educate a court about their particular beliefs and the social practices which flow from those beliefs.[39] It is easy to give instances of cases where expert evidence has been adduced and believers have succeeded or where the courts can be shown to have gained experience of the religious beliefs of a particular religious group over a series of cases and, as a consequence, ameliorated their treatment of that group.[40] However, the adversarial trial process is not the best site for

[38] There were, for example, a number of cases in which believers were successful in claiming exemption from closed-shop trade union arrangements. See Bradney, *supra* n. 6 at 142.

[39] Although sometimes obdurate believers may benefit from judicial ignorance. In *Holmes* v. *Attorney-General* Walton J observed that the disciplinary practices of the Exclusive Brethren, which involve the use of ostracism, might have been put in "a much more charitable light than it wears in reality" by the Brethren who gave evidence (*The Times*, 12 Feb. 1981). The inference in his judgment is that, had he known more about these practices, he might have found that the group failed to pass the public morality test for charities found in *Thornton* v. *Howe* ((1862) 31 Beav. 14).

[40] For example Ellis Cashmore, a sociologist, gave evidence about the new religious movement, the Rastafarians, in a successful Industrial Tribunal attempt to have them treated as an ethnic group

education. The rules relating to the calling of expert witnesses are designed to facilitate the progress of a trial and to provide detailed technical information about pertinent issues.[41] They do not easily allow for the broader educative effort involved in learning about an unfamiliar religious culture. Moreover such education demands not just the acquisition of information but a period of time spent in reflection on that information. In his judgment in *Re ST* Ward LJ notes that the case took 75 days to hear and that he spent nearly one year preparing his judgment. This unusually long period of time spent preparing the judgment properly reflects the intellectual difficulties inherent in coming to terms with the views of obdurate believers. However, lengthy trials, involving many expert witnesses and prolonged deliberation by the judiciary, are not conducive to the smooth running of a legal system already burdened with over-long court lists. Judges already receive training in awareness of racial and ethnic differences.[42] Training in religious differences would have an equal value allowing those holding judicial office to meet and discuss the problems that arise from the clash between the obdurate believer and the court in an atmosphere free of the immediate pragmatic and pressing concerns of an individual case.

RELIGION AND VALUES IN BRITISH COURTS

The factual ignorance about matters of religious belief and practice, which is illustrated in *Chauhan* and is found elsewhere in a much wider range of cases, is an important matter in its own right. However, it also serves to mask a more profound problem about the relationship between religion and law in British courts.

In the widely cited case of *C* v. *C*, a child custody decision, Balcombe LJ held that judges, when exercising their discretion, should "start on the basis that the moral standards which are generally accepted in the society in which the Judge lives are more likely than not to promote . . . [the child's] welfare".[43] Such an approach characterises not only the area of law relating to child custody disputes but also many other areas of law where the religion of a litigant may

for the purposes of the Race Relations Act 1965: *Crown Suppliers* v. *Dawkins* [1991] IRLR 327 at 328. This decision was later overturned on appeal: *Dawkins* v. *Department of the Environment* [1993] IRLR 284. In *Buckley* v. *Buckley* (1973) 3 Fam. Law 106 a Jehovah's witness parent lost custody of her three daughters in large part because she lived in the witness manner which the court regarded as socially isolating the children. By the time of *Re T* (1981) 2 FLR 239 the courts had come to accept that it was reasonable for a parent to teach their children the tenets of the witness faith and to give care and control of children to witness parents, albeit with access conditions which enabled the children to celebrate Christmas and have their own birthday parties (things which Jehovah's witnesses regard as being theologically unacceptable).

[41] Thus, for example, see Tapper's comment that "the guidance [of expert evidence] must also be sufficiently relevant to a matter in issue": C. Tapper, *Cross and Tapper on Evidence* (8th edn., London, Butterworths, 1995) 558.

[42] See, for example, *Judicial Studies Board Report for 1987–1991* (London, HMSO, 1992) 17–18.

[43] [1991] 1 FLR 223 at 230.

become part of the legal issue before the court. "[M]oral standards which are generally accepted in society" are both an evidentiary test of the *bona fides* of the litigant, as for example in *Chauhan*, and a normative standard to which the believer must adhere, as, for example, in the *Thornton* v. *Howe* morality test in the law relating to charities.[44] A failure to live by such standards frequently becomes, in the law's eyes, a failure to live in an acceptable manner. In a society such as Great Britain, dominated as it is by secular liberal *mores*, obdurate believers will invariably live by standards which are different from those which are general in society or take the standards which are general and apply them in a more rigid and unwavering manner. There is thus, at root, an incompatibility between the law and the believer.

In *Re ST* when NT pleaded with Ward LJ not to denigrate the beliefs of The Family rather than pleading for care and control of her child Ward LJ asked "[w]here is her sense of priorities?". It is this question which lies at the heart of the failure of British courts to understand obdurate believers. What perplexes the court is not only the character of the beliefs of believers but the very obduracy with which those beliefs are held. Yet historically there is nothing unusual in the fervour with which believers adhere to their religions. In the tradition of three major world religions, Christianity, Islam and Judaism, God told Abraham to sacrifice his only son Isaac. And Abraham was willing to obey.[45] In Ward LJ's court Abraham would be asked where was his sense of priorities? In the Christian tradition Christ said he came to put mother against daughter.[46] In advocating the division of families Christ, like Abraham, could be asked to justify his priorities. In the Hindu tradition male householders should, towards the end of their lives, abandon their families.[47] Where, once again, are their priorities? In each case the answer is with their religion. In following their religion Chauhan and Janaway lost their jobs; NT risked losing care and control of her son. They were willing to sacrifice that which most people in Britain see as being central to their lives, work and family. But had they acted otherwise they would have lost all of that which gave their lives purpose, shape and direction. For each of these litigants, as with any obdurate believer, their religion, with its values and duties, is the organising principle that makes everything else, including work and family, possible.

Within modern civil society there is an all-pervasive notion of balancing conflicting rights and principles when making decisions. Through balance comes moderation as principles play upon each other. Balance and moderation lie behind all of the judgments discussed above and are an important part of Balcombe LJ's "generally accepted moral standards". But for obdurate believers balance is an anathema. For them there is only the priority and primacy of faith.

[44] *Thornton* v. *Howe* (1862) Beav. 14.
[45] Genesis 22: 2–12.
[46] Matthew 10: 35.
[47] *Laws of Manu, supra* n. 19, Lecture IV.

It has been argued that "identity is not a singular but rather a multifaceted and context-specific construct".[48] In modern Britain for most people this will be so. Most people, if they are an adherent to a particular faith, will also have a social class, an ethnic background, an education, a job, a nationality and so forth which will cumulate to make them what they are. The balance that the individual strikes between these competing sources of identity amounts to their identity. But for the obdurate believer it is their religion and their religion alone which makes them what they are.[49] For most people giving up or changing one part of that which gives them their identity makes little overall difference to them. Since their identity comes from so many sources blocking off one source is of limited consequence. For the obdurate believer, however, their identity comes from just one source. To block that source, to ask them to doubt or ignore their religious belief, is a radical attack on their sense of self. They are who they are only so long as they are firm in their religion. It is their religion which gives them the ability to be the employee or indeed the mother that they are. In his judgment in *Re ST* Ward LJ says of NT:

> "she could, of course, leave . . . [The Family] but I cannot require her to do that—that is a matter for her choice according to her conscience and her love for her son."

This division between conscience and parental love is one which, for the obdurate believer, does not make sense: "I could not love thee (deare) half so much/ Loved I not honour more".[50] Religion does, and for such believers logically must, come first, making all other things possible. Balcombe LJ's "moral standards which are generally accepted in the society" are, literally, of no account to the obdurate believer.

The efficacy of Balcombe LJ's test in *C v. C*, both in relation to its precise use in the law relating to child custody and in relation to its reflection of more widespread legal practice, is debatable in any society which pretends to liberal aims. A pluralistic, multi-racial, multi-religious society is one which has to accommodate a wide range of social practices. A liberal society is one which does not make value choices for its members.[51] That which is commonly done is not necessarily that which is right. It is not necessarily the only thing that is right. This has been recognised by the courts. In *C v. C* Balcombe LJ, having enunciated his

---

[48] A. Brah, *Cartographies of Diaspora* (London, Routledge, 1996) 47.

[49] The discussion here is a discussion of the psychology of how people see themselves. These psychological beliefs may be mistaken. I have argued elsewhere that any attempt to assert a priority of anything over the existential fact that individuals makes choices (so that someone says I *had* to do something or I *must* believe something because of my religion) is philosophically inaccurate: see Bradney, *supra* n. 6 at ch. 2. Nevertheless, even if such beliefs are inaccurate they can still be the things which dominate and govern people's lives. Equally, even in an obdurate believer others will see the effect of class, gender and so forth in the believer's values and actions. But this will not affect the believer's own very different sense of self.

[50] Richard Lovelace, "To Lucasta, Going to the Wars".

[51] J. Rawls, "The Priority of Rights and Ideas of the Good" (1988) 17 *Philosophy and Public Affairs* 251 at 262.

general morality test, immediately went on to add that "standards may differ between different communities" within British society.

Obdurate believers will be members of a "different community" where "standards may differ" and should be treated as such by the courts.[52] Yet, whilst a liberal society does not prescribe the values that its citizens adhere to, it does not allow for complete freedom of choice in values. "Standards may differ" but not infinitely. Value choices by one member of the society which impinge upon the ability of others to make value choices will not be permitted. I may not, for example, in the name of racial superiority, claim the right to practise *apartheid*. An obdurate believer may thus come from a community whose values are both different and also unacceptable in a liberal society. But in showing that a value choice is not acceptable in a liberal society a heavy burden is put on those who wish to forbid the choice. For example, when it is argued that a value choice will be unacceptable if it causes "harm" to others, the notion of harm ought to be seen in a strong sense. Any choice I make, any action of mine, even the very fact of my being, has consequences for others in society. For liberalism to have operational effect, for there to be a multi-cultural, multi-religious community with diverse value choices, it must be a matter of considerable effort for me to show that a consequence for others has become a harm to others and that a value choice is thereby prohibited. If courts are to show that obdurate religious believers are not simply from a community where values differ but from a community whose values are to be forbidden, judicial practice ought to pay less attention to the question of which social practices are commonly accepted and more attention to the need to show that the social practices which flow from particular religious beliefs are positively, strongly and directly harmful to people other than the believers. Judicial practice must acknowledge that difference and damage are not the same things.

TOLERANCE, NON-DISCRIMINATION AND AFFIRMATION

Raz has traced three successive liberal responses to the phenomenon of multiculturalism in modern society. First there is tolerance, permitting minority cultures to pursue their ends providing they do not interfere with the majority culture. Secondly, there is non-discrimination, giving individuals rights against discrimination manifested in particular ways. Finally there is affirmation which seeks to create a variety of respected and flourishing cultural groups.[53] Raz argues for the superiority of the third approach.[54] Raz's argument seems to offer

---

[52] If the believers are not themselves tolerant of others value choices in their theology then they have no right to claim such toleration but must nevertheless be treated with such tolerance: J. Rawls, *A Theory of Justice* (Oxford, Oxford University Press, 1972) 216–21.

[53] J. Raz, "Multiculturalism: A Liberal Perspective" in J. Raz, *Ethics in the Public Domain: Essays in the Morality of Law and Politics* (Oxford, Clarendon Press, 1994) 174–5.

[54] For similar arguments see B. Parekh, "Britain and the Social Logic of Pluralism" in *Britain: A Plural Society* (London, Commission for Racial Equality, 1990) particularly at 68–79.

succour to those religious minority communities who see themselves ignored or oppressed by the state.

Raz's specific argument for the superiority of affirmation over tolerance or non-discrimination seems untenable since it rests on the proposition that "it is in the interest of every person to be fully integrated in a cultural group" because "[o]nly through being socialized in a culture can one tap the options which give life meaning".[55] Gidden's discussion of modernity, noted at the beginning of this essay, suggests that such an experience of deep-rootedness in a single culture is unusual in modern complex societies. Rushdie's observation that:[56]

> "the very experience of uprooting, disjuncture and metamorphosis (slow or rapid, painful or pleasurable) that is the migrant condition . . . can be . . . a metaphor for all humanity"

is a more accurate description of the experience of the majority. In modern-day Great Britain most people "tap the options which give life meaning" from various sources in a very different way from that envisaged by Raz. Nevertheless, full integration within one community *can* be a way of giving life meaning and, if a liberal society is to live up to its claim not to select values for its members, the existence of this possibility, albeit that it is a considerably more limited position than that advanced by Raz, will be sufficient to justify his argument for the superiority of affirmation over tolerance or non-discrimination. Obdurate believers wish to live in a single community, wish to take their values blindly from that source, and, because of this, liberalism demands that the state affirm the importance of their community and its values providing it and they do not impinge on the value choices of others.

CONCLUSION

There is an inevitable conflict between the secularism of the argumentative rhetoric in the British courts and the faith-based vision of the obdurate believer. Greater judicial knowledge about religion may ease some of these difficulties. However, a court which declares itself "agnostic" about the truth of the religious beliefs of those who appear before it will always clash with those who see questions of right religious conduct as necessarily permeating all aspects of human life.[57] The new Human Rights Act 1998 is likely dramatically to increase litigation about rights in the same manner that the introduction of the Canadian Charter of Rights and Freedoms increased such litigation in Canada.[58] Litigation about infringement of religious beliefs will be a part of that increase.

[55] Raz, *supra* n. 53 at 177.
[56] S. Rushdie, "In Good Faith" in S. Rushdie, *Imaginary Homelands* (London, Granta Books in association with Penguin, 1992) 394.
[57] *Varsani* v. *Jesani* [1998] 3 All ER 273 at 280.
[58] H. Arthurs, "The Political Economy of Canadian Legal Education" (1998) 25 *Journal of Law and Society* 14 at 25.

Greater numbers of obdurate believers will appear before the courts. A greater weight of cases will make the gap between the kind of religious beliefs seen above and the nature of modern British legal discourse ever clearer. Even where believers win their cases, they will win not because of their beliefs but because, fortuitously, their beliefs or the social practices that result from their beliefs fit within the legal order. Even Raz's concept of affirmation does not involve accepting the validity of beliefs; merely their importance and value in believers' lives. Even if obdurate believers are cherished by the British legal systems and the state they and their form of belief will lie outside modernity. Believers can never win on their own terms and, wanting to live their lives only on their own terms, will always be disappointed in the law. Paradoxically, implementing a new legal mechanism to protect religious susceptibilities may highlight the necessary limitations that there are to the law's attempt to appreciate and protect the religious conscience.

6

A Comfortable Inauthenticity: Post-Theological Law

VICTOR TADROS

"The confession has spread its effects far and wide. It plays a part in justice, medicine, education, family relationships, and love relations, in the most ordinary affairs of everyday life, and in the most solemn rites; one confesses one's crimes, one's sins, one's thoughts and desires, one's illnesses and troubles; one goes about telling, with the greatest precision, whatever is most difficult to tell."[1]

INTRODUCTION

IN her famous *Panorama* interview, Princess Diana made a bizarre use of the ancient practice of confession. This confession did not reveal the truth of Diana. It did not recount acts, the history of which we were unaware. It was not used to ask for forgiveness. Nor was it used to purify. Finally, it was not used as a forum to receive interpretation or instruction. Rather, it transformed a media icon which had been carefully sculpted for over a decade. Its sole aim was a masterstroke in the æsthetic manipulation of the image of Diana. The gradual process through which the chocolate-box plump prettiness of her early years of marriage was transformed into an independent, tortured, twisted modern beauty was finally completed in that unforgettable broadcast that enthralled the nation. Princess Diana had taken charge of her self-presentation, she resisted the attempts of the royal family to construct her. She regarded herself as a project to be transformed through strategic action, and particularly in the realm of sex. To use Drucilla Cornell's words, Diana's confession was an example of "the renewal of the imagination as we come to terms with who we are and who we wish to be as sexuate beings".[2]

This is one way of presenting the Diana myth: Diana is nothing more than a media icon, an element of unreality, an image that never "really" happened and whose conflicts were entirely phoney and artificial, conducted only for our, the real spectators', pleasure. However, this representation of Diana's confession as

[1] M. Foucault, *The History of Sexuality: Volume 1: An Introduction* (London, Penguin, 1978) 59.
[2] D. Cornell, *The Imaginary Domain: Abortion, Pornography and Sexual Harassment* (London, Routledge, 1995).

an act in the field of æsthetics is insufficient in itself. The manipulation of the image did not just have æsthetic results. It was felt politically and the political consequences were difficult to anticipate, not least for Diana herself. The very transformation of the image, even more than the criticisms that were implicitly made of the monarchy, was a mark of resistance, and this was so keenly recognised that speculation that she had been killed by a royal conspiracy was commonplace following her death. The control of the image is at the heart of monarchist power; once its direct political and religious power declined, the control of the image became the most important way in which the monarchy could sustain itself and continue to be socially effective. This is why Diana's image was both effective and dangerous. If politics is war pursued by other means, as Foucault suggested, then this war is conducted through control of the images. And its potency in no way diminished its "unreality". The general acceptance that we had not seen the "real Diana", or even the recognition that there was no "real Diana", did not diminish the effect of her confession.

In his televised confession concerning the Monica Lewinsky affair, or "zippergate" as it has affectionately been termed, President Clinton attempted to tread the thin line between apologising for a relationship that was already public knowledge and avoiding the legal charge of perjury. Like the case of Diana, Clinton's confession marked a particular break with tradition, both stylistically and substantially. Traditionally one's confession was supposed to reveal one's sins in the most explicit and detailed form, a revelation that was also the manifestation of one's true self. Clinton's confession, on the other hand, was full of euphemisms and oblique references. For example, that he was suggesting *fellatio* rather than fornication was not mentioned explicitly; it was implicit in the statement that he had not committed perjury. As with implicit sense could be easily deduced: both the content of the statement and its interpretation were correctly anticipated by the press before the confession was even made. Again, the ancient rite of confession was used for the most political purposes. Rather than reveal the true self of the President through a revelation of his sins, confession was used as a strategic manœuvre in the political game.

It seems that Foucault's diagnosis that we have become a singularly confessing society has never been more true than it is today, if in a way that he did not anticipate. The social role of confession has changed considerably as we have entered what has been called the "post-modern" or "post-industrial" era, an era in which our faith in authenticity has taken a severe battering. In a world in which statements such as "there is no truth" and "there is no reality" are commonplace, we should not expect confession to be treated with any greater reverence than any other statement. The traditional role of confession—to reveal the authentic subject—has dwindled as we increasingly accept and respond to our own scepticism both with regard to the sincerity of confessions and their capacity to reveal untainted, de-politicised representations of "internal" truth. Such scepticism has led to a panorama of unpredictable social effects, not least in law. However, this has not diminished the importance nor the effect of confession. On the contrary it is more widespread than ever.

Perhaps part of the space left by the critique of authenticity has been filled by an ethics that is closely aligned with æsthetics. In this account the term "confession" no longer represents the expulsion of internal truth into the social world, it represents the moment at which the subject takes hold of itself æsthetically, a moment of self-creation that has become possible only through the radical acceptance of inauthenticity. The critique of authenticity ought not to lead us to ethical disempowerment. It ought to lead to a radical empowerment, the empowerment to construct ourselves as æsthetic/ethical beings. The contingency of subjectivity leads more or less automatically to a free space in which the subject can manufacture itself spontaneously and resist political structures, most notably the law. Even Luhmann buys into this optimism to some extent:[3]

> "The question is no longer 'what should I be?' but rather 'How should I be?' . . . This diagnosis should not be too quickly labelled as pessimistic. It can also be taken as an allusion to the prospect of trying new combinations, new differentiations, for which functional simplification remains an indispensable prerequisite."

Nevertheless, we might counter, scepticism about truth and reality is now widespread. And yet the result has not been a transformation of the social world, only a marked return to conservatism. This is true not least in law. The radical critique of the legal subject has not undermined the legal system; it has been incorporated into it. These comments reveal two related problems which it is the purpose of this essay to discuss. What happens when the legal system presents its own inauthenticity to itself? And what does this mean for legal ethics?

Consequently, this analysis puts into question the work of those thinkers, including Jacques Derrida and Drucilla Cornell, who attempt to construct or describe an effective "post-modern" ethics following the recognition that it is impossible to overcome cognitive contingency and the supposition that there is no "unified subject" that can be neutrally represented. My argument will be that neither of these thinkers anticipates the legal response to its second-order observation of these epistemological problems. Derrida's account of aporia[4] and ethics is insufficiently sensitive to the extent to which the legal system is comfortable with its paradoxes. The equation of deconstruction with justice is naïve, not because a lack of ethics follows naturally from deconstruction but because the opposite is also untrue. The recognition that paradox cannot be overcome can be utilised strategically and the effects of such strategies are difficult to predict. Paradoxes are just much more mundane but also potentially more vicious than Derrida assumes. Recognition of paradox has not resulted in an immediate and direct ethical crisis; it has resulted in an exploitative repetition.

---

[3] N. Luhmann, *Observations on Modernity* (Stanford, Cal., Stanford University Press, 1998).

[4] J. Derrida, "The Force of Law: The Mystical Foundation of Authority" in D. Cornell, M. Rosenfeld and D. Carlson (eds.), *Deconstruction and the Possibility of Justice* (London, Routledge, 1992) 3.

In a sense, Cornell is more aware of these political difficulties. For her, the recognition that there is no universal subject entails the necessity for individuals to be given the freedom to construct their identity in way they deem right or pleasing. Consequently she argues that the practice of "self-creation" can be protected by a rights-based scheme. My point in response to Cornell is not that self-creation is an illusion, nor that it cannot emerge as a positive force, but rather that self-creation is as imbued with strategies of power as self-discovery, and that it consequently needs to be treated with an equally sophisticated critique. For example, whilst Cornell's claim that a woman who aborts her child should have "narrative power over her decision"[5] provides an important contribution to that particular ethical and legal problem, the control over the way in which individuals narrativise themselves cannot be regarded as a precondition of freedom in general. Narrativisation, or statements of self-presentation, to be more accurate, can be used strategically in a variety of ways and to achieve a variety of effects. And the same is true for the theory that the self is narrative. As Gunther Teubner puts it in a slightly different context, "who can decide in advance what political camp makes use of which version of autopoiesis and how!".[6]

This creates a problem for "post-modern ethicists". Propositions that are grounded adequately in theory can result in unanticipated effects. In order to understand the significance of this claim it is necessary to trace the history of our modern "loss of authenticity". I will do this by discussing Foucault's account of the history of confession. Foucault's account of modernity is made up of various devices or mechanisms (*dispositifs*) that construct relatively stable forms of subjectivity. Two of the most important in Foucault's work are confession and discipline. However, the stability of the subject that Foucault finds in confession has been replaced by the contingency of the narrative subject. The confessing subject has already been surpassed, and not just in the realm of theory. Social systems have begun to realise that the subjects with which they deal are contingent discursive moments. The experience of contingency has not resulted in the substitution of radical æsthetic self-creation for the liberal conservative subject. It has resulted in a boring repetition of fragmentary experiences. The upshot of this is that Foucault's critique is no longer timely. Critique in general, as Foucault defines it,[7] is no longer timely.

---

[5] *Deconstruction and the Possibility of Justice* (London, Routledge, 1992) 35.

[6] G. Teubner, *Law as an Autopoietic System* (Oxford, Blackwell, 1993) 64. For the view that Foucault's analysis of the "care of the self" provides an example of autopoiesis *avant la lettre*, *cf.* A. Schutz, "The Twilight of the Global Polis: On Losing Paradigms, Environing Systems and Observing World Society" in G. Teubner (ed.), *Global Law Without a State* (Aldershot, Dartmouth, 1997) 269.

[7] See M. Foucault, "What is Enlightenment?" in M. Foucault, *Ethics: The Essential Work: 1* (London, Penguin Press, 1997).

In Foucault's later work, confession is described as one of a series of practices that he termed "technologies of the self". The orientation of his project, he claimed, was to determine the transformations that had occurred in the techniques through which one could exert force upon one's self in order to achieve a certain ethical state. Technologies of the self were defined as techniques:[8]

> "which permit individuals to effect by their own means, or with the help of others, a certain number of operations on their own bodies and souls, thoughts, conduct, and way of being, so as to transform themselves in order to attain a certain state of happiness, purity, wisdom, perfection, or immortality."

This project seems (or at least once seemed) peculiar in relation to Foucault's earlier work. He had long been associated with the proposition that the subject was a derivative of power and discourse. Confession, in this earlier work, appeared simply to be a way in which one individual could control the meaning given to the statements of another. However, this later project suggests that individuals play a role in their own formation. In order to understand this difference and its reorientation of Foucault's project I will consider the confession in relation to both discourse and power.

If technologies of the self have a complex relationship with relationships of power, this is primarily because of the discursive possibilities that they raise. The statements produced in technologies of the self are of the kind that are called "self-presentation" in modern German theory,[9] statements where at least traditionally, the sincerity with which they are pronounced and the consistency with which they are acted upon rather than their correspondence to a state of affairs in the world[10] determines whether they are accepted as true or rejected as false. In the statement "I believe x", for example, the rationality of the statement depends upon the reasons available for believing x. The truth of the statement, on the other hand, depends only upon the sincerity of the speaker and the extent to which he acts upon it. It matters not whether x is actually true, nor that there are reasons for believing that it is true. Consequently, the truth of such statements cannot be established simply by providing reasons. Their truth, as Habermas puts it, "cannot be *grounded* but only *shown*".[11] For most beliefs, that is true for him who states the belief as much as for him to whom it is stated.[12] However, if the truth of such statements is determined by their

---

[8] M. Foucault, "Technologies of the Self" in *ibid*.

[9] *Cf.* N. Luhmann, J. Bednarz and D. Baecker, *Social Systems* (Stanford, Cal., Stanford University Press, 1995) 156 and J. Habermas, *Theory of Communicative Action: Reason and the Rationalization of Society Vol.1* (Cambridge, Polity, 1984) 15.

[10] Habermas, *supra* n. 9 at 41.

[11] *Ibid.*

[12] For example, the statement "I am not afraid of heights" is only true for me if I am able to put that statement into practice and not just if I am sincere. *Cf.* also L. Wittgenstein, *Philosophical Investigations* (Oxford, Blackwell, 1953) 154. As Wittgenstein points out, such a belief can be tested

relationship with sincerity and action, that is not true of their meaning. It is this precarious difference between truth and meaning that makes technologies of the self particularly open to involvement in power relationships. For example, Foucault shows that the meaning of statements in confession is not ultimately determined by the speaking subject himself. Meaning is determined by the one to whom he confesses. For example, Foucault wrote of the nineteenth-century psychiatrist that:[13]

> "with regard to the confession, his power was not only to demand it before it was made, or decide what was to follow after it, but also to constitute a discourse of truth on the basis of decipherment."

The meaning of the statement "I believe x" can be made the subject of hermeneutic interpretation, unlike the truth of that statement.

As a result of the truth conditions of these statements, a certain form of subjectivity is produced. The confessing subject is not, for Foucault, a unity that produces a multiplicity of statements whose meaning must be determined. Rather, the process of confession forms a particular kind of statement which determines a particular form of subjectivity.[14] Consequently, Foucault's analysis is a reversal of the form of interpretation at play in confession. In the art of confession the task is to determine the unity of the subject hidden behind the surface of statements, the subject which produced them. For Foucault, on the other hand, it is the statements themselves that produce the subject as a derivative of them, and at each moment that the statement is articulated.[15] This draws on Foucault's meticulous analysis in *The Archæology of Knowledge*[16] of a field of statements or "enunciative domain" that "is described as an anonymous field whose configuration defines the possible position of speaking subjects". There Foucault encouraged us to see different forms of subjectivity as "effects proper to the enunciative field".[17] The subject is not hidden transcendental consciousness that founds all knowledge; it is an effect, a way of organising consciousness that is peculiar to the discourse that produces it.[18]

by the speaking subject hypothetically. To some extent this is also true of the subject to whom one speaks. The speaking subject is encouraged to answer questions of the "what would you do if . . . ?" kind.

[13] Foucault, *supra* n.1 at 67. Confusingly Foucault uses the terms "truth" and "meaning" interchangeably.

[14] *Cf.* also G. Teubner, "How the Law Thinks: Toward a Constructivist Epistemology of Law" (1989) 23 *Law and Society Review* 727 at 730, for a similar idea in relation to law: "it is not human individuals by their intentional actions that produce law as a cultural artefact. On the contrary, it is law as a communicative process that by its legal operations produces human actors as semantic artefacts."

[15] *Cf.* A. Pottage, "Power as an Art of Contingency: Luhmann, Deleuze, Foucault" (1998) 27 *Economy and Society* 1 at 18–19: "Discourse, or each discontinuous discursive process, is articulated by "subject-functions" which do not exist as replicas of some abstract "master-function", but which subsist only in the particular enunciative performance which "machines" them. In other words, discursive roles and functions are processual."

[16] M. Foucault, *The Archaeology of Knowledge* (London, Routledge, 1972).

[17] *Ibid.*, 122.

[18] For further clarification of the idea that the subject, for Foucault, is a derivative of the statement see G. Deleuze, *Foucault* (London, Athlone, 1988) 6–7.

The particular form of subjectivity that is produced in confession is a subjective double. As Foucault put it, "the confession is a ritual of discourse in which the speaking subject is also the subject of the statement".[19] It is this double nature of the confessing subject that ensured the peculiar value that was attached to statements of confession. Confession involved making statements which only the subject himself could know, information to which the confessing subject had sole access. The importance of confession in criminal law, for example, is linked to the concept of *mens rea*. It is only the acting subject himself who can know his true intention. Whilst inferences can be made from the external appearance of his act, it is only the subject himself who can know the mental state that accompanied those appearances. Hence the metaphor that the defendant must have "had the intention", which suggests the presence of a hidden internal monologue which the defendant "held", is commonplace rather than a statement that he "acted intentionally" or "acted voluntarily", statements the truth of which can be objectively observed.[20] As we shall see, confession became an integral part of the process through which the law managed to organise its power relations. It was only through confession that the law could determine the meaning of the criminal act and consequently discover the correct mode of punishment or treatment.

From Foucault's two major works on power, *Discipline and Punish*[21] and *The History of Sexuality: Volume 1*,[22] it might appear that the subject plays no part in its own formation. Rather, the subject emerges simply as a derivative of operations of discourse and power. This position was summed up by Foucault's use of the term *assujetissement*.[23] This term, which has been translated as "subjectification", has a double meaning. On the one hand it refers to the way in which an individual is subjected to operations of power. On the other hand it refers to the way in which the individual is made a subject by operations of power. For example, psychiatry utilised a series of techniques through which an individual was made to behave in a particular way, to say and do certain things. These techniques were utilised on him. But at the same time, and through the same processes, he was formed as a psychiatric subject which could then be acted upon and which had a certain experience of his own subjectivity. In Foucault's work of the 1970s, the experience which the subject had of himself appeared to be entirely determined through practices such as discipline and confession that emerged from within pedagogical or theological institutions.

[19] Foucault, *supra* n.1 at 61.
[20] *Cf.* Wittgenstein, *supra* n. 12 at 165, where he writes: "what is the natural expression of an intention? Look at a cat when it stalks a bird; or a beast when it wants to escape."
[21] M. Foucault, *Discipline and Punish* (London, Penguin, 1977).
[22] *Supra* n.1.
[23] I retain the original French term in order to distinguish it clearly from the term "*subjectivation*" which designates the way in which the subject forms himself as a subject through action upon himself (see M. Foucault, "Le Retour de la Morale" in M. Foucault, *Dits et Ecrits* (Paris, Gallimard, 1994) 696 at 706).

In his later work, Foucault was critical of this limitation. Was it not the case that the individual played a part in his own development? How could this self-evident fact be incorporated into his "anti-subjectivist" scheme? Through a particular series of processes, Foucault thought, first, that certain experiences of oneself could occur and, secondly, that through those experiences subjectivity could be formed. This made it possible to consider the extent to which the subject could engage in its own formation and transformation without giving up the earlier analysis that subjectivity is not unified. Subjectivity was still considered as an effect, but such an effect could be self-reflexive. Subjectivity was not the condition for the possibility of experience; experience was the rationalisation of a process through which subjectivity could be formed and through which it could act upon itself. For this process Foucault used the term *subjectivation*.

The possibility of reflexive self-formation is often considered to be the key to freedom in Foucault's work, a way of escaping the all-pervasive network of power and knowledge that he had meticulously analysed in *Discipline and Punish*. This statement, despite its inaccuracy, has some truth to it. On the one hand, reflexive self-formation could not be considered to be the condition for freedom. This would merely be to posit the old liberal opposition between freedom and power that Foucault had already rejected in his work of the 1970s. In fact, freedom had never been absent from Foucault's earlier work. For Foucault, it is power that is the condition of freedom, and this is not because it imbues a pre-existing subject with a choice, but rather because subjectivity is only produced as immanent in action. Freedom is strategic action; strategic action produces subjectivity. And it is this fact that allows one to distinguish power[24] from violence.[25] This is a rejoinder to the suggestion that for Foucault the proliferation of power relations entails the repression of freedom. Freedom is a product of power rather than an ontological condition of subjectivity that is repressed by power. Furthermore, techniques of the self are not free from power relations. Techniques of the self are not mere interpretations of the self. Nor are they nar-rativisations of the self.[26] They are practices, the exercise of force upon oneself to transform oneself. In other words, techniques of the self take the form of a power relation that one has with oneself, a "folded force" as Deleuze put it.[27] Such practices can occur in private but they can also occur in relation to another who determines their content and effect. Consequently, practices of the self can occur as exercises of freedom or within relationships of domination, that is, relationships in which one or both of the individuals involved cannot act strategically upon the power relationship itself.[28]

---

[24] It should be noted that the word "power" is a translation of *pouvoir* from Foucault's work rather than *puissance*.

[25] M. Foucault, "The Ethic of Care of the Self as a Practice of Freedom" in J. Bernauer and D. Rasmussen (eds.), *The Final Foucault* (Mass., MIT, 1988) 12.

[26] As *per* Cornell, *supra* n. 2.

[27] Deleuze, *supra* n. 18.

[28] Foucault, *supra* n. 25 at 18.

However, whilst these techniques of the self did not automatically result in subjective freedom, they did give Foucault the opportunity to provide a site for the critique of the all-encompassing network of power relations that he had analysed particularly in *Discipline and Punish*. Critique could be conducted by attempting to establish the extent to which the knowledge and power permit us to transform ourselves as individuals. For example, in his essay "What is Enlightenment?" Foucault argued that historical critique would be "oriented toward the "contemporary limits of the necessary," that is, toward what is not or is no longer indispensable for the constitution of ourselves as autonomous subjects".[29] Techniques of the self, once they were freed from the idea that there is a kernel of subjectivity between our appearances to be unearthed, could be utilised to oppose systems of repression and to direct personal and political strategies. They were not pure examples of freedom but they could be used strategically to resist the application of power. What is required is not the affirmation of technologies of the self, not the statement "technologies of the self rule OK", but their critique and transformation in particular sites of action. Such a critique, Foucault argued, could not be conducted at the general level of society but only in specific domains.

The implications of this analysis of technologies of the self are important for liberal political and legal theory. Liberal theory has long been based around liberating the true and authentic subject from political oppression. The subject is considered as that upon which discourse and power act. Foucault's analysis shows that this is an inadequate way to ground political critique. The subject is not only that which power and discourse act upon; it is also that which is produced by power and discourse. Attempts to ground political critique upon some core meaning of subjectivity, or in lay terms "human nature", risk having that "nature" harnessed for unanticipated political ends. In a discussion with Noam Chomsky, Foucault put forward the example of the Soviet Union, which utilised an idealised version of the nineteenth-century liberal individual for political ends that were anything but liberal. Foucault put the relationship as follows: "the universalisation of the model of the bourgeois has been the utopia which has animated the constitution of Soviet society".[30] This is the starting point for Giorgio Agamben's analysis of the concentration camp. For Agamben, the biopolitical complicity of the camp and liberal democracy is established through a particular subject:[31]

> "the spaces, the liberties, and the rights won by individuals in their conflicts with central powers always simultaneously prepared a tacit but increasing inscription of individuals' lives within the state order, thus offering a new and more dreadful foundation for the very sovereign power from which they wanted to liberate themselves."

[29] Foucault, *supra* n. 7 at 315.
[30] N. Chomsky and M. Foucault, "Human Nature: Justice versus Power" in F. Elders (ed.), *Reflexive Water: The Basic Concerns of Mankind* (London, Souvenir Press, 1974) 174.
[31] G. Agamben, *Homo Sacer: Sovereign Power and Bare Life* (Stanford, Cal., Stanford University Press, 1998) 121.

Foucault makes a similar critique of psychoanalysis.[32] The psychoanalytic project attempted to liberate the subject from repression but actually resulted in the production of forms of identity (homosexuality, for example) which could be utilised for all sorts of political motives. Psychoanalysis suggested that homosexuality was "really" all about the opposition between certain natural drives and their repression. The aim was to liberate the "true" from the discourse that represses. Foucault's analysis, on the other hand, proceeds from the principle that sexuality, and consequently (though Foucault is sometimes less explicit about this) sexual experience, is produced by the discourse itself.[33] This posits a problem for political theory: the subject cannot be liberated from discourse and power, it can only be produced through discourse and power. A consequence of this is that political philosophy loses its traditional site of critique: the unified, free subject.

The solution to this problem has often been made in terms of æsthetics, both by Foucault and by others. However, if the anti-liberal implications of the theory are not taken on board with sufficient rigour, such an æsthetics will merely be subjected to a similar critique. Drucilla Cornell's book, *The Imaginary Domain*, provides an interesting example of this problem. Cornell agrees with Foucault that liberal philosophy would be wrong to base political strategies around the idea of a unified and stable subject. The self, she suggests, is not a pre-given whole that pre-exists experience and action. Rather it is a project that one is continually in the process of working on. Liberalism portrays a model of the individual which she criticises for:[34]

> "failing to come to terms with the full legal significance of the self as a fragile and continuing process of internalisation of a projected self-image which has been recognised by others in its coherence and bodily integrity."

Because the individual gains her sense of self from the community with which she engages, a critique that just posits spaces of freedom fails to engage with the ethical need for recognition in the continuing process of attaining selfhood. Consequently, she argues, ethical action ought to be directed not only at creating the conditions of free choice (over one's sexuality for example) but also at giving individuals the power over their "imaginary domains", the power to narrativise their existence. One could put the argument in Foucauldian terms: once it is accepted that the individual is the derivative of discourse, an ethical critique must attempt to establish the control of the individual over the discourse from which he is constructed. However, Cornell derives from this argument a project which, according to her, can be realised within the framework of Rawlsian liberalism. The key to this solution concerns the establishment of a space in which the individuals will be free to exercise their imaginary power

---

[32] Foucault, *supra* n. 1, Part III.
[33] *Ibid.*, 18.
[34] Cornell, *supra* n. 2 at 60.

over their own existence: the protection of what Cornell calls "the imaginary domain".[35]

Cornell plays out this strategy in three different legally contested areas in her book: abortion, pornography and sexual harassment. Let us take the example of abortion. The question whether or not a pregnant woman ought to be permitted to abort is often argued in terms of competing rights: the rights of the woman against the rights of the unborn child. Cornell's argument against limiting the right to abort stems from the question of what is required for an individual to create her own sense of self. To quote Cornell:[36]

> "The denial of the right to abortion enforces the kind of splitting that inevitably and continuously undermines a woman's sense of self. Her womb and body are no longer hers to imagine. They have been turned over to the imagination of others, and those imaginings are then allowed to reign over her body as law. The wrong in denial of the right to abortion is often thought to be that the woman is forced to turn over her body to the foetus as an invader. The wrong as I reconceive it involves a woman, at a crucial moment, having her body turned over to the minds of men."

There are different ways in which the relationship between a mother and her unborn child can be narrativised. Consequently, the denial of the right to abortion not only imposes a course of action upon pregnant women, it imposes a certain narrative identity upon them. This implies that they do not have the necessary psychic space to construct their lives in the way that they deem right or desirable. Cornell's account is distinctly anti-essentialist. The purpose of the rights that she recommends is not to redeem the secret of womanhood from beneath masculine repression; it is to create the space necessary for women to be allowed to develop themselves as an ongoing project.

In this way Cornell attempts to utilise what has been identified here as the loss of authenticity for ethical and political ends. The fact that we can posit the end of the authentic subject of confession is attached uncritically to a politico-ethical programme, a programme which replaces the authentic subject with the æsthetic subject. The problem with an æsthetic solution to the loss of authenticity is that it fails to engage with the extent to which narrativising the self is implicated within structures of power and consequently used strategically. As we saw in the opening paragraphs of this essay, statements of self-presentation can be used for a variety of political purposes. We ought not to presume that such statements are beyond the scope of rational critique. That is not to deny the importance of self-expression; it is just to take seriously its political nature.

Furthermore, once we understand such expressions as a part of social structures, we are confronted with the following problem: it becomes difficult to predict the response of such structures to the loss in authenticity attached to this version of the self. Just as the Soviet Union, in Foucault's argument, could use

---

[35] *Ibid.*,184. For a "Foucauldian" critique of the liberal distinction between power and free spaces see V. Tadros, "Between Governance and Discipline: The Law and Michel Foucault" (1998) 18 *OJLS* 75 at 82–6.

[36] *Ibid.*, 47.

the ideal of the bourgeois individual for anti-liberal ends, so modern social systems can utilise the idea of the social construction of reality for unanticipated purposes. Again I refer to Teubner's claim that we cannot predict which political camp will use the theory of autopoiesis for its own ends and in which way.[37] The political bite of this statement is made out once we consider that there are instances in which the legal system becomes aware that the confessing subject is no longer the mimesis of the authentic subject but recognises confession as a contingent practice through which a particular subject is formed. And this has political consequences. The legal system, according to this thesis, not only thinks by constructing reality through concepts. It is also capable of doubting those concepts and responding to those doubts.

In a sense, Foucault's philosophy is no longer timely. We have moved so far beyond authentic subjects that we can take inauthenticity for granted. We have become accustomed to our inauthenticity. We are bored with it. We have reached the point that Deleuze and Guattari, at the beginning of *A Thousand Plateaus*, hoped that we would reach: "not the point where one no longer says I, but the point where it is no longer of any importance whether one says I".[38] And yet this has not resulted in the exciting multiplicities that they envisaged, but only in new forms of repetition that have no space for authentic selves and have no time for their laborious production. The experience of contingency has already been executed and stabilised. Modern systems are comfortable with their own contingency and the contingency of the subjects that they produce. Contingency does not result in radicalism but only in a series of substitutable and more or less stable alternative distinctions: "stability is . . . guaranteed in that only limited possibilities of substitution exist for everything we encounter".[39] This is the condition of freedom: the construction of limited possible substitutions. This is what one can make out of Foucault's network of power relations. It determines the condition that power and freedom are not, or at least are no longer, opposites.

These problems cannot be adequately addressed by utilising a system of rights. Such rights themselves, as I hope to show, can be appropriated by the legal system for the purpose of its own repetition. Freedom and power are not opposites as rights rhetoric presupposes. Power networks constitute freedom. A consequence of this is that the experience of freedom does not automatically preclude both the existence of domination and the corresponding experience. This is no less true for narrative freedom. Narrative freedom is produced systemically and can be controlled systemically. The idea of a blank page upon which one can narrativise one's existence is meaningless as a tool for political

---

[37] Cornell harnesses autopoietic theory to her own political ends in her article "The Philosophy of the Limit: Systems Theory and Feminist Legal Reform" in D. Carlson, D. Cornell and M. Rosenfeld, *Deconstruction and the Possibility of Justice* (London, Routledge, 1992).

[38] G. Deleuze and F. Guattari, *A Thousand Plateaus: Capitalism and Schizophrenia* (London, Athlone, 1988).

[39] Luhmann, *supra*, n.3 at 20.

theory. The subject is not produced spontaneously; it is produced through a constant process of discursive reproduction. A consequence of this is that the loss of authenticity and the freedom that goes with it are far more boring than they once appeared.

"The problem, of course, is that a minimum of 'synthesis of imagination' (to use Kant's own term) which (re-)creates its object is necessary for sexuality to function normally. This 'imagined part' becomes visible in an unpleasant experience known to most of us: in the middle of the most intense sexual act, it is possible for us all of a sudden to 'disconnect'—all of a sudden, a question can emerge: 'What am I doing here, sweating and repeating these stupid gestures?'; pleasure can shift into disgust or into a strange feeling of distance."[40]

To suggest that law is like sex is to risk one's credibility both as a lawyer and sex-god. Nevertheless, Zizek's account of sex can tell us something important about how law manages to sustain itself even when it recognises the contingency of its cognitive operations. The point is not that law sustains itself *despite* recognising that its effects are unpredictable within social reality and that the individuals that it deals with are merely shadowy representation of real individuals. The point is that the law can sustain itself *because of* such a recognition. In this case it is the representation of unreality itself that "is the minimum idealisation the subject needs in order to be able to sustain the horror of the Real",[41] a variation on Zizek's account (and fortuitously suggesting that the law is the opposite of sex, which may go some way to restoring my credibility). As we shall see from the way in which the legal system has dealt with the question of infanticidal mothers, the problem for the law is not so much that it can appear to be ridiculously impotent in its repeating operations but rather that it can appear to be ridiculously potent. The horror that the law is confronted with, and wishes to desublimate, is not so much that it does not have the erotic power that it symbolises but rather that it *has* that erotic power. Consequently, the law fantasises not because it is afraid of its impotency but because it is afraid of its potency. In order to maintain its potency and reproduce its operations, then, it constantly gives up its power, only ultimately to retain it. Let me elaborate on this remarkable phenomenon by beginning with the problems of self-mastery.

The ethical problem of self-mastery, as it was discussed in stoic philosophy, involved a certain set of operations through which the individual could act upon himself in order to produce himself as an ethical being. Christian confession radically reinterpreted this practice, shifting the problematic from æsthetic creation to hermeneutic interpretation. This is, for Foucault, the most important shift in

---

[40] S. Zizek, *The Plague of Fantasies* (London, Verso, 1997) 65.
[41] *Ibid.*, 66.

what he calls "technologies of the self". Foucault's critique attempts to show that the subject that is produced by confession is not authentic, and for two reasons: first because subjectivity is not the unity that lies behind discourse but is an effect of discourse, and secondly because confession is never spontaneous, it occurs within a power relationship. For Foucault, the idea that we can "get back" to our authentic selves through either religion or psychoanalysis is problematic, both politically and theoretically. Consequently, he regarded self-creation as a form of resistance to technologies of self-discovery.

However, as far as social systems are concerned, confession has begun to play an entirely different role. Rather than constituting a reflexive action, confession plays a key moment in the legal constitution of the person. From the point of view of the psychic system, confession is a moment of second-order observation *and* reflexive action. The moment when the individual reveals himself is also the moment that he purifies himself. From the point of view of the legal system, and despite its continuing importance in the law of evidence, confession is simply one of a series of operations through which the law can construct legal persons. This draws upon the insight that the "persons" whom the law deals with are "mere constructs, semantic artefacts produced by the legal discourse itself".[42] The moment of legal confession simultaneously plays a function within two systems. In Luhmann's terms, confession provides an example of interpenetration between the social and psychic systems. What is, for our purposes, one event (confession) produces a series of self-reflexive communications within two systems; the psychic system and the social system. And, as each system constructs reality in a different way, the meaning that is attached to this event can be entirely different.

Now, both the legal system and the psychic system can, and have, become aware of this difference. The legal system, with which we are primarily concerned, responded to the problems of systemic difference by creating a theoretical model for the presentation of the psychic system in law, what we might call "legal psychology". The confession played an important role in developing this model. Let us take, as the starting point for this discussion, Foucault's essay "The Dangerous Individual".[43] In that essay Foucault describes a series of cases that were decided in the early nineteenth century concerning crimes for which no motive could be discovered. These cases usually involved murders of individuals close to the defendant which were not performed for any apparent gain and which could not be attributed to the ordinary motives of revenge, jealousy and so on. On the other hand, they seemed to have been performed with full cognition and understanding. There was no question that they could be excused under an ordinary insanity defence. Nevertheless, the newly developing science of psychiatry did become involved in these cases. The concepts of monomania and moral insanity were invented in order to describe them—the bizarre inter-

---

[42] Teubner, *supra* n. 14 at 741.

[43] M. Foucault, "The Dangerous Individual" in L.D. Kritzman (ed.), *Politics, Philosophy, Culture: Interviews and Other Writings: 1977–1984* (London, Routledge, 1988) 125.

vention of psychiatry into cases which would once have been considered to be at the core of law.

In these cases it appears that the legal system had become dissatisfied with its interpretations of the legal act. In order fully to understand the act it became necessary to discover the underlying nature of the individual that produced it. As Foucault put it:[44]

> " 'What must be punished, and how?' That was the question to which, it was believed, a rational answer had finally been found; and now a further question arose to confuse the issue: 'Whom do you think you are punishing?' "

The legal system became aware that the meaning of the act as far as it was concerned, simply an illegal act for which the defendant was culpable, was different from the meaning that emerged for the defendant himself. In order to understand this second meaning, and consequently to ensure that he was punished correctly, a model of the individual's internal workings had to be constructed. The meaning of the act, it seems, could only be understood by understanding its meaning *for the defendant*, in our terms, within his psychic system. Of course the legal use of psychological terminology was still very primitive; that terminology had hardly developed itself. Nevertheless, this primitive attempt was important in the development of a series of questions concerning the nature of the criminal.

The statements from which this psychological reality could be created were statements of the confession. Confession had long been used in law to determine that the defendant was responsible for the act. Even if it was extracted by the most violent methods, confession was considered an essential part in determining that the act had been committed and that the legal response to it was just.[45] Here, however, confession came to play a different role. Rather than determining that the act had been committed, it created a narrative in which the *meaning* of the act could be established. The narrative of confession provided a set of statements which could be interpreted psychologically to determine the nature of the individual who could produce such a horrific act. Confession ensured that the law did not just construct its own interpretation of the act. It ensured that the law constructed an interpretation of the *defendant's* interpretation of the act.

Of course, the legal system very quickly became aware that this new introduction of psychological constructivism could be strategically manipulated by defendants. Awareness that the legal interpretation of acts was dependant upon the narratives of defendants naturally encouraged defendants to produce narratives that would have the mildest legal consequences. The legal anticipation of this problem is widely regarded as one of the reasons for the narrow interpretation of the term "insanity" in the insanity defence in English law.[46]

---

[44] *Ibid.*, 128.

[45] Foucault, *supra* n.1 at 59.

[46] *Cf.* A. Norrie, *Crime, Reason and History: A Critical Introduction to Criminal Law* (London, Weidenfeld and Nicolson, 1993) at 184 for one of many examples.

Consequently, the legal-psychological method of interpretation began to be disrupted. If the material produced during confession was strategic, the law could no longer determine the meaning that the criminal act had through its construction of the defendant's psychology. This was because the confession no longer appeared to be a neutral representation of the individual. It appeared as an account that was tempered for particular purposes. Despite the attempts to ensure that confessions were made in what Habermas would call "ideal speech situations"[47]—situations which are devoid of power—it was not possible to return to a situation where confession would once again reveal the individual in his neutral state.

This awareness that confession was inevitably strategic is just one example, though an important one, of the law's acceptance of its own epistemological constructivism. The law becomes aware that as information is only available for particular purposes, and therefore selected, it is contingent and can no longer be relied upon either as a representation of reality or to direct the application of power. The recognition that the information that is produced about an individual is strategic also implies that it is not neutral. The fact that it is not neutral entails that the traditional legal ambitions of "just consequences" and "effective solutions" appear to be unrealisable. Law becomes a precarious enterprise when it recognises that it has limited access to "the real world" or, in particular, the individual "as he really is". Judgment is made upon the narratives that law presents to itself, narratives that may bear limited relation to the narratives constructed in other systems. Consequently the ability of the law either to create just consequences or to regulate the world becomes hampered. Strategies which are effective for the construction of the world produced by the legal system are not necessarily effective in other systems. Despite the fact that legal communication is also social communication, the possibility of strategic intervention is limited. "Legal communications reliably motivate only legal communications. It is well known that their capacity to motivate general social communication is relatively limited",[48] as Teubner puts it.

The recognition of the cognitive contingency of the law has led to two different strands in what we might unflatteringly call "post-modern ethics". For Jacques Derrida, the legal recognition of its own cognitive contingency seems to be the condition of a justice that goes beyond law. Derrida attempts to retrieve deconstruction from the charge that it must inevitably lead to the end of ethics, the claim that "deconstruction ruins the very possibility of justice".[49] On the contrary, he argues, the acceptance of paradox is the key to the utterance of an unutterable and even impossible justice. For it is only through justice that deconstruction finds its motivation. This line of argument is problematic.

---

[47] J. Habermas, *The Theory of Communicative Action: Volume 1: Reason and the Rationalisation of Society* (Boston, Mass., Beacon Press, 1984) ch. 3.

[48] Teubner, *supra* n. 6 at 91.

[49] J. Derrida, "The Force of Law: The Mystical Foundation of Authority" in Carlson, Cornell and Rosenfeld, *supra* n.37 at 4.

Whilst deconstruction opens the space of freedom and responsibility, overcoming the account of deconstruction that would leave it in ethical paralysis, it can give that space little content. Derrida himself is aware that the paradox at the foundation of the law is precarious: "Left to itself, the incalculable and giving idea of justice is always very close to the bad, even to the worst for it can always be reappropriated by the most perverse calculation".[50] Although elsewhere Derrida states the somewhat arrogant equation of deconstruction and justice:[51]

"[J]ustice in itself, if such a thing exists, outside or beyond law, is not deconstructible. No more than deconstruction itself, if such a thing exists. Deconstruction is justice."

The problem for Derrida is that the law is familiar with its own paradox and is full of strategic devices to deal with it. In fact, for Luhmann, this operation of dealing with paradox is one of law's most ordinary operations:[52]

"[T]he problem [for law] is now to suppress or attenuate the paradox which an observer with logical inclinations or with a sufficient degree of dissatisfaction could see and articulate at any time."

To the verbs "suppress" and "attenuate" we might add "utilise" and "mobilise".

In *The Imaginary Domain* Cornell's solution to cognitive contingency is confined to the question of self-constitution and self-narrativisation. Given that acts can have multiple meanings, she argues, the meaning given to the individual ought to be determined by the individual herself. Rights ought to be attached not to the specific qualities of human nature but to the spaces in which one can realise oneself as an individual. However, numerous problems emerge from this strategy as well. It is not clear that it is possible to create a neutral space for self-realisation outside legal intervention. And surely this is not possible within the legal system. The meaning that is given to a particular set of statements will always be determined within what Wittgenstein and Lyotard call language games (discourses for Foucault, social systems for Luhmann and Teubner—let us not get into too many nice distinctions). This is no less true for statements of self-presentation than it is for any other type of statement. But language games are by their nature strategic, and these strategies are always multi-directional. As Foucault puts it:

we must make allowance for the complex and unstable process whereby discourse can be both an instrument and an effect of power, but also a hindrance, a stumbling block, a point of resistance and a starting point for an opposing strategy.[53]

Strategy and discourse are intertwined. It is not possible to predict in advance which types of statements will be used for which purpose and by whom. Narratives are contested within the legal system, for example, and the protection

[50] *Ibid.*, 28.
[51] *Ibid.*, 14–15.
[52] N. Luhmann, "The Third Question: The Creative Use of Paradoxes in Law and Legal History" (1985) 15 *Journal of Law and Society* 153.
[53] Foucault, *supra* n.1 at 101.

of such narratives by rights will not necessarily be effective in ensuring justice. It is not only the individual but also the law that can use narratives strategically.

For example, a series of nineteenth-century criminal cases concerned mothers who murdered their own children. It was widely recognised that these murders were carried out for particularly oppressive reasons, both social and financial. (A typical narrative involved a woman in service who became pregnant by her master, either through rape or voluntary intercourse.) If they kept their children, such women faced social exclusion and unemployment with the extra financial requirements resulting from the care of the child. It was clear from the cases that there was a large measure of sympathy for these women and in most cases, despite overwhelming evidence that they had committed the act in question, the jury acquitted. Now, this presented the law with a problem. The narrative which was constructed both inside and outside the courtroom meant that juries were faced with a dilemma. The application of the law appeared to be manifestly unjust given the social situation of these women. On the other hand, the introduction of such social pressures as a valid legal excuse for murder would lead to all sorts of problematic inconsistencies in the law as well as a degree of complexity which the legal system could not cope with. In short, the appearance of the "reality" of crime into the courtroom led to a legal dilemma. The courts were presented with the unreasonable potency of the law, its power to affect the lives of individuals in the most unjust and disproportionate manner. The legal solution to this problem was to re-narrativise the event. An excuse was provided for infanticidal mothers on the basis of an extremely dodgy psychiatric analysis of the effects of childbirth.[54] An alternative narrativisation of events was created strategically in order to preserve the unity of the law in the face of the manifest injustice of the application of its principles without disrupting its traditions or its coherence.

The effects produced by the relationship between discourse and power are difficult to predict in advance. We should not imagine that the freedoms associated with a system of rights are a solution to this problem. It is not only through the explicit creation of new narratives for strategic purposes that the law can utilise its recognition of cognitive contingency. It can also utilise contingency indirectly by providing defendants with a choice of narratives. This involves governance not by interdiction but by the provision and control of alternatives in which either result preserves the coherence of the law. In such cases a choice of narrative is placed in the hands of the defendant. However, this in turn results in strategic effects that are manifestly unjust.

[54] The Infanticide Act 1938 s. 1(1) states that "where a woman by any wilful act or omission causes the death of her child being child under the age of twelve months, but at the time of the act or omission the balance of her mind was disturbed by reason of her not having fully recovered from the effect of giving birth to the child or by reason of the effect of lactation consequent upon birth of the child, then, notwithstanding that the circumstances were such that but for this Act the offence would have amounted to murder, she shall be guilt of felony, to wit of infanticide, and may for such an offence be dealt with and punished as if she had been guilty of the offence of manslaughter of the child."

Let us take another example from the criminal law. Recently, the criminal law has been presented with a series of cases involving women who have killed their husbands after suffering years of abuse.[55] Traditionally such women attempted to reduce their convictions from murder to manslaughter through the defence of provocation. However, such attempts were often unsuccessful. In order to rely on the defence of provocation it is essential that the response was provoked by a particular act that led to the immediate loss of self-control. However, in these cases such a loss of self-control would not have been effective due to the imbalance of physical strength. Because the killings occurred after these women had the time to "cool off", the defence of provocation was not available. Again, the traditional application of the criminal law can be shown to be unjust to women who respond to their detrimental social situation with rational or justified violence. And again the courts responded by providing an alternative defence to the act rather than disrupting the traditional principles of criminal law. This was done by making the defence of diminished responsibility available to such defendants on the grounds that they were suffering from battered women syndrome at the time of the killing.

Unlike the example of infanticidal mothers, in this case the legal system does not respond to its self-observed cognitive contingency by choosing to narrativise. It responds to contingency by placing that decision in the hands of the defendant. To this extent, the defendants choose the legal construction of reality for the legal system. Either defendants choose to construct themselves as women who have justifiably lost control as a consequence of continued abuse, in which case a defence will be limited to those defendants who acted immediately, or they construct themselves as suffering from mental disorder as a result of their abuse. The defendant is given a measure of control over her "imaginary domain" as Cornell calls it. However, as far as the legal system is concerned, this freedom is not made available for ethical reasons; it is a structural response to the particular problem of injustice that had been introduced by these cases. It is difficult to argue that this has resulted in an increase in justice. Rather, women who kill their husbands for the acceptable reason that they have suffered years of abuse are encouraged to construct themselves as mad, the problems of which have been well recounted.[56] The legal system responds to narrative contingency by putting the choice of narrative into the hands of defendants: more than one type of self-presentation statement is appropriate and the legal system does not attempt to determine in advance which is most appropriate. But at the same time the system anticipates its response to each type of statement. It reorients its operations to deal with the disappointment of its failure to anticipate and

---

[55] The two most prominent cases are *R.* v. *Ahluwalia* [1992] 4 All ER 889 and *R.* v. *Thornton (No.2)* [1996] 2 All ER 1023. Scots law has utilised the ability of the jury to ignore unjust directions to achieve a similar result. See *HMA* v. *Greig* (1979) (unreported). *Cf.* C.H.W. Gane and C.N. Stoddart, *A Casebook on Scots Criminal Law* (2nd edn., Edinburgh, W. Green & Son, 1988) 526.

[56] For an introduction to the extensive literature, see N. Lacey and C. Wells, *Reconstructing Criminal Law* (London, Butterworths, 1998) at 589–97.

control action by creating options rather than imposing narratives. This is also the nature of rights.[57] But, in this instance, the principle of rights is not used for the purposes of justice and freedom to the pre-existing subject, it is used to orient the system to be more effective in coping with the failure to control.

My critique of Cornell's position is not that creating rights which protect the "imaginary domain" will necessarily lead to "negative" consequences, but rather that its consequences are unpredictable. In using the language of rights Cornell reproduces the unimaginative opposition between spaces of freedom and structures of power. This opposition is inadequate. As I argued earlier, Foucault's critique of power relations shows the ways in which freedom and power are mutually constituted. Spaces without power simply do not exist. Consequently, statements of self-presentation must operate within networks of power. This entails the recognition that the use of these statements is politically complex and unpredictable. This is not to denigrate the importance of self-creation, it is to recognise the dynamic political scenario in which self-creation operates. It is for this reason that Foucault's historical presentation of technologies of the self is important. Foucault was at pains to describe the complex set of interactions between self-self and self-others in the culture of the Ancients. Such interactions, as he was well aware, cannot be transposed uncritically into modern society. A critique of self-creation needs to be as complex and sophisticated as a critique of power relations. Positing self-creation as an end might be an effective strategy for some purposes and not for others. Furthermore, self-creation can be utilised for unanticipated strategic reasons. This is a problem for rights-based theories. Such theories simply fail to recognise the imaginative uses to which rights can be put.

CONCLUSIONS

The "post-modern age" is characterised by epistemological scepticism. This scepticism has been particularly disruptive in the field of legal ethics. In the light of cognitive contingency, it becomes difficult to argue for ethical solutions based on the principle of human nature. This has led to an unfortunate turn towards ethical solutions that fail to anticipate the reality and the potential of legal operations. Legal recognition of its own epistemological contingency does mitigate the need for political strategy. In fact, the discovery and use of paradox can itself be problematised as a strategically contested operation. And it leads to all sorts of unanticipated strategic results, the justice of which cannot be guaranteed. But solutions which assimilate æsthetics into the language of rights are equally problematic. Such solutions create a simple opposition between the power of the law and the freedom of the individual. They do not anticipate the way in which freedom can be utilised by the legal system within the "rights" discourse to attain ends that are directed against those anticipated by rights-strategists.

[57] Cf. Teubner, *supra* n. 6 at 94.

This difficulty is a new example of an interminable problem: the relationship between theory and practice. The importation of ethical theory into operationally closed systems has unpredictable consequences. The difficulties which law has when it attempts to regulate society or other social systems are also faced by theoretical advances which attempt to regulate law. For whereas ethical questions are powerfully motivational for ethically inclined actors, to the legal system they can appear as irritants: the application of justice to the individual is not the only motivational factor for the legal system. But the legal system does not respond to this problem merely by prohibitions. It also finds ways in which it can utilise ethical language for other purposes.

This leads me to a position of unmitigated cynicism that has become unpopular in recent times, not least among supposedly anti-ethical critical legal scholars. The optimism that characterised some early "post-modern" writings—that the destruction of traditional theories of the subject would lead to ethical results—has not been realised. Nor should we hope that such results can be realised by more adequate theorisation. The proposal of solutions to practical problems is a risky business, a business which two of the thinkers which I have considered here, Foucault and Luhmann, refused to engage in despite their sophisticated attempts to conceptualise and problematise the social history of modern society.[58] The extent to which Foucault wavered from this refusal towards the end of his life, and it was only a very limited extent,[59] can only be considered unfortunate. Theory is much better at discovering social problems than it is at solving them.

---

[58] As Luhmann has written, "like Foucault, I am not interested in finding some nice, helpful theory oriented towards the "Good", and much less in basking in indignation at the current state of affairs": N. Luhmann, *Love as Passion* (Cambridge, Polity, 1986) at 4. Unlike Luhmann, I am quite happy basking in indignation.

[59] See discussion in Foucault, *supra* n. 7.

7

Faith and the State of Jurisprudence

MALEIHA MALIK*

"F AITH"-based arguments, so often associated with theism, can also be
understood as covering a wider field. The term faith usefully captures
the sense of unquestioning confidence which underlies commitments
associated with not only religion, but also race, nationality and cultural tradition which may be important in the life of an individual. Contemporary concern
with social pluralism and diversity will ensure that understanding the status of
these commitments in the life of agents will remain a key issue. Discrete areas of
law—especially constitutional theory and discrimination law—have responded
to the problems which arise when faith-based arguments are used by agents to
justify belief and action. This essay considers the broader implications for law
by addressing this issue in two inter-related ways, with a view to undertaking an
exploration rather than reaching a conclusion. First, it examines the way in
which recent changes to our political culture—the State—have put issues of
faith back on the agenda. Secondly, it discusses the implications of this change
for the way in which we approach the study of law—the present state of
jurisprudence. It is suggested that contemporary changes in our political culture
which have put faith back on the agenda raise matters of relevance to our delib-
erations about law and legal institutions.

I

Current debates on the contemporary political culture of Western liberal
democracies have typically focused on two features. They have highlighted the
fact of "reasonable pluralism": that individuals in contemporary liberal democracies are committed to a range of different and often contradictory conceptions
of the good. In addition, they have been concerned with the "politics of recognition (and identity)": that a person's identification with a group characteristic
may be an important component of his or her well-being. These themes recur

* Previous drafts of this essay were presented at the King's College Legal Theory Seminar (Dec.
1997) and the International Law and Society Conference (June 1998). I am grateful to all the participants for their comments. I would particularly like to thank Neil Duxbury, Frank Reynolds,
Larry Rosen and Winnie Sullivan for their comments on an earlier draft. I remain solely responsible
for the contents.

in the many discussions of the problems faced by liberal multicultural states.

The problems of social pluralism have preoccupied a number of disciplines. The challenge is to develop an adequate response to the diversity of heterogeneous—and often incompatible—beliefs, practices and customs which are adopted by individuals as part of their comprehensive conception of the good. John Rawls' recent discussion in *Political Liberalism* is a good example of reflection on this issue. It labels the dilemma facing modern liberal democracies as the problem of "reasonable pluralism". These diverse religious, political and moral doctrines have two features: they are—simultaneously—incompatible and reasonable. No one comprehensive doctrine is adopted by citizens as their conception of the good. In fact, the structure of modern liberal democracies ensures that this "reasonable pluralism" is inevitable: the liberal state's commitment to autonomy, freedom of belief and expression ensures the creation and maintenance of this diversity. For Rawls, this is the natural outcome of the exercise of human reason under conditions of freedom.[1]

This acceptance of reasonable pluralism is an important modification to Rawls' previous work in the influential text, *A Theory of Justice*. It represents a concession that not all the members of a liberal democratic regime will endorse the underlying principles of his "Justice as Fairness" as their comprehensive doctrine. The "burdens of judgement" under which human reason operates ensure reasonable disagreement between different comprehensive doctrines which include conceptions other than liberalism. The sources of reasonable disagreement among reasonable persons arise from the "many hazards involved in the correct (and conscientious) exercise of our power of reason and judgement in the ordinary course of political life".[2] The most obvious sources include, *inter alia*: limits of evidence, disagreement on the relevance and weight of considerations, inherent indeterminacy which allows disagreement on judgements and interpretations, the influence of a citizen's total experience, and incommensurability between values.[3]

The contrast between faith and reason is one way of categorising the range of arguments which characterise social pluralism. If—as Rawls suggests—there

---

[1] J. Rawls, *Political Liberalism* (New York, Columbia University Press, 1993). Rawls states at xvi:

> "A modern democratic society is characterised not simply by a pluralism of comprehensive religious, philosophical, and moral doctrines but by a pluralism of incompatible yet reasonable comprehensive doctrines. No one of these doctrines is affirmed by citizens generally. Nor should one expect that in the foreseeable future one of them, or some other reasonable doctrine will ever be affirmed by all, or nearly all, citizens. Political liberalism assumes that, for political purposes, a plurality of reasonable yet incompatible comprehensive doctrines is the normal result of the exercise of human reason within the framework of the free institutions of a constitutional democratic regime. Political liberalism also supposes that a reasonable comprehensive doctrine does not reject the essentials of a democratic regime. Of course a society may also contain unreasonable and irrational, and even mad, comprehensive doctrines. In their case the problem is to contain them so that they do not undermine the unity and justice of society."

[2] *Ibid.*, 55.
[3] *Ibid.*, 57.

are limits to the ability of reason to resolve these issues, then one way of categorising the resulting diversity is by reference to faith-based justifications. Not only religious dogma, but also a wider field of beliefs, practices and customs which appeal to non-reason-based modes of knowledge can be understood as sources of "reasonable pluralism". Of course this simple opposition and tension fails to do justice to the complexity inherent in any contrast between reason and faith. It could be argued that Rawls' idea of public reason is based in large part on faith in the power of reason; and that those who base their beliefs and actions on faith may be able cite cogent arguments to support and justify their position.

However, the "reasons" for their belief and conduct are likely to be internal to the tradition.[4] Many faith-based commitments are justified by reference to facts not amenable to the standards of proof and evidence typically employed in reason-based analyses. These arguments are based on tradition, narratives, custom and culture which provide the basis for legitimation. These sources perform important functions for individuals and their communities. They provide a set of pragmatic normative guides for belief and conduct which generate evaluative criteria. These norms also provide the individual's terms of membership and the social bonds of his or her community. In this way, faith-based narratives are a key aspect of social regulation for these sub-communities. Moreover, faith-based forms of knowledge characteristically determine their own criteria of validity, competence and application. For the individual, they define what can and should be said and done. Legitimacy is provided by the fact that people within a tradition listen to the narratives, recount them, give them authority and use them as the basis for their beliefs and conduct.[5] In addition these normative criteria provide the background context for the exercise of choice in a wide range of matters for the individual. Commitments of faith may be critical, not only in relation to pragmatic choices about what to do and how to act, but also to the whole range of æsthetic and emotional experiences of the agent.[6] In these ways, a feature of faith-based arguments is their influence on the motivations and inner states of consciousness which guide belief and conduct in important areas of the agent's life. As I argue below, greater clarity in appreciating these features becomes a prerequisite for analysing the importance of faith for agents.

Of course it will be possible to challenge the legitimacy of faith-based arguments using the familiar criteria associated with scientific proof and practical reason. Where faith is based on prejudice, error or misinformation, one response will be to ask the individual to re-evaluate his belief and the authority which he is giving to narratives in the hope that this will lead to some

---

[4] See G. Postema, *Bentham and the Common Law Tradition* (Oxford, Clarendon Press, 1996) 76.

[5] J.F. Lyotard, *The Postmodern Condition: A Report on Knowledge* (Manchester, Manchester University Press, 1986) 18–23.

[6] See the discussion of Hume on human nature in Postema, *supra* n. 4 at 92–7. See also C. Taylor, "Self-interpreting Animals" in his *Human Agency and Language, Philosophical Papers, Vol. 1* (Cambridge, Cambridge University Press, 1985) 45.

modification. A move along these lines may lead to some unanimity and agreement concerning belief, but it will not deplete the range or status of faith-based arguments. John Rawls' argument based on the "burdens of judgement" which are a source of reasonable disagreement is a recognition of the limits of reason-based analysis to resolve disagreements.[7] In any event, the truth or falsity of the arguments by reference to rationality does not exhaust the relevance of these issues for our analysis. It is the fact that faith is important in the life of the individual which makes it relevant for analysis. In this sense, justification of faith-based beliefs—rather than their truth or validity—is agent-relative. An individual may be justified in continuing to believe in the arguments—which make sense given the whole of his belief structure—even if they are false given other evidence and using criteria of practical reason.[8] This agent relativity is a key feature of the present analysis which has focused on the relationship between faith and the identity, self-respect and well-being of agents.

For Rawls, "public reason" will ensure that these differences do not manifest themselves in the public sphere and that all citizens will accept the value of reaching an agreement based on his principles as the public principles of justice, thereby forming a *modus vivendi*—an "overlapping consensus"—irrespective of their notion of the comprehensive good. This analysis is compatible with the idea that membership of groups is important for individuals but suggests that these communal attachments are relevant in the private rather than the public sphere.

The second feature of contemporary liberal culture—the "politics of identity" issue—focuses attention on a number of recurring themes in contemporary political writing. Writers such as Raz, Taylor and MacIntyre have all addressed these topics. Although there remain important differences between them, their work highlights a number of common concerns. These theorists reject an atomistic picture of individual freedom as radical detachment. Their work recognises an important link between individual freedom and identity on the one hand, and social practices and community on the other. A number of consequences follow from these connections. First, we are forced to notice that an important source of the well-being and self-respect of agents arises out of their sense of who they are; through their identification with important beliefs, groups and attachments. Secondly, where these beliefs, attachments and groups are denigrated this in turn undermines the sources of self-respect and well-being of the agent. Raz states this in terms of "alienation from society" and the "pivotal importance of self-respect to the well-being of people".[9]

[7] *Supra* n. 2 and accompanying text.

[8] See Raz's account of the coherence of belief (which he distinguishes from the issue of coherence of legal norms etc.): "[t]he justification of each person's beliefs is relative to that person's totality of belief. This makes it possible for two people to be justified in holding beliefs that contradict those of the other. As justified beliefs may be false, there is no problem about that": J. Raz, "The Relevance of Coherence" in his *Ethics in the Public Domain* (Oxford, Clarendon Press, 1994) 288.

[9] See e.g. J. Raz, "Duties of Well Being", *ibid.* at 27. See also "Multiculturalism", *ibid.*, 170 and C. Taylor, *Multiculturalism and the Politics of Recognition* (Princeton, NJ, Princeton University Press, 1992).

The fact that important aspects of identity are formed "dialogically", and the resulting importance of respect and recognition, makes issues of identity and group membership important for the public sphere.[10] The link between recognition by others and individual well-being raises the stakes in the "politics of identity" debate. Taylor, for example, argues that an important additional feature of the "politics of identity" is the idea that the failure to grant recognition, or the misrecognition of the other, is characterised as a harm which can cause damage to the well-being of the individual. In this second sense—as the recognition of identity—the argument moves the "politics of identity" debate from the private to the public sphere. If recognition by others is important for individuals, then the failure to grant recognition and reflecting back to agents a demeaning picture of themselves or the group from which they draw their sense of self can be categorised as a serious matter which has implications for their well-being and autonomy.[11] Where the state and its institutions are implicated in creating and sustaining this distorted image, there is a strong case that the requirements of the politics of identity and recognition have been breached.

II

"Reasonable pluralism" and the "politics of identity" have been, and are destined to remain, important issues for understanding contemporary political culture. Do they also raise questions for the enterprise of jurisprudence?

It is sometimes assumed that jurisprudence as an enterprise is—and should be—immune from contemporary fashions and changes in our political culture. A powerful set of assumptions underlies this view. Analytical jurisprudence, it is argued, should concern itself with factual and descriptive accounts of the concept of law and our legal practices. The argument is that an analysis of the nature of law should proceed solely on morally neutral and non-evaluative criteria. On this account the social fact of multi-culturalism and pluralism does not raise questions for jurisprudence, for there is ultimately no real choice about how we should study the nature of law. What is important is the search for stipulative definitions which will assist in theorising. Lyons, for example, argues that before we can enter into a discussion concerning the merits or demerits of law we must first reach some agreement concerning the relevant concept.[12]

---

[10] For a discussion of the untenability of Rawls' distinction between private and public reasons for action see J. Finnis, "Natural Law Theory and Limited Government" in R. George (ed.), *Natural Law, Liberalism and Morality* (Oxford, Clarendon Press, 1996) 9.

[11] Taylor, *supra* n. 9 at 25–7. The importance of "recognition" finds an analogy in Hume's idea of the importance of "sympathy" which is a "fellow feeling or other-regarding concern establishes the essential link between the individual and the community": see Postema's discussion of Hume, *supra* n. 4 at 97.

Despite differences, there must—at any one moment in time—be sufficient agreement concerning our use concepts to allow such analysis to proceed.

Relying on this starting point, one view of the agenda for jurisprudence may suggests that reflection on the nature of law must proceed without any concern for the social and practical context within which law operates. This line of argument assumes a sharp distinction between analysis and evaluation, often discussed in the context of the positivism and natural law debate. The view that reflection on the nature of law should be wholly unconcerned with issues of social and political context is not necessarily synonymous with positivism. It is not inconsistent to recognise a different vision whilst at the same time remaining within the central commitments of positivism. This possibility becomes clear once we recognise a crucial distinction between two sets of propositions which can be identified with positivism. First, it is possible to argue—as positivists do—that there are limits to the criteria which are used to determine the validity of propositions of law. However, this is distinct from the argument that there is a range of arguments (which may include evaluative criteria) which can be used to justify this conception of law. There is no inherent contradiction in supporting both propositions.[13] Joseph Raz states:[14]

> "The [positivist] doctrine of the nature of law yields a test for identifying law the use of which requires no resort to moral or any other evaluative argument. But it does not follow that one can defend the doctrine of the nature of law itself without using evaluative (though not necessarily moral) arguments. Its justification is tied to an evaluative judgement about the relative importance of various features of social organisations and these reflect our moral and intellectual interests and concerns."

Some theorists push the relationship between theoretical concepts and practical context even further. As stated, natural law theorists such as Finnis challenge the possibility of separating theory and data in an unproblematic way which enables description without evaluation. Others set out an analysis between theory and practice which suggests a more complicated and nuanced relationship. Postema, for example, argues for a "normative" jurisprudence which he sets up as a contrast to a strict "analytical" position which assumes that jurisprudence must proceed solely through *a priori* analysis of legal concepts without any concern with the social context in which these concepts operate.[15] His argument

---

[12] See D. Lyons, "Moral Aspects of Legal Theory" in P.A. French, T.E. Uehling and H.K. Wettstein (eds.), *Mid west studies in Philosophy VII: Social and Political Philosophy* (Minneapolis, Minn., Univeristy of Minnesota Press, 1982) 223–54; J. Coleman, "Negative and Positive Positivism" (1982) 11 *Journal of Legal Studies* 139–64.

[13] Coleman, *ibid.*, states: "the argument for ascribing certain tenets to positivism in virtue of the positivist's normative ideal of law is to commit the very mistake positivism is so intent on drawing attention to and rectifying" (quoted in Postema, *supra* n. 4 at 330).

[14] "The Problem of the Nature of Law" in Raz, *supra* n. 8 at 209. The adoption of positivism "on moral grounds" has also been discussed by N. MacCormick, "A Moralistic Case for A-Moralistic Law" (1985) 20 *Valpariso L. Rev.* 1 at 9–10.

[15] Postema, *supra* n. 4 at 332. The argument that conceptual analysis must be attentive to the social context within which concepts emerge raises related points, but is a different argument, from

challenges the possibility and use of universal and general concepts, which can be divorced from the social context within which these concepts operate, as the basis for jurisprudential theory. He argues that conceptual analysis—gaining an understanding of the nature of law—needs to be linked to, and is not sharply delineated from, gaining an understanding of the practices and forms of life in which concepts exist and operate.[16] This is not just an issue about whether theory or data should control our enquiries. Theorists such as Postema rely on a more complex and subtle relationship between theoretical concepts and the social context within which they arise and operate.[17] Conceptual analysis in jurisprudence and legal theory cannot, he argues, concern itself solely with stipulative definition and description. Rather, the subject matter—human belief and conduct—requires a process of characterisation and interpretation of the data by the theorist: it cannot be understood without an understanding of the point or meaning attributed to the behaviour and social practice.[18]

This vision of the relationship between theory and social practice raises a number of issues. If it is accepted that description of human conduct is insufficient and what is required is an analysis of the beliefs and meanings which underlie human conduct and social practices, then this will inevitably introduce uncertainty. Rather than yielding certain and absolute definitions, these concepts and their common meanings will invariably be the subject of controversy and debate. Where there is a dispute concerning the characterisation or interpretation of a social practice, pointing to facts and evidence will not exhaust the limits of a dispute concerning its "meaning" or "point". Descriptions of meaning and point do not present themselves in the same way as the description of a physical object: as a factual description which can attribute absolute properties to a physical object, and which can be tested by the usual proofs, causation and evidence. Accepting a particular characterisation as valid is dependent on accepting the plausibility of the sense, point and significance attributed to it by those who are involved as participants. A theory which postulates a certain characterisation of behaviour as correct is always open to challenge by those who do not accept its underlying assumptions concerning the point or meaning

---

the claim by those who advocate a "social theory" or "sociological" approach to the subject. Roger Cotterell e.g. distinguishes between normative legal theory and empirical legal theory. He writes:

> "By normative legal theory I mean theory that seeks to explain the character of law solely in terms of the conceptual structure of legal doctrine and the relationships between rules, principles, concepts and the values held to be presupposed or incorporated explicitly or implicitly within it. By empirical legal theory I mean theory that seeks to explain the character of law in terms of historical and social conditions and treats the doctrinal and institutional characteristics of law emphasised in normative legal theory as explicable in terms of their social origins and effects."

See R. Cotterell, *Law's Community* (Oxford, Clarendon Press, 1995) 24.

[16] Postema, *ibid.*, 328–39; Raz, *supra* n. 4 at 209.

[17] For a general discussion, see Postema's account of "normative jurisprudence", *supra* n. 4 at 328–36. See also N.E. Simmonds, *The Decline of Juridical Reason: Doctrine and Theory in the Legal Order* (Manchester, Manchester University Press, 1984) 9–11.

[18] C. Taylor, "Interpretation and the Sciences of Man" in his *Philosophy and the Human Sciences, Philosophical Papers, Vol II* (Cambridge, Cambridge University Press, 1985) at 15.

attributed to the social practice. In order to command legitimacy and agreement, characterisations of meaning and significance will need to draw on common meanings, which are not just the beliefs of individual actors, but should be understood as a constitutive set of ideas and norms which are the common property of the society.[19]

Recent Anglo-American legal theory, especially the work of Ronald Dworkin, has revived the importance of community, which was an important feature of common law theory. However, the argument—introduced earlier— that law is a social institution which is constituted by, and draws on, common meanings develops the idea of community in a much stronger form. It suggests that there are certain social practices and institutions which rely on and sustain inter-subjective meanings, which can be understood by all participants, and which allow the development of a common language and vocabulary.

Common meanings and beliefs are embedded in and constitutive of the social and political culture, the community, and its institutions. These cannot be understood by merely noting their impact on, or importance for, individual agents. These are not just shared beliefs and attitudes of all the individuals in a society. Rather, they form the basis for a common understanding of these social practices and institutions which cannot be understood as anything but communal. The common meanings which are associated with law and legal institutions, and which they in turn sustain, are the basis for community. People have to share and participate in a language and understanding of norms which allows them to talk about these institutions and practices.[20] If the view that there is a stronger—constitutive—relationship between law and social practices is accepted then this goes beyond seeing a link between law and the community whereby law must attend to communal values. This connection suggests that law has an important function to play not only in reflecting, but also in creating and sustaining, social life and shared values.

Those who emphasise these constitutive features attribute an important function to law and legal institutions which goes beyond that of regulating disputes. They argue that law functions as an institution which constructs behaviour, gives it sense and meaning, and influences the self-interpretation of beliefs and conduct of participants. This complex social function assigns to law and its institutions an important public role, as a bank of collective wisdom, and as a public "ritual". Postema has made this point most forcefully in his work on the common law:[21]

[19] C. Taylor, "Interpretation and the Sciences of Man" in his *Philosophy and the Human Sciences, Philosophical Papers, Vol II* (Cambridge, Cambridge University Press, 1985) at 32–4. See also the discussion of communitarian approaches to legal theory which are presented as an alternative to the "individualism" of traditional Anglo-American legal theory. Classical common law thinking and Ronald Dworkin's legal theory (e.g., *Law's Empire* (London, Fontana, 1986)) suggest that law has an important role to play in creating and maintaining common meanings and community. See Cotterell, *supra* n. 15 at 222–34.
[20] See Taylor, *supra* n. 18.
[21] See Postema, *supra* n. 4 at 73.

"One might say that the processes and practices of Common Law, on this view, define a kind of secular public ritual. . . . The Common Law, then, not only defines a framework for social interaction, a set of rules and arrangements facilitating the orderly pursuit of private aims and purposes, but it also publicly articulates the social context within which the pursuit of such aims takes on meaning. It is the reservoir of traditional ways and common experience, and it provides the arena in which the shared structures of experience publicly unfold."

The metaphor of "public ritual" could also very comfortably be applied to the procedures which are a prelude to passing legislation.

If this metaphor is apt, and law performs a public function in the creation and interpretation of beliefs and attitudes, then it is clear that this has important implications for our analysis. The complex relationship between law and social practices (such as those based on faith) suggests that an "error" in theory can have a substantial impact on the practices themselves. In describing a physical object, where theoretical analysis fails to "get it right", it still leaves the subject matter unchanged. However, with more complex social practices where a theoretical concept fails there is a risk that it will distort the subject matter in a more fundamental way: it may influence the way in which the social practice is understood even by participants and those whose conduct and beliefs are being described. Where there is a failure of theory in relation to these types of beliefs, which fails to capture the full range of relevant data or uses methods of analysis which are likely to be distortive, this has serious consequences for the underlying subject matter. Theorising in this context has an important role in setting the context within which not only outsiders but also insiders come to understand the practices: "it does not leave the phenomenon unchanged".[22] If it fails to accurately capture the practice, it will distort also the underlying reality which is the object of analysis. Reflecting back to agents a distorted or demeaning image of themselves will influence not only the perception of outsiders but it will also impact on the self-understanding of "insiders". This may explain why insiders care so passionately whether or not their beliefs are presented accurately. Given the importance of law and legal institutions in the public sphere, it is not surprising that a major part of the struggle for "recognition" has focused on the reform of legal provisions and institutions, which have such great symbolic and rhetorical significance for individuals.

---

[22] Simmonds notes this causal connection between theory and the social reality which it seeks to describes in the following terms:

"The wide separation between theory and reality rests above all on a failure to appreciate the extent to which 'a man's social relations with his fellows are permeated with his ideas about reality.' For changes in theory and belief are not sources of truth or error about reality: by transforming the significance of human practices, they may work a transformation in the nature of social reality itself."

See N.E. Simmonds, *supra* n. 17 at 12. An alternative view, one which views the social reality as "brute facts", would suggest that any error at the level of theory and in formulating definitions will not impact on the substance of the underlying phenomenon, and that the choice of definitions does not have any practical consequences.

Nudging analysis in a direction which ensures an undistorted and accurate understanding of faith-based arguments presents a considerable challenge. Reflection upon the nature of law and legal institutions requires attention to relevant facts about human belief and conduct. Where this includes behaviour and conduct based on faith, how should we understand these facts accurately and without distortion?

There is an inherent tension in any attempt by liberal institutions to respond to faith-based arguments.[23] Although the changes in our political culture make it important to understand faith-based arguments, existing concepts and models based on practical reason and rationality are not the ideal starting point for such an analysis. Theoretical analysis which proceeds via precise definition and rational demonstration does not very easily accommodate faith-based arguments. An adequate response to faith requires an understanding of a realm of experience and consciousness which fits uneasily with practical reason and its concomitant model of truth and cognition. Michael Oakeshott suggests that this is an intractable conflict. He characterises reason-based modes of politics as "the enemy of authority, of the merely traditional, customary or habitual".[24] For Oakeshott, the "rationalist is essentially ineducable" in relation to issues of tradition and narrative—which we have characterised as faith—because they require from him an "inspiration which [is regarded] as the great enemy of mankind".[25] In addition, and more worrying, is the risk that the effort to articulate, analyse and subject to critical scrutiny a tradition by "outsiders" may be incompatible with preserving the full meaning of the tradition as understood and experienced by "insiders".

The usual tools of neutrality and objectivity seem at first sight to be a particularly attractive method for understanding faith in the context of social pluralism. These allow the theorist to bypass problems of choice of evaluative criteria. The claim to neutrality and certainty is achieved by avoiding any subjectivity or "bias" of the theorist, and by focusing on data which can be understood in absolute terms and without reference to the experiences of the subject. In this way the theorist is encouraged to break free of his own perspective and to adopt

---

[23] See e.g. the discussion of Stephen L. Carter in "Evolutionism, Creationism and Treating Religion as a Hobby" (1987) 6 *Duke Law Journal* 977. Although Carter's discussion deals specifically with religious belief his discussion in Part II (Liberalism and Religion) could be applied to all faith-based arguments which are relevant to this discussion. See also *ibid.*, 993, n. 44, where Carter quotes Unger: "[w]herever liberal psychology prevails, the distinction between describing things in the world and evaluating them will be accepted as the premise of all clear thought . . . The contrast of understanding and evaluation is foreign to the religious consciousness, for its beliefs about the world are simultaneously descriptions and ideals."
[24] M. Oakeshott, "Rationalism in Politics" in his *Rationalism in Politics* (London, Methuen, 1962) at 1.
[25] *Ibid.* , 32. See also Hume's discussion of the limits of reason and the importance of imagination in Postema, *supra* n. 4 at 128–31.

a neutral point of view as a prerequisite to study; thereby using a method for the study of human conduct which avoids the dangers of uncertainty, evaluation and subjective interpretation. All of these ensure that faith-based arguments are on an equal footing between each other and in relation to other types of arguments.

However, a closer look at this model suggests that it is not hospitable to faith. The appropriateness and success of this analysis require that the subject matter is amenable to study using the techniques of neutral observation and description: human conduct needs to be made more manageable to enquiry of this type. This is usually achieved through a number of moves. First, this model gives priority to those features of human agency which can be correlated with absolute properties: that is, which can be described without the dangers of uncertainty and relativity. In this way the focus of analysis is steered towards the external conduct of the agent. The importance of inner motivations, beliefs and states of consciousness is ignored, or at the very least marginalised.[26] Even where theory gives priority to this internal attitudes they are treated as "brute facts" which can be stated unproblematically in neutral and objective descriptions, rather than as inherently subjective "meanings" which need to be understood from the perspective of the relevant subject who experiences them.[27] Secondly, the appropriate temporal unit for analysis tends to be the basic action. Instead of concentrating on the history of the individual or the origins of the social practice which

[26] Traditionally, John Austin's attempt to develop a "science of jurisprudence" sought to develop the subject along the lines of the natural sciences. The fact that reflection on the nature of law is concerned with human conduct was not seen to be a significant barrier to the application of description and observation as the appropriate tools for understanding these facts. Contemporary jurisprudence has of course broken free of the naïve assumptions of Austin's model, although the methods and assumptions concerning human agency which underlie this approach continue to present themselves as an attractive option. Arguably, the attraction of Economic Analysis of Law is explained (in part) by the way in which its assumptions concerning human agency (focusing on Man as a rational maximiser of desires) successfully avoids questions of motivation. All questions concerning value are either avoided or equated with what people want using a criterion of efficiency which is amenable to calculation. This type of analysis emphasises weighing between values rather than any investigation of a qualitative contrast between them. For a discussion of these features of Economic Analysis of Law see A.A. Leff, "Economic Analysis of Law: Some Realism about Nominalism" (1974) 60 *Virginia L Rev*. 451.

[27] Hart's work breaks from the naïve techniques which focus on outward phenomenon, towards a method which attends to the inner states of subjects. He states, in relation to understanding law as a rational and empirical science :

"My main objection to this reduction of propositions of law which suppress their normative aspect is that it fails to mark and explain the crucial distinction that there is between mere regularities of human behaviour and rule-governed behaviour. It thus jettisons something vital to the understanding not only of law but of any form of normative social structure. For the understanding of this the methodology of the empirical sciences is useless; what is needed is a "hermeneutic method" which involves portraying rule governed behaviour as it appears to its participants, who see it as conforming or failing to conform to certain shared standards."

H.L.A. Hart, *Essays in Jurisprudence and Legal Philosophy* (Oxford, Clarendon Press, 1993) 15. However, despite giving priority to the internal attitude, Hart's account remains within a tradition which treats motivations and meanings as facts to be described rather than inter-subjective meanings to be interpreted by attending to the experience of the subject. Therefore, it is argued by Simmonds that Hart's theory remains within the empiricist paradigm rather than adopting a genuinely alternative "hermeneutic approach". See Simmonds, *supra* n. 18 at 104–5.

provides the context within which the act is performed, conduct tends to be studied as an isolated and one-off act.[28] Difficult questions of evaluation and comparison are avoided. On this model there is no problem of distortion of the other; there is merely a description of conduct about which it is not possible to be wrong. No viewpoint is given priority; neutrality and objectivity ensure accurate and unbiased understanding.

The attraction of this method as a way of overcoming any problems of "ethnocentricity" or bias when confronted with the multifarious traditions, cultures and viewpoints which flourish in contemporary pluralist societies is obvious. However, there are important ways in which this method is inappropriate when it comes to faith-based arguments. Its focus on external conduct and the basic action is likely to distort the full value of these practices as experienced by participants. What is missed altogether—or at the very least rendered marginal—are the crucial motivations and inner states of consciousness which underpin these types of beliefs and conduct. Understanding these actions fully will require reference to their meaning, as understood and experienced by the participants. A descriptive method often ignores these altogether. Where they are considered, these aspects are treated as facts to be described: by merely noticing that a belief is held or by delineating causal connections between beliefs and conduct and attributing these to specific individuals. These techniques are not ideal for analysing inner states from the perspective of the subject who experiences them, which is of critical importance in this context. In addition, this emphasis on the basic action and an ahistorical analysis of conduct means that the agent's history cannot be a focal point of the analysis. The action may take on its meaning in the context of the whole of the life of the agent; or it may be linked to a longer narrative tradition or social practice which gives the act its justification, meaning and significance. Attention to the act, without any reference to inner states and this wider temporal context, is therefore likely to miss important features of faith-based conduct.

The shift towards understanding conduct from the perspective of the subject is problematic in the context of social pluralism. How is it possible to take into account all the different motivations and beliefs which underlie these different and various perspectives? It is tempting to fall back on description and observation in this context, in the hope of avoiding internecine disputes about intention, thereby providing some potential for understanding and consensus through theory. However, any advantages of this method are illusory. Rather than complying with the requirements of neutrality, in the context of faith this strategy is unlikely to yield a useful and accurate understanding of the other. The "point from nowhere" neutrality towards which this method aspires as the basis from which to understand is not—from the perspective of faith-based arguments— neutral. What seems to be a neutral starting point, and objective method, does not facilitate an undistorted understanding of faith. On this analysis, faith-

---

[28] A. MacIntyre, *After Virtue* (London, Duckworth, 1981) ch. 15.

based conduct which is alien and different is likely to remain inexplicable and will continue to seem irrational to the theorist.

Recent post-modern scholarship tells us that this problem of "ethnocentrism" arises whenever we seek to understand a tradition as outsiders by applying an evaluative criterion, which is often a universally applicable standard external to that tradition. In fact, one of the main concerns of the advocates of the "politics of recognition" in contemporary liberal democracies has been to expose as delusory and ethnocentric the claim to neutrality made by this universalist model.

The alternative to ethnocentrism is to avoid evaluation altogether, thereby side-stepping the need to choose criteria. Some post-modern scholarship, particularly the work of theorists who invoke Nietzsche, and arguments derived from the writing of Foucault and Derrida, emphasise the importance of "diversity" as a value. These writers often insists that any evaluative criteria used are ultimately derived from existing power structures.[29] To impose evaluative criteria from the outside is to do "violence" to the other. On the whole, these theories avoid the problem of choice of evaluative criteria in one of two ways: either by arguing that there are no evaluative criteria to apply in this context, or that all evaluative criteria are equally valuable. Neither of these is ideal for understanding faith-based arguments. The first claim—which denies the legitimacy of applying evaluative criteria—sits uneasily with faith-based arguments. Although these types of arguments rely on narrative and tradition, and often invoke their own criteria for legitimacy, they remain committed to the position that these are valuable options. This first strategy, which seeks to avoid evaluation, is unlikely to provide a useful model for understanding the full implications of the claims made by those who rely on faith. The second option, which concedes that all evaluative criteria are equally valid, seems to be more attractive. It coheres with the claim to respect and recognition which is sought. However, on closer examination this strategy is also problematic. If all positions are granted "equal respect" without any enquiry into what they are or why they are valued, then—arguably—this is a "hollow" version of recognition. The respect and recognition sought—and the argument that there should be a better understanding of faith-based arguments—require some attention to the claim by insiders that these have value. An endorsement on demand, without any investigation or appreciation of the true value of the faith for "insiders" does little to advance understanding in this context. In any event, rather than being an act of respect and recognition, an automatic grant of approval on demand could be construed as an act of condescension.[30]

To gain a better grasp of faith, what is required is an approach which explicitly shifts the focus from external conduct to the inner motivations and beliefs which underlie this conduct. Those theorists who insist that it is an essential rather than a contingent fact about human beings that they not only desire and

---

[29] See, e.g., I.M. Young, *Justice and the Politics of Difference* (Princeton, NJ, Princeton University Press, 1990) especially ch 4.

[30] Taylor, *supra* n. 9 at 70.

act, but also undergo a process of reflection about their conduct, provide some of the resources for such a move.[31] This alternative method forces us to notice that not only do human agents have first-order desires (brute desires), they also have second-order desires (where they rank these desires according to evaluative criteria). In this way, some desires and actions of the agent are ranked by him according to his conception of value as being higher, noble and an aspect of an integrated way of living, whereas others are deemed to be unworthy, base and associated with a fragmentary life. These second-order desires necessarily entail not only a quantitative assessment of what and how much is desired, but they also require a qualitative assessment of whether these desires fit in with the agent's sense of what makes his life valuable. This method presents a more attractive way of capturing all the data relevant for an understanding of faith-based arguments which give particular weight to these features of human agency.

Once this different view of human agency is accepted, it becomes clear that a full understanding of conduct cannot rely solely on observation and description. Reflection—motivations, beliefs and intentions—cannot be communicated in certain, absolute and objective terms. This emphasis necessarily introduces sub-jectivity, as we are required to understand these features by referring them to the experience of the agent. Moreover, these features require a focus on a temporal unit for analysis which extends beyond the basic action. Understanding mean-ings, motivation and the inner states of consciousness necessarily requires plac-ing these features within the context of the whole history of the agent. Where the agent relies on faith-based arguments this may also require attention to the historical background of the tradition within which these arguments develop and take on their significance.

Three modifications need to be made to incorporate these aspects. First, moti-vation, belief and the "meaning" of practices take on a central rather than a peripheral role in this enquiry. Secondly, the conduct needs to be placed within the wider context of the experiences of the agent. This shift in focus means that the methods of neutrality and observation need to give way to techniques which focus on the data from the perspective of the agent. Objectivity will need to be supplemented by some attention to the viewpoint of the subject, as the theorist attempts to understand belief and conduct from this perspective. Thirdly, the nature of these types of commitments set important constraints on the degree of certainty and the type of understanding which the theorist should seek. It is often assumed that understanding in these contexts requires reaching an agree-ment on shared values which can be endorsed by both—or all—relevant parties.

---

[31] See e.g. C. Taylor, "What is Human Agency?" in his *Human Agency and Language, Philo-sophical Papers, Vol. 1* (Cambridge: Cambridge University Press, 1985) 15; H. Frankfurt, "Freedom of the Will and the Concept of a Person" (1971) 67 *Journal of Philosophy* 5–20. I. Murdoch discusses these issues at length in *Metaphysics as a Guide to Morals* (Harmondsworth, Penguin, 1992). See also M. Oakeshott, "On the Theoretical Understanding of Human Conduct" in his *On Human Conduct* (Oxford, Clarendon Press, 1990) 1.

However, this is not a helpful way of setting up the goal of analysis in these types of cases. There is an alternative way of approaching study in this context which proceeds very differently. Rather than seeking agreement on absolute and neutral criteria, this alternative method suggests that "understanding the other" is about making that person and his or her self-understanding more intelligible.

IV

Philosophical hermeneutics provides some of the resources necessary for making the experiences of agents amenable to analysis in this way.[32] This approach enables an understanding of a perspective which is different and alien. The "interpretative turn in theory" is not free of its own difficulties and it has been the subject of powerful and well-rehearsed criticism. However, it has a number of advantages in the context of faith-based arguments.[33] It does not rely on the adoption of a model of neutrality, which, as we have seen, is inappropriate in the context of faith. Nor does it adopt a sceptical or relativist approach to the claims of value made by agents who rely on faith. Rather, this alternative approach seeks to mediate the tension between attention to the perspective of the subject relying on faith on the one hand, and the needs of a theorist who is seeking greater understanding and clarity on the other. Gadamer's work is particularly useful because of its explicit discussion of the problems of understanding in these contexts. Gadamer's insight is that knowledge of the other—who is different and alien—is only possible if we use rather than suspend our pre-existing insights into the human condition: "[o]nly the support of familiar and common understanding makes possible the venture into the alien, the lifting out of something out of the alien, and thus the broadening and enrichment of our own experience of the world".[34] For Gadamer, a pre-existing attitude towards experience is precisely what allows a meaningful experience of the new and different.

Emilio Betti has discussed this alternative approach in the context of legal theory. For Betti, the task of understanding the other requires attention to the "representative value" which is implicit in this type of practical activity. The theorist needs to reflect upon this value and to make it explicit and therefore uncover the "marks of personality" of the subject. For Betti, this activity of making the "representative value" explicit is a cognitive act of interpretation: "interpretation as

[32] I am grateful to Dr Janet Martin Soskice for her Stanton Lectures (1998) (unpublished), especially her analysis of the work of F. Schleiermacher, which allowed me to appreciate the importance of philosophical hermeneutics as a resource for analysing faith-based arguments.

[33] The problems which are faced by "interpretative approaches" to the human sciences are addressed by Taylor, *supra* n. 18, especially 20–9. For a trenchant criticism see M. Moore, "The Interpretative Turn in Modern Theory: A Turn for the Worse?" (1989) 41 *Stanford Law Review* 871.

[34] H.G. Gadamer, "The Universality of the Hermeneutical Problem" in D.E. Linge (ed.), Philosophical *Hermeneutics* (Berkeley, Cal., University of California Press, 1976). I would like to thank Sohail Nakhooda (Nottingham) for his assistance on this point.

action whose useful outcome is understanding".[35] This method relies on a special relationship between the subject and object, which recognises the unique nature of the phenomenon which is being studied: "[a]t one head of the process is the living and thinking spirit of the given interpreter. At another is some spark of the human spirit, objectivised in representative form . . ."[36] This method seeks to accomodate the greater need for subjectivity and understanding the experiences of the other which may be important in the context of faith-based arguments. Betti states:

> "On the one hand, the interpreter must respond to the requirements of objectivity; his rethinking of the object, his reproduction of it, must be faithful and as close as possible to the expressive or characteristic value possessed by the representative form he seeks to understand. . . . Two things are thus held in opposition: one, the subjectivity that is inseparable from the spontaneity of understanding; the second, the objectivity, or otherness so to speak, of the sense which interpretation seeks to elicit in the object. Upon it, one may construct a general theory of interpretation, which, in allowing critical reflection upon that process, can serve as the basis of an account of its ends and methods. This theory is hermeneutics."[37]

At first sight, it may seem that such a strategy will raise insurmountable problems when it comes to understanding faith in the context of social pluralism. How can such a range of diverse perspectives—many of which rely on beliefs radically different from, and often incompatible with, the normative "home understanding"[38]—be studied in this way? Inner motivations will vary according to different subjects; they will be impossible to delineate with any degree of precision; and in the face of such diversity there is a danger of fragmentation and conflict rather than a better comprehension of the "other". Giving priority to the home perspective will mean that these divergent belief structures will be deemed to be wrong and erroneous, thereby invariably breaching the requirements of the "politics of recognition".

Despite its inherent limit, such a pessimistic reaction underestimates the potential shift in understanding which can result from this alternative approach. As Taylor—commenting on this hermeneutical method in the human sciences—notices, understanding the other with radically different beliefs and practices requires placing these against analogous "home" beliefs and practices. Understanding in this context necessarily requires a contrast. This may seem problematic. In the context of faith-based practices, the immediate outcome of this comparative process will be to notice that the faith is radically different from the home beliefs and practices with which the theorist is familiar. The theorist will apply his own home value system to judge the practice as clearly different and wrong. There will be a clear attribution of error to the beliefs and

---

[35] E. Betti, "On a General Theory of Interpretation: The *Raison D'Etre* of Hermeneutics" (1987) 32 *The American Journal of Jurisprudence* 245.
[36] *Ibid.*, 248.
[37] *Ibid.*, 249.
[38] I.e., from the perspective of the theorists own beliefs and culture.

practices of the other, who will be missing some critical feature of social reality. Bias and the application of an external criterion will be explicit using this approach.[39]

However, the analysis does not end there. The fact that the theorist has been forced to make the contrast has consequences which go beyond the simple conclusion that the faith-based arguments are wrong. Understanding the very different practices of another through comparison takes a special form. By placing the practices against a home understanding, and most importantly using a method which looks beyond merely external acts, the theorist is forced to notice a range of factors which often remain obscure when the "neutrality" model is used. The theorist is forced to notice that the other person is acting out of inner beliefs, motivations and states of consciousness to advance what—from his perspective—is a social practice with value. The theorist uses rather than neutralises his own home understanding of his motivation, belief and conduct. This pre-existing knowledge acts as a modular frame within which faith-based practices are placed, contrasted and made more intelligible. In this way the act of making a comparison contains within it the seeds of its own success. Using this method, there is some possibility that the theorist will come to see and appreciate that the faith-based conduct is underpinned by motivation and belief; that it has point, value and meaning from the perspective of the agent; and that the agent is engaged in a process of reflection which seeks to make sense of these features within the context of his whole personal history.

There are obvious limits to the extent of agreement concerning values which we can expect using this method. However, once it is recognised that the task is to make the other more intelligible, it becomes meaningful to claim that the act of comparison has led to a shift in understanding the other. In Betti's terms, "[k]nowledge in this instance has a singular trait, not given or to be confused with knowledge of physical phenomena: it recognises and reconstructs a human spirit, communicating with the interpreter through the forms of its objectivization, and causing him to sense an affinity with it through their common humanity."[40]

In this way, there is some potential for making sense of what seems to be irrational faith-based conduct. Rather than merely noticing that the action is different and alien, the theorist can attempt to comprehend the meaning of the action from the perspective of the subject. It is only from this perspective—trying to grasp the significance of the external conduct for the agent- that the action can be made more intelligible. This does not mean that the action is now accepted as being valid or as meeting some objectively agreed criteria of what is rational. The action may still remain puzzling but it is now seen as one of a range of possibilities for human agents who wish to realise meaning, point and value in their lives. The action is now characterised as a part of a stream of

[39] C. Taylor, "Comparison, Truth and History" in his *Philosophical Arguments* (Cambridge, Mass., Harvard University Press, 1995) 146.
[40] See Betti, *supra* n. 35 at 249.

behaviour of an agent who will reflect upon it in order to make sense of his personal history.

One obvious outcome of this method will be that this shift in understanding is necessarily accompanied by a judgement that the faith-based conduct is wrong. It could be argued that this is a breach of the requirement to grant recognition to others. Should those who rely on faith-based arguments insist that this is a fatal flaw? Such a hasty dismissal should be avoided for a number of reasons. The usual models on offer—analytical neutral description or difference-sensitive post-modern theory—are inhospitable to faith-based arguments. A method which provides some potential for an appreciation and accommodation of the value of faith for participants—as they experience it and without distortion—is a substantial advance on these approaches. Moreover, under conditions of reasonable pluralism, reasonable comprehensive doctrines which rely on faith may be forced to conclude that they cannot insist on the truth of their conception of the good as the basis for organising political co-operation in the public sphere.[41] Faced with a choice between insisting that the absolute truth of their doctrine is acknowledged, and the prospect of communicating the value that their faith has for them to others, "insiders" have good reason to prefer the latter. In addition, the concern in the present analysis has been with understanding faith because it is agent-relative, that is, because it has value and importance from the perspective of the agent. Therefore, theorists who are "outsiders" also have good reasons to prefer an undistorted understanding of the value of faith for participants over any analysis or recognition of its claims to absolute truth.

There are limits to this type of enquiry. Of course, a method which is dependent for success on the "home" understanding of the theorist will raise problems of subjectivity in an acute form. This approach is dependent on the theorist reviewing and re-examining his own perspective. Success in this enterprise will be dependent on the ability of the theorist to remain open to the possibility of a change and shift in his perspective. Self-understanding and the ability to analyse his or her own "home understanding" will be as important as the ability to describe and observe. The subjectivity of this approach, with the resulting lack of certainty, clarity and predictability, sits uneasily with methods of verifiable description and observation which are usually applied in these contexts. The obvious criticism will be that this approach leads us to a "hermeneutical circle", which we cannot enter if we do not share the home understanding of the theorist, and which we cannot break out of if we lack objective criteria which we have discarded because of their "ethnocentricity". The accusation that this

---

[41] Rawls discusses this in terms of the "overlapping consensus" which will command the support of all reasonable comprehensive doctrines, and which will be the basis for organisation in the public sphere. See Rawls, *supra* n. 1. A critique of Rawls' arguments in this context, which are also relevant to the present argument that the "truth" of the faith-based arguments need not be the focus of the analysis for political theory, is J. Raz, "Facing Diversity: The Case of Epistemic Abstinence", *supra* n. 8 at 60.

model is flawed because of its subjectivity, uncertainty and arbitrariness has some force and validity in this context.

Especially relevant to the present discussion will be cases where the faith-based conduct is so very different or irrational that it is not possible for the theorist to place it against any analogous "home" practice. In these cases, the home understanding may operate as an absolute barrier to understanding, and it is unlikely that the method will assist in understanding faith. The practices of the other will remain irrational and inexplicable, along with an absolute judgement that these are based on error. These may be cases which fall within Rawls' classification of the "irrational" which he states are "unreasonable and irrational, and even mad, comprehensive doctrines. Here the challenge is to contain them so that they do not undermine the unity and justice of society."[42] It could be argued that this approach will fail in exactly those situations where there is the most urgent need to make faith-based practices intelligible.

These intractable difficulties and risks may suggest that a sterner response is preferable, one which openly acknowledges that it is not possible to do justice to the ideal of reason which underpins liberal politics and the claims of those who rely on faith. Rather than presenting itself as neutral between rational enquiry and faith, theory should resolve the tension by clearly advocating the former. On this view, faith-based arguments fail to meet the prerequisite conditions of rationality which are the basis for organising public life and institutions. Although relevant in private life they should have nothing to do with the public sphere. Therefore they need not concern discussion about contemporary political and legal theory.

v

There are good reasons to resist such a quick dismissal. The resurgence of the "politics of recognition" and "identity politics"—permanent aspects of our contemporary political culture—confirms that this dismissal will be seen to carry within it an implicit dismissal of those individuals for whom these beliefs are of great significance and value. In addition, it is a distinguishing characteristic of faith-based reasons that they have significant status for the relevant individual. One way in which they will operate on the reasoning of the individual is as a theoretical authority, and this will have implications which go beyond the private realm. There is a potential for divergence and conflict between these sources of authority and law's claim to act as a practical authority. Where individuals are faced with conflicting demands—between the requirements of theoretical (faith-based) authority on the one hand and compliance with a legal rule on the other—differing beliefs may lead to a barrier to understanding, creating a conflict and a refusal to act according to the requirements of law. In these

---

[42] Rawls, *supra* n. 1 at p. xvii.

circumstances it becomes necessary to overcome resistance and resolve this conflict. The agent's understanding of his situation will need to be replaced by a decision by an impartial third party (i.e the judge or legislator). Another option is to ensure that the prospect of these types of disputes is minimised, so that there is a greater convergence between all the various institutions which provide the sources of normative guidance in the daily and practical lives of individuals. In order to fulfil these tasks adequately it will be important to ensure that the judge or legislator is in touch with, and has an accurate understanding of, the customs and practices of the individuals and sub-communities who rely on faith-based arguments. This will be especially important if the link between individual well-being, identity and recognition is accepted. In this context, minimising such conflicts is not just a matter of expediency and efficiency; it becomes an important part of the conditions necessary to allow individuals to flourish and lead fully autonomous lives.

A vision of law which sees it as not only a system for regulating conduct, but also as a source of creating and sustaining common meanings in a community, makes it especially important to take seriously the sincere feelings of those who rely on faith-based arguments. The self-perception of these individuals that their views have been considered and given some weight by legal institutions becomes important in order to ensure their identification with the legal system.[43] This analysis suggests that where, as with prevailing conditions of reasonable pluralism, individuals draw their beliefs from a wide variety of sources, law needs not only to be factually comprehensible but also to "speak" to people's beliefs and attitudes.[44] The prospect of a greater coalescence between the experience of individuals in their daily and practical lives and their experiences of normative legal and political institutions—and therefore of meaningful identification and a higher degree of willing co-operation with these institutions—would justify such an effort.

If one of the features of the contemporary political culture is the presence of faith as the justification for belief and conduct, then this has implications for our discussions of law and legal institutions. The challenge is not to justify these beliefs and attitudes as true or seek absolute objective criteria on which to base a legal system. Nor that our reflections concerning the nature of law should take the faith-based beliefs and attitudes of these insiders as the starting point for analysis or as true facts on which to build a legal system. This is not about coming up with a natural law theory out of which to build a true or perfect account

---

[43] See the discussion of the "common meanings" and the constitutive function of law and legal institutions in Section II. In addition, theorists who adopt a social theory or sociological approach to jurisprudence have highlighted the importance of these issues. Cotterell argues that we need to focus on law's image of *community* rather than *imperium* which predominates in the English tradition. He suggests that this vision is more likely to yield inter—personal trust and a reduction in the "moral distance" between the individual and the legal system. See Cotterell, *supra* n. 15 at ch 15.

[44] For a discussion of the relevance of this issue in the specific context of criminal liability see R.A. Duff, "Law, Language and Community: Some Preconditions of Criminal Liability" (1998) 18 *OJLS* 189.

of law based on objective facts. Rather the challenge is that theorists must understand these facts about human agents accurately, treat them as serious and important matters and, where relevant, take these participant beliefs into account. These are matters which are important not only for those "insiders" who rely on faith, but also for all those concerned with understanding law and legal institutions.

Index